Women, Ethnicity and Nationalism
The politics of transition

D0451853

This new study documents the processes of political transition in countries steeped in 'old' nationalist rivalries or which have experienced the 'revival' of ethnic nationalism. Each of the book's contributors describes and explains how recent constructions of national identities disadvantage women in what has been trumpeted as the 'new world order'. An extensive introductory chapter and a discussion of gender, nation and nationalism are followed by case studies on post-apartheid South Africa, Northern Ireland, Yemen, post-Soviet Russia, the former Yugoslavia, the Lebanon and Malaysia. The contributors each challenge the mooted 'newness' of the respective gender orders and identify communities of resistance among women and feminists in the continuing struggle to achieve citizenship.

The book concludes that despite being only too aware of the relegation of women to the status of second-class citizens in societies that have gone through profound transition in earlier decades of the twentieth century, women in the societies covered by this volume find themselves moving almost inexorably towards the same status. The imperatives of economic development and political/cultural nationalism are conspiring together to impose profound obstacles to women's equitable participation in the societies under investigation.

Rick Wilford is Reader in the Department of Politics, The Queen's University of Belfast. **Robert L. Miller** is a Senior Lecturer in Sociology at The Queen's University of Belfast.

Women, ethnicity and nationalism

The politics of transition

Edited by
Rick Wilford and Robert L. Miller

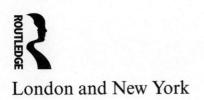

London and New York

First published 1998
by Routledge
11 New Fetter Lane, London EC4P 4EE

Simultaneously published in the USA and Canada
by Routledge
29 West 25th Street, New York, NY 10001

© 1998 selection and editorial matter Rick Wilford and Robert L. Miller;
individual chapters the contributors

Typeset in Times by Routledge
Printed and bound in Great Britain by MPG Books Ltd, Bodmin

British Library Cataloguing in Publication Data
A catalogue record for this book is available from the British Library

Library of Congress Cataloging in Publication Data
Wilford, Rick, 1947–
    Women, ethnicity and nationalism: the politics of transition / Rick
    Wilford and Robert L. Miller.
  1. Women–social conditions. 2. Women–political activity. 3. Ethnic relations.
  4. Nationalism. I. Miller, Robert L., MA. II. Title.
HQ1121.W55 1998   98-9381
305.42–dc21   CIP

ISBN 0–415–17136–9 (hbk)
ISBN 0–415–17137–7 (pbk)

Contents

Contributors

Rick Wilford is a Reader in the Department of Politics at The Queen's University of Belfast. He is the co-author of ten books including *Women and Political Participation in Northern Ireland* (Avebury 1996). He is currently editing two books, one on women and politics in Ireland and another on politics in Northern Ireland, to be published by Westview Press in 1998.

Robert L. Miller is Senior Lecturer in the Department of Sociology and Social Policy, The Queen's University of Belfast and in 1996–1997 was visiting Professor at the National University of Malaysia. He is co-author of *Women and Political Participation in Northern Ireland* and has undertaken a number of policy-relevant research projects, including a major study of religious discrimination in the Northern Ireland Civil Service. He is currently involved in further research on social mobility, employing a life history approach.

Rosalind Marsh is Professor of Russian Studies at the University of Bath. She formerly taught at The Queen's University of Belfast and at the University of Exeter where she was Director of the Centre for Russian, Soviet and East European Studies from 1989 to 1991. Among her numerous publications are *Images of Dictatorship: Stalin in Literature* (Routledge 1989) and *History and Literature in Contemporary Russia* (Macmillan 1995). She also edited *Women in Russia and Ukraine* and *Gender and Russian Literature: New Perspectives*, both published in 1996 by Cambridge University Press. In 1997 she became President of the British Association of Slavonic and East European Studies.

Sheila Meintjes lectures in Gender and Politics, African Politics and Feminist Theory at the University of Witswatersrand, having previously held teaching posts at the universities of Cape Town, Natal and Durban. She has been active in a number of organizations since the early 1980s, including the Women's National Coalition in which she coordinated the Research Supervisory Group between 1993 and 1994; the Natal Organization of Women and the United Women's Organization in Cape

Town. Most recently she was a member of the Gender Equality Commission's sub-committee on Policy, Planning and Research. She is currently writing a chapter, 'Gender and the Truth Reconciliation Commission', to appear in M. Turshen (ed.) *Women and Conflict in Africa* (Zed Books 1998).

Maxine Molyneux is a political sociologist who has published widely on politics and policy with a focus on gender issues in socialist and post-socialist states. Her most recent article, 'Women's Rights in the International Context', was published in M. Threlfall (ed.) *Mapping Women's Movements* (Verso 1996). She is a Senior Lecturer at the School of Advanced Studies, University of London.

Norani Othman is Associate Professor in the Department of Anthropology and Sociology at the National University of Malaysia and a Research Fellow at its Institute of Malaysian and International Studies. Her publications include articles on Islamic law and the Malaysian social science tradition as well as others on the politics of Islamization.

Elisabeth Porter lectures in Sociology and Women's Studies at the University of Ulster. Her research interests encompass feminist social, political and moral theory and her publications include *Women and Moral Identity* (Allen & Unwin) and *Building Good Families in a Changing World* (Melbourne University Press).

Tanja Rener is Assistant Professor in the Social Science Faculty at the University of Ljubljana, teaching family sociology, women's studies and the sociology of everyday life. She is currently working on a study of youth at risk.

Kirsten Schulze lectures in the Department of International History at the London School of Economics. She has published widely on women in the Middle East and is currently embarked on a project concerning loyalist paramilitarism in Northern Ireland. Her most recent article 'The Northern Ireland political process: a viable approach to conflict resolution?' appeared in *Irish Political Studies* in 1997.

Mirjana Ule is Ordinary Professor of Social Psychology at the University of Ljubljana and Director of its Centre for Social Psychology, which she founded. She is currently working on life course analysis, identity formation and women's and youth studies.

Nira Yuval-Davis is Professor and Post-Graduate Course Director in gender and ethnic studies at the University of Greenwich. She has written widely on nationalism, racism, fundamentalism and gender relations in Israel and other settler societies as well as in Britain and other European states. Her latest book, *Gender and Nation*, was published by Sage in 1997.

Preface and acknowledgements

The idea for this edited volume grew out of a series of research seminars held in Northern Ireland during 1993 and 1994. The original theme of the series was 'The Economic and Political Participation of Women' but, as it unfolded, the focus of the seminars narrowed towards that of gender and neo-nationalisms. This change occurred as the various contributors reflected on the lived experiences of women in countries that had either recently undergone or were undergoing political transition. Indeed, these countries seemed to include Northern Ireland as the IRA's ceasefire was announced towards the end of the series in the late summer of 1994. Progressively, the linkages among women, ethnicity and nationalism came to dominate the proceedings, which were enlivened by the contributions of those (mostly female) participants drawn from ethnically divided societies and those with active research interests in such societies.

While the intellectual climate at the time was still influenced by the 'end of history' thesis, the participants at the seminars were, to say the least, less than persuaded that the eruptions of ethnic conflicts presaged new worlds of equality for women. What the disorders of the moment made plain – or plainer – was that the generally unhappy relationship between women and nationalism showed little sign of being reconciled. Certainly the changes wrought in South Africa and the prospect of a transformation in Israeli–Palestinian relations and latterly between Unionists and Nationalists in Northern Ireland gave grounds for some guarded optimism. However, past experience supplied a corrective to an unexamined belief that a mantle of peace, stability and gender equality was about to settle in the midst of ethnic nationalist revivals. At a time, too, when feminist discourse was preoccupied increasingly with identity politics, celebrating rather than denying 'differences' among women, ethnic nationalism threatened to create new barriers among women both within nations embarked upon transition and those witnessing the regime changes from afar. This apparent contradiction was acutely felt by the participants at the seminars and generated a great deal of introspection among us, some sense of which we hope is captured in the contributions to this book.

We would like to express our thanks to the Economic and Social Research Council for funding the seminars: without that support the opportunity to explore our ideas would have been unrealized. Thanks are also due to the British Council for supplementary funding, especially to Peter Lyner its representative in Northern Ireland, and to Queen's University which hosted three of the seminars, and the University of Ulster which hosted the fourth of them. We are grateful to all who participated and played an important role in helping each of us to continue our education, sometimes in public. In particular, we would like to acknowledge the part played by the discussants at the series: Vicky Randall, Sylvia Walby, Valentine Moghadam and Kathy Glavanis-Grantham, and those who presented papers, not all of whom could be included in this volume.

The organization of the series was a formidable undertaking and was greatly eased by the unseen work of the late Betty Donnelly and Eileen McNeill. We would also like to thank the publishers of *Ethnic and Racial Studies* and of *Middle Eastern Studies* for permission to include revised versions of articles by Nira Yuval-Davis and Maxine Molyneux that first appeared in their pages. Ruth Dilly is owed special thanks for ensuring that the technical specifications for the book were fully complied with. Finally, thanks to James Whiting and Vicky Smith at Routledge: their patience was sorely tested in bringing this project to fruition.

Rick Wilford and Robert Lee Miller
Queen's University of Belfast, July 1997

1 Women, ethnicity and nationalism

Surveying the ground

Rick Wilford

> ... as a woman I have no country. As a woman I want no country. As a woman my country is the whole world.
>
> (Virginia Woolf 1938)

INTRODUCTION

In surveying the relationship between women and nationalism it is difficult to escape the conclusion that it turns on male-crafted conceptions of nation and national identity. As Pettman (1996: 49) observes, 'In a complex play, the state is often gendered male and the nation gendered female'. Women, that is, are commonly constructed as the symbolic form of the nation whereas men are invariably represented as its chief agents and, with statehood achieved, emerge as its major beneficiaries.

The ground upon which the nexus among women and nationalism is based is, though, littered with controversy. Bystydzienski (1992: 209), for instance, while not uncritical of national movements, takes a more sanguine view of nationalism than Pettman: [it has] 'empowered millions of women . . . created pride in indigenous cultures, a demystification of innate superiority of foreign oppressors, and a recognition of community'. Such conflicting assessments hint at the extent of disagreement that exists. Contesting theories of nationalism, debates about the relationship between ethnicity and 'race', ambivalence about the celebration of 'difference', together with the problematization of 'women' as an organizing construct, all combine to lay a conceptual and political minefield. It would be misleading to claim that this book settles these controversies. At a time of rapid political transitions each of the contributors does, though, help to negotiate a course across the contested terrain guided – as this introduction is – by the proposition that 'All nationalisms are gendered' (McClintock 1993: 61).

The inclusion of internally divided or settler societies lends a sharp focus to this edited collection. Territorial conflict imbues the politics of such societies with a zero-sum rather than a positive-sum character. While all societies are internally differentiated those within which there is conflict over territory may become highly segmented and potentially, if not actually, violent (Horowitz 1985, 1994). Thus, while nationalism is propelled by an 'us and them', insider/outsider, inclusive/exclusive dynamic, this can be carried to exaggerated and dangerous extremes in divided societies: barriers – whether physical, social, material and/or psychological – are erected and inter-ethnic differences can spiral into violence as self-consciously distinctive groups take up arms in order to realize their claims to autonomy. Though such barriers or cleavages, whether structured by region, religion, ethnicity or class, may be bridged – by power-sharing and provision for segmental autonomy (consociationalism), decentralization (regional or local government), the devolution of powers (federalism) and/or an array of public policies that promote, or at least accommodate, multi-culturalism – the politics of divided societies are likely to be unstable.

MILITARISM, NATIONALISM AND FORGETTING

Where measures designed to manage conflict do fail and violence does erupt, martial values are prized and symbols of separate nationalist identities exalted. In such contexts women are invariably marginalized by a condition of 'armed patriarchy' (McWilliams 1995: fn 7). Enloe (1989: 44) makes the broad point eloquently in discussing anti-colonial nationalism: 'typically [it] has sprung from masculinised memory, masculinised humiliation and masculinised hope', only rarely taking 'women's experiences as the starting point for an understanding of how a people becomes colonized or how it throws off the shackles of that material and psychological domination'. Enloe also declares that 'When a nationalist movement becomes militarized . . . male privilege in the community usually becomes more entrenched' (1989: 56) and, with near deadening finality, states: 'militarization puts a premium on communal unity in the name of national survival, a priority which can silence women critical of patriarchal practices and attitudes; in so doing, nationalist militarization can privilege men' (1989: 58).

Chazan (1989: 5) shares this general judgement in reflecting on the consequences for Israeli women of the particular circumstances of the Arab–Israeli conflict, noting that 'a [divided] society . . . in a prolonged period of conflict inevitably develops values which underestimate the role of women and [their] essential contribution to the social order'. Moreover, even where conflict is succeeded by a peace (of sorts), or at least a condition of non-war, the exclusion of women is sustained. For instance, Sharoni's analysis (1996: 121) of the gendered discourse that structured the fragile Israeli–Palestinian Accord of 1993, documents how the voices of women and feminists were silenced by the 'masculinisation' of the peace process: 'This process of exclusion . . . is gendered. [P]eople, practices, symbols and ways of thinking coded as 'masculine' mark the centre of politics, while what is rendered 'feminine' is relegated to the margins'.

Moreover, fighting alongside men to achieve independence does not provide a guarantee of women's inclusion as equal citizens. Jayawardena's (1986: 259) magisterial survey of feminism and 'third world' nationalism makes the general point: 'Once independence had been achieved, male politicians who had consciously mobilized women in the struggle, pushed them back into their "accustomed place"'. Similarly, in post-revolutionary Algeria the 'delegitimization of the heroine' (Cherifati-Merabtine 1994) was symptomatic of the side-lining of women after independence was achieved. As Glavanis-Grantham (1996: 175–6) observes, the Algerian experience is understood in salutary terms by Palestinian women activists, who: 'warn of the dangers of subordinating the social struggle to the national struggle to the extent that women may have the gains of the Intifada subverted and be forced to return to the domesticity of former years'.

While others (Abdo 1994; Holt 1996) argue that the politicization of Palestinian women has created a determination to make certain, as Abdo puts it, that there will be 'no going back', there is a keen awareness that a tension exists 'between women's needs and rights and perceived national needs [which] has led some to wonder whether the national struggle is retarding the efforts for women's equality' (Najjar 1992: 14). However, challenging a nationalist movement on the grounds that it neglects gender equality can incur high risks: women can all too easily be labelled as subversive or treacherous, or as succumbing to the blandishments of foreign and hence unwelcome ideas such as feminism. As Enloe (1989) states:

> Women who have called for more genuine equality between the sexes . . . have been told that now is not the time, the nation is too fragile . . . [they] must be patient; they must wait until the nationalist goal is achieved; then relations between women and men can be addressed. 'Not now, later' is the advice that rings in the ears of many nationalist women.
>
> (Enloe 1989: 62)

While many women will reply 'If not now, when?', the broad lesson appears to be that not only do revolutions devour their children but also that nationalist movements have a disagreeable habit of swallowing their women. Pettman (1996: 136–7), in cataloguing the experiences of women from a variety of revolutionary and nationalist struggles, notes the occurrence of 'an uneven but very widespread pattern of regression in terms of women's claims and participation after the state is won'. Men, the charge runs, suffer a collective and convenient memory loss about the contribution made by women to national liberation struggles: '"forgetting" . . . appears to be a frequent effect of reconsolidating centralised control of authority . . . [it] is part of the process of legitimising privilege, including gender privilege' (*ibid.*: 138). Such was the case in culturally homogeneous Ireland.

Buoyed by the 1916 Proclamation's commitment to guarantee equal rights and equal opportunities to all citizens, the women who fought and otherwise assisted in the Easter Rising were later subjected to such forgetting by the Irish Constitution of 1937. The handiwork of Eamon De Valera, the Constitution embodied his unswerving patriarchy which was foreshadowed by his singular refusal to allow women to fight alongside the men he had commanded in 1916. Together with the special status accorded to the Catholic Church, subsequently removed following a referendum in 1972, the Constitution underwrote the spirit of the Papal Encyclical, *Casti Connubii*, by declaring that 'In particular, the State recognises that by her life within the home, woman gives to the State a support without which the common good cannot be achieved' (Article 41 (2) 1). Hanna Sheehy-Skeffington, a co-founder in 1908 of the Irish Women's Franchise League, was to the fore in exposing De Valera's 'mawkish distrust of women' and in criticizing the Constitution's 'Fascist proposals endangering [women's] livelihood, cutting away their rights as human beings' (Ward 1995: 165). Despite a concerted and spirited campaign of opposition, this and other offending articles were implemented following the ratification of the Constitution by plebiscite.

More recent casualties of this forgetting include the 20,000 or so women who fought in the Marxist Eritrean People's Liberation Front. Demobilized after freeing their land from Ethiopian rule in 1991, they have been decanted back into a deeply patriarchal society that has done little to reward their warrior status. As one of them commented, 'It was better when we were in the field – we were equal with the men and we got good treatment' (McKinley 1995).

FUNDAMENTALISM AND BARGAINING

Anti-colonial struggles have been the spur to much of the literature concerning the gendered nature of nationalism, including those within which Islamic fundamentalism (or revivalism) has been resurgent. In such regimes the wearing of *hijab* (modest dress) may be construed not as an act of induced submission but as a pragmatic, if not entirely voluntaristic, response among women.

On this view *hijab* represents a form of negotiation with patriarchy enabling women to move freely in public spaces, hidden from the 'male gaze' (see, for example, Afshar 1996; Mir-Hosseini 1993, 1996). One Palestinian activist, Lilly Feildy (see *The Guardian*, 8 February 1996), suggests another motive, *viz.* the adoption of propriety as a badge of commitment: 'There were no veiled Palestinian women before the Intifada: it became an expression of identity'. Kandiyoti (1988: 283) goes further, suggesting that the donning of 'traditional modesty markers' by women signifies a 'patriarchal bargain', indicating to their menfolk that they continue to be 'worthy of protection'. Azari makes the same point in relation to young women in Khomeini's Iran: 'the restriction imposed on them by an Islamic order was . . . a small price that had to be paid in exchange for security, stability and presumed respect this order promised them' (quoted in Kandiyoti 1988).

There is a certain plausibility in this latter reading of women's motives: that at a time of political crisis or transition they seek to renew a classic patriarchal bargain as a coping strategy intended to afford some security in an uncertain present and as a hedge against an unpredictable future. Tansu Ciller, Turkey's first woman prime minister, appears to have struck her own contract in response to the electoral advance of the pro-Islamic Welfare Party (WP). Prior to the 1996 election she committed herself to continuing the process of Westernization and to upholding the tradition of secular government bequeathed by Ataturk, explicitly ruling out a partnership between her own True Path Party and the WP. However, following the election she negotiated a coalition with the Welfare Party, acquiring the deputy premiership in the process and now often appears in public wearing *hijab*. Whether or not Ciller's *volte face* was merited, her bargain was structured by the bounds of patriarchy: it isn't, to borrow a cliché, only stone walls that a prison make. As Anthias and Yuval-Davis (1993: 108) observe, while 'Femininity may be seen as a coping mechanism', it can also be interpreted to mean that 'women can be both individually and collectively active agents in their own subordination'.

In societies based upon either a religion or a political doctrine that is consummatory in character, any attempt to oppose or subvert its tenets courts danger. Other than embracing scripturally based values and beliefs, there are few options available to women: perhaps exegesis, seeking in effect to reinterpret, and liberalize, the relevant text to their relative advantage (Afshar 1996); or, alternatively, either silence or exile. The capture of Kabul by Taliban in September 1996 demonstrates vividly the constraints that can issue from unreconstructed fundamentalism. While men have not escaped unscathed from its zealotry – they must cover their heads and grow beards, especially if employed in the public sector – Taliban's advance led to the enforcement of an unflinchingly patriarchal interpretation of Islam. This is manifested by the imposition of the all-enveloping and shroud-like *burqa*; the closure of schools for girls over the age of 10, and of women's universities; and the prevention of women from undertaking paid employment, or even working for the international aid agencies upon which many rely for food, medical aid and shelter.

The extremes of Taliban, the excesses of Islamic vigilantes in Algeria who murder women adopting a secular lifestyle, the custom of so-called 'honour-killings' of women who are accused of adultery by their male relatives in Palestine and Iraq (see Helie-Lucas 1994), do seem to label Islam as the most patriarchal of religions. Yet, as Moghadam (1993: 7) observes, the diversity of Islamic practice throughout the Middle East (and elsewhere) is such that the status of women in Muslim societies is 'neither uniform nor unchanging nor unique' but varies with class, ethnicity, level of educational attainment and age.

What matters here is not whether a fundamentalist interpretation of Islam, Hinduism, Judaism or, for that matter, Christianity (see Klatch 1994) is more or less oppressive of women, but the role(s) women are assigned as cultural markers of national identity and propriety. The compulsory veiling of women by nationalist movements in Sudan, Iran or Afghanistan, whether they are seeking to shore-up existing regimes or fashion new ones, is but a graphic representation of women's subordination that elsewhere may assume more subtle forms but which are, nevertheless, integral to the processes of defining a national identity. The wider and more germane point is that the limits to self-actualization by women are, as Allen (1994) notes, culturally and historically specific.

Allen's remark made in relation to 'heterogeneous societies' is perhaps even more appropriate when applied to those that are divided and within which mutually exclusive identities are accentuated: *viz.*, 'identity denies and suppresses differences *within* socially created categories and emphasizes differences *between* them' (1994: 96, Allen's emphases). With the former Yugoslavia and other recent ethnic conflicts in mind, she quotes Young (1990: 98) to underline the point: 'Identity turns the merely different into the absolutely other'. *Inter alia*, such 'other-ing' deters dialogue and interaction across the relevant lines of cleavage – whether among women or men – and also disguises or deflects attention away from the gendered inequalities that exist within ethnic groups. Where ethnic identity is mobilized into an exclusivist nationalist movement, the limits to self-actualization for women can be profound. If we needed to be reminded of this, events in the former Yugoslavia supply the required jolt, whether in the nauseating incidence of systematic rape as policy, or the construction of new pro-natalist constitutions in Slovenia and Croatia. (On the former Yugoslavia see Drakulic 1993 and Milič 1993.)

It is, of course, possible to draw admittedly value-laden distinctions between 'good' and 'bad' nationalist movements in the same way as one may differentiate 'good' from 'bad' revolutions. Moghadam (1993: 71ff) engages in just such an enterprise by distinguishing between two types of revolution and national-identity construction: a 'Women-in-the-Family' or patriarchal model; and a 'Women's Emancipation' or modernizing model. The former (encompassing, in her view, the French, Algerian and the Iranian revolutions of 1789, 1962 and 1979 respectively), commonly stressing sexual difference, relegated women to a subordinate status, while the latter (including the Russian, South Yemen and Afghan revolutions of, in turn, 1917, 1967 and 1978) were those within which 'national progress and societal transformation were viewed as inextricably bound up with equality and the emancipation of women'. Pettman (1996: 56), by contrast, is far less buoyant, arguing that 'In comparing nationalist struggles internationally, we discover specificity, but also remarkably similar constructions of women in relation to nation – a reminder that nationalism is always gendered'.

PLUS ÇA CHANGE

The resurgence of nationalism in central and Eastern Europe and its tenacity elsewhere, offer the (unwelcome) opportunity to recognize anew the ways in which constructions of national identity are gendered. While it is the case that many recent political transitions have been in a liberalizing if not a democratizing direction, all develop through what Pridham (1993) terms 'zones of uncertainty', whether precipitated by a programme of reform or a break with the past. Some aspects of the transitional process do, however, appear to be more predictable than others. Though there is, for instance, little evidence of organizational continuity in Eastern Europe, where pre-communist parties have not been electorally successful following the collapse of communism, there is ample evidence of cultural continuity: patriarchal attitudes have proved resilient, and not only where the Catholic Church retained its sway, as in Poland (see Regulska 1992).

The ideological commitment to gender equality asserted throughout the former Soviet bloc turned out, as we now know, to be little more than an exercise in doctrinal hubris. Any lingering pretence concerning the solving of 'the woman question' was jettisoned as the new, post-communist regimes sought to effect both a rapid political transition and a swift economic transformation. In that respect Gorbachev's (1988: 117) invocation to female citizens in the former Soviet Union to 'return to their purely womanly mission' has proved to be remarkably prescient. The slump in female representation in the public sphere, the decanting of women out of the formal economy and their consequent loss of job security, together with the widespread adoption of pro-natalist policies, indicate that throughout much of central and Eastern Europe women have borne the brunt of the costs of political and economic change. (See, for example, Bridger *et al.* 1996; Funk and Mueller 1993; Rai *et al.* 1992.)

Just as there was/is an unhappy marriage between feminism and Marxism, events in the former Soviet Union demonstrate an equally miserable relationship between feminism and neo-nationalisms. As Pettman notes (1996: 140), 'In old East Europe and the ex-Soviet Union, democratisation and liberalisation appear to mean masculism'. This assessment was prefigured by Enloe's (1993) engaging autocritique prompted by the ending of the cold war. She woke up 'the morning after' with a nasty hangover caused by her recognition that, far from heralding a brave new world of sexual politics, the ending of superpower rivalry merely fortified her understanding 'of the ways in which men have used nationalism to silence women [and] conscious of how nationalist ideologies, strategies and structures have served to update and so perpetuate the privileging of masculinity' (1993: 229)

DIFFERENCE AND DIVERSITY

Such a judgement may now seem commonplace but it underlines the fact that mainstream texts on nationalism have ignored the significance of gender, a neglect that feminist scholars have sought to remedy by demonstrating that gender is central to the project of fashioning national identity. The renaissance of nationalism and the allied processes of regime transition – more properly, transitions – have, though, coincided with two other trends in feminist thinking: first, the shift from a recognition of differences among women to their celebration; and second, the deconstruction by post-structuralists of the category 'woman'. As Stacey (1993: 64) puts it: 'Rather than assuming "woman" to be a given category of feminist analysis . . . these feminists highlight the fluidity of the meaning of that category across time, place and context'.

This understanding of 'woman' as 'a constantly shifting signifier of multiple meanings' (*ibid.*), together with the legitimization of differences among women, supplies a necessary corrective to the ethnocentrism of the earlier phases of second-wave feminism which postulated the existence of a global sisterhood – most notoriously in the slogan 'women are the niggers of the world'. What the more recent understandings prize is an attention to diversity explored through cultural and identity politics, allied to the recognition that subjective identities – including ethnic identities – are themselves malleable, conflicting, fluid. Such an open-textured perception of identities not only rejects all forms of determinism or notions of essentialism but enables one to unpack the gendered processes by which they are constituted.

Therapeutic though these insights are, as Maynard (1994: 10) notes, the concentration on diversity among women is not problem-free. She argues that the stress on 'difference' risks 'masking the conditions that give some forms of "difference" value and power over others. In the context of race and ethnicity, this can lead to the marginalization of issues such as racism, racial domination and white supremacy'.

Adams (1989: 27–8) also sounds a cautionary note about the preoccupation among some feminists with 'a politics steeped in identity', warning that this can create the singular pursuit of autonomy among clusters of small groups 'constantly negotiating the tension between respectful diversity and fragmentation and rarely pooling their strengths'. To reinforce her admonition she quotes with approbation the earlier injunction voiced by Zimmerman (1985): 'There is a price to pay for a politics rooted so strongly in consciousness and identity. The power of diversity has as its mirror image and companion the powerlessness of fragmentation'.

There is, then, a felt ambivalence among some feminists about the weight attached to difference, while yet others articulate outright opposition. This is not to imply that the significance of difference should be denied, not least because it does arrest the unreflective universalism of the earlier women's movement. On the other hand, it may generate timidity on the part of 'first world' feminists. Stung by criticisms of their ignorance of, and historic complicity in, the oppression of 'third world' women they may feel unable to do little more than organize around their own oppressions, perhaps abandoning those, no matter that they are valued as different, deemed to be 'other'.

More worryingly, as Comaroff remarks (1995: 246), 'the postmodernist insistence on the polymorphous [could be] merely perverse, a product of Euro-American bourgeois consciousness obscuring its own politics of indifference in respect of the powerless and the truly poor'. Similarly, Norval's (1993: 137) exploration of the conceptual tension that exists between universality and particularity, between, that is, the denial and the privileging of difference, stresses the need to avoid both 'the politics of the enclave' and 'a simplistic reassertion of universality': 'At stake' she argues 'is the kind of politics that can recognize and legitimate difference while resisting fragmentation into discrete and local identities'. The conjuncture of cultural analysis, identity politics and the re-ascendancy of nationalism is, therefore, problematic. Viewed in this light, Norval's somewhat nervous comment (*ibid.*) seems highly appropriate *viz.*, 'just when marginal and oppressed groups are asserting their rights as political subjects is no time to deconstruct these identities'.

THEORIZING NATIONALISM

It isn't only because of its gendered character that one has to tread carefully in discussing nationalism. As Anderson (1983: 12–13) observes: 'Nation, nationality, nationalism – all have proved notoriously difficult to define, let alone to analyse . . . plausible theory about [nationalism] is conspicuously meagre'. It is, though, less that the theoretical gruel is thin, more that it is multi-grained. As Smith (1991: 72) notes, 'nationalism' has been deployed in a variety of ways, including: the whole process of nation building; a sense of national consciousness or sentiment; a symbolic and linguistic representation of the nation; an ideology; and a movement intended to realize the national will.

Cutting something of a (jagged) swathe through the literature, theories of nationalism can be said to fall into one of two camps, sometimes called 'traditionalist' and 'modernist' or, in Comaroff's case (*op. cit.*: 247), 'primordialist' and 'constructionist'. Exponents of the former present nations as natural and universal entities that, even if dormant, can be roused from their slumbers when conditions allow. It is akin to a 'genie in the bottle' understanding of nationalism: once the cork is removed – whether, for instance, through revolution, economic crisis, war, conquest or the collapse of empire – the hitherto trapped essence of national identity is released and quickly assumes its 'given' shape. Constructionists, though their exact positions vary, dismiss this atavistic understanding of nationalism, instead presenting it as a by-product of the wider modernization process associated with the rise of industrial capitalism. Here nationalism is perceived in contingent or pragmatic terms: as, for example, the invention of the 'thinking classes' during the latter part of the eighteenth and early nineteenth centuries. Viewed from this perspective nationalism was contrived by intellectuals and political elites to ensure cultural homogeneity within a growing and increasingly urbanized population, thereby protecting the instrumental needs of a modernizing industrial society against its neighbours and competitors.

Smith (1986: 15) occupies an intermediate position between these camps by focusing upon 'the ethnic foundations and roots of modern nations'. His concern is with 'the cultural forms of sentiments attitudes and perceptions as these are expressed and codified in myths, memories, values and symbols'. While this is not to adhere to a fixed or essential belief in the naturalness of nations, neither is it to dismiss the effects of modernization upon nationalism. It is, though, the sense of continuity and descent expressed by the 'myth-symbol' complex which interests him: the idea that there are pre-existing, that is pre-modern, ethnic or 'collective loyalties and identities' which nationalist ideologues consciously tap into rather than merely conjure out of the ether. Smith marks out his theoretical niche by dovetailing two usages of nationalism *viz.* as both an ideology and as a movement intended to realize the national will. Thus, nationalism is 'an ideological movement for attaining and maintaining autonomy, unity and identity on behalf of a population deemed by some of its members to constitute an actual or potential "nation"'.

This approach has proved attractive to some feminists concerned with nationalism (see, for example Anthias and Yuval-Davis 1993; Racioppi and See 1995), primarily because he understands self and social identity to consist of a repertoire of categories and roles: territory, class, religion, ethnicity and gender. Most pertinently, he presents gender as standing 'at the origin of other differences and subordinations', but contends that its very universality and pervasiveness 'makes it a less cohesive and potent base for collective identification and mobilisation' than either ethnicity or religion (Smith 1991: 4). Hence: 'Geographically separated, divided by class and ethnically fragmented, gender cleavages must ally themselves to other, more cohesive identities if they are to inspire collective consciousness and action'.

Smith's insistence that gender is relatively impotent as a basis for collective mobilization is, if not entirely welcome, nevertheless a point well made: it is, after all, consistent with the discomfiting recognition that 'sisterhood' was/is not the global, nor indeed national, force many feminists earlier believed it could be. In prioritizing ethnicity – and its 'twin circle' of religion – as the mobilizing force of nationalism Smith underscores the importance of 'a sense of continuity' among 'successive generations of a cultural unit of population', the 'shared memories of earlier events in the history of that unit and to notions entertained by each generation about the collective destiny of that unit and its culture' (1991: 25).

Racioppi and See, while acknowledging Smith's recognition of gender as the fount of self and national identity, berate him for undervaluing its significance. As they point out (1995: 17) 'if ethnic identity and ethnic group formation are rooted in notions of descent and familiality' – which Smith does claim – 'then gender is necessarily at their heart . . . yet it is only gender that disappears entirely from [his] theoretical and empirical analyses of ethno-nationalism'. In their critique of leading theorists of nationalism Racioppi and See conclude that 'for none [of them] does national identity have to do with our intimate relations. For none does it have to do with gender' (*ibid.*: 32).

Among the targets of their criticism is Benedict Anderson, whose *Imagined Communities* (1983) falls squarely into the modernist camp. He argues that nationalism, which he understands as the 'product of the ruptures of the late eighteenth century', supplies the felt need for continuity and immortality within communities confronted by the rational secularism of the Enlightenment, the corollary of which was 'the ebbing of religious belief'. In these circumstances: 'What was required was a secular transformation of fatality into continuity, contingency into meaning . . . few things were (are) better suited to this end than the idea of a nation' (1983: 19).

Anderson's key proposition is that nationality and nationalism are 'cultural artefacts' that were created, imagined, at the end of the eighteenth century. What distinguishes communities, whatever their scale, is 'the style in which they are imagined' by their members, and the substance and form of style is itself rooted in culture: '[N]ationalism has to be understood by aligning it not with self-consciously held political ideologies, but with the large cultural systems that preceded it, out of which – as well as against which – it came into being' (1983: 19).

RE-IMAGINING THROUGH SELF-EMPOWERMENT

Anderson's suggestive idea of an 'imagined community' has appealed to some feminists seeking to explore and explain the gendering of nationalism. It has in effect set an agenda, though not one envisaged by Anderson himself, that poses a series of decidedly rhetorical questions, including: 'Who, exactly, does the imagining?'; and 'What roles are assigned to women in the nationalist project?' It is, then, the heuristic value of the imagined community that has been recognized in feminist critiques of nationalism. It has, for example, been used with effect by Radcliffe and Westwood (1996: 134–5) in their analyses of the relationships between gender and national identities throughout Latin America, where 'nations and associated modernist discourses of democracy have been filtered through ideologies of gender' and where '[W]omen are not "imagined" . . . to be national citizens'.

Employing the familiar dichotomy between *machismo* and *marianismo* they demonstrate the ways in which men and women are imagined to embody 'the national', noting the ubiquity with which 'the strongly maternal component of Marian identities is frequently recirculated' (*ibid.*: 141):

> As expressions of national imaginings and myths as well as fact, histories of [Latin American] nationhood are markedly gendered in their templates, often highlighting hegemonic masculinities and emphasized femininities. . . . Men appear in the histories of battles, governments and monarchs, whereas women appear as icons of national domesticity, morals and 'private' sociality.
>
> (*ibid.*: 147)

But not all women. As Radcliffe and Westwood (*ibid.*: 151) stress, female images are invariably 'racialized'; white creole, urban women and those from influential families, often linked to male national heroes, tend to predominate as role-models. Notwithstanding such racial/ethnic and also class differentiation, 'female subjects remain associated with maternal attachments and private spaces' (*ibid.*: 158). Indeed, they tend to occupy an ambiguous status in relation to national communities in Latin America. On the one hand they 'enjoy' symbolic importance emblematized in *marianismo*, yet on the other they are consigned to the realm of the *casa* (home). In that respect they are simultaneously 'at both the centre and at the margins of the national imagined community' (*ibid.*: 159): venerated as icons, yet disempowered in the public realm (*calle*).

However, as Radcliffe and Westwood (1996) and Waylen (1992, 1996) among others have shown, women in Latin America have proved adept as 'mothers of political invention' and imagining in both *status quo* and oppositional movements. They have, in effect, created 'opportunity spaces' that 'can be used to alter the existing pattern of gender relations' (Waylen 1996: 16), whether defining these spaces in terms of 'practical' or 'strategic' interests (Molyneux 1985). Women are, thus, not simply hapless victims in even the most seemingly inclement of patriarchal contexts, a point made equally strenuously by Afshar (1996) and Tohidi (1991, 1994) in relation to Iran, and Abdo (1994) in the case of the Palestinian struggle.

This capacity for self-empowerment is evident from the following two examples, each of which meshes both practical and strategic interests. Early in 1996 with the peace threatening to unravel in the wake of the IRA's breach of its ceasefire, a number of women in Northern Ireland took the strategic decision to contest the election to a new 'Forum', empowered to delegate representatives to the planned peace talks. This decision was only taken after the region's major political parties had failed to respond to requests from a variety of women's groups to gender-proof their candidate selection procedures, and in the light of the failure of the British Government to introduce such a requirement for the purpose of the election. Following a series of hastily convened meetings among women already active in a wide variety of community and cross-community organizations, a 'Northern Ireland Women's Coalition' emerged committed to:

Working for a solution
Offering inclusion
Making women heard
Equity for all
New thinking

Within six weeks the Coalition's candidates, all of whom were women, were urging voters to 'Wave goodbye to the dinosaurs' in order to promote dialogue, accommodation and compromise and thereby maintain the peace. This was accomplished with some effect as they succeeded in getting two of their candidates elected and thus were able to participate in the ensuing talks process.

Another instance of self-empowered imagining can be drawn from Iran. In 1995 its parliament rejected a proposal to establish a committee concerned with women's issues. This spurred feminists to renew their attempts to liberalize the regime, a campaign encouraged by the success of Faiza Hashemi Rafsanjani who came second in the country's 1996 parliamentary elections. Interviewed in *Zanan* (*Women*) magazine she is reported to have said that 'Women should now be getting to the higher levels, including the executive level, the presidency. There is no religious bar to this, for Islam only says women cannot be judges' (Evans 1996).

Rejecting cosmetics and clothed in a black *chador*, Faiza seems an unlikely reforming figure. A possible presidential candidate, she has endorsed the right of women to wear colours other than the officially sanctioned black, brown, grey and blue and has also supported the proposition that women be allowed to ride bicycles and motor cycles, outraging more conservative clerical elements as a result. Such an agenda may seem small beer but nevertheless does indicate the preparedness of some women to step out of the long shadow cast by patriarchy – although in Faiza's case, she is aided by the fact that her father is the current Iranian president.

In Latin America the readiness of women to devise strategies of self-empowerment and to exercise their own imaginations is documented by Radcliffe and Westwood:

As women's sphere of activities and their social interactions changed during periods of economic crisis and political repression, so the ways that they imagined themselves – and the ways in which others imagined them – were subtly yet powerfully transformed. No longer were women simply domestic, maternal figures [with] . . . no wider community [but] active and majority participants demanding changes to . . . gender relations.

(Radcliffe and Westwood *op. cit.*: 159)

Mohanty (1991: 4) in mapping 'third world' feminism also appropriates the concept of 'imagined communities' in an inventive way, likening them to 'communities of resistance', whose creative power resides in their potential to form political alliances opposed to male domination. Such imaginings and their related empowerment strategies (see Bystydzienski (ed.) 1992) represent a counter-culture among women, inspired perhaps by sheer practical necessity and/or the recognition that 'all ethnic identities are historical creations' (Comaroff *op. cit.*: 247).

An awareness that 'all identities are not "things" but relations: that their content is wrought in the particularities of their ongoing historical construction' (*ibid.*), creates both the opportunity and the motive for women to engage in projects designed to remake identities in their own images. The proposition that 'there cannot be a "theory" of ethnicity or nationalism *per se*, only a theory of history and consciousness capable of elucidating the empowered production of identities' (Comaroff *ibid.*: 249), captures the gist of feminist critiques of nationalism. Its internalization affords the conceptual space within which women can engage in their own imagining, or rather re-imagining, in order to reconstitute their own national identities. Yet, bereft of power and authority in the public realm women cannot act to ensure that such reconstructed identities will become fully embedded in the state. Without public power women will remain 'the subjected territory across which the boundaries of nationhood [are] marked out [and not] active participants in the construction of nations' (Hall *et al.* 1993b: 162).

NATIONALISM AND FORGETTING

Mosse's analysis of the alliance between nationalism and bourgeois respectability confirms this proposition. Moral renewal, religious revivalism, romanticism and the promotion of heterosexual orthodoxies were, he insists (1985: 16ff), the accompaniment to the stoking of national consciousness in England, Germany, France and Italy:

> Nationalism and respectability assigned everyone his place in life, man and woman. . . . Alongside the idealization of masculinity as the foundation of the nation and society, woman . . . was at the same time idealized as the guardian of morality and of public and private order. The roles assigned to her were conceived of as passive rather than active . . . guardian, protector and mother. . . . Woman as a national symbol was the guardian of the continuity and immutability of the nation, the embodiment of its respectability.

Nationalism's 'special affinity for male society' allied to 'the concept of respectability' legitimated men's control of women. Mosse's analysis is echoed by Parker *et al.*. (1992: 6) who contend that nationalism can be abbreviated as a 'virile fraternity . . . which favors (*sic.*) a distinctly homosocial form of bonding', a perception also shared by Anderson (1983) who conceived of the nation in terms of a horizontal and *brotherly* comradeship.

Enloe (1989: 54), reflecting on the linkage between nationalism and masculinity, senses its significance by noting the ideological weight men assign to the dress and sexual purity of women:

> [It is] because they see women as the community's or the nation's most valuable *possessions*; the principal *vehicles* for transmitting the whole nation's values from one generation to the next; *bearers* of the community's future generations – crudely, nationalist wombs; the members of the community most *vulnerable* to defilement and exploitation by oppressive alien rulers; and most susceptible to *assimilation* and cooption by insidious outsiders (Enloe's emphases).

Failure to address such patriarchal orthodoxies results in women losing the struggle for common and equal rights once a nation-state is established. This is why Bystydzienski (1992: 10) places the onus on women to ensure that their claims are entrenched in the agendas of nationalist movements: 'unless women themselves question and organize and press for change within nationalist movements, they are not likely to achieve recognition'. Taken too far, however, this implies that women are the authors of their own fates, which appears to place undue stress on agency and not enough on structure. Pushing against the grain of patriarchy within a nationalist movement requires not just a feminist consciousness, but power.

CONCLUSION

Women can and do participate in ethnic and national processes in a number of ways, as Yuval-Davis and Anthias (1989) make clear: as biological reproducers of the ethnic community; as reproducers of the boundaries of ethnic or national groups; as key actors in the transmission of the community's values; as markers of ethnic or national distinctiveness; and as active participants in national struggles. But even where women have been active as warriors in such struggles they invariably are left holding the wrong end of the citizenship stick, which is itself 'gendered and racialised' (Anthias and Yuval-Davis, 1993: 127). Differences of class, status and ethnicity exert varying influences upon discrete categories of women, not least in relation to the labour market (see Moghadam 1994c).

The intermeshing of sexism and racism is, as Anthias and Yuval-Davis stress, of particular relevance for ethnic minority women (see also Sahgal and Yuval-Davis 1992). Lying beyond the nation's boundaries of identity they possess only limited citizenship rights, leaving them exposed to exploitation in the employment process. The status of female migrant workers in 'Fortress Europe' or of Filipino 'domestics' in the Middle or Far East are instructive examples. Pettman (1996) has developed this aspect of gendered disadvantage in her discussion of the 'international political economy of sex' which appears in a variety of guises, including institutionalized prostitution around military bases, 'sex tourism', domestic service, and the market in mail-order brides.

On balance the relationship between women and nationalism can be likened to an unhappy marriage, or at least one that has not yet been joyfully consummated. This may seem a harsh judgement, partly because nationalism is itself a capacious doctrine and one normally found in association with other secular or religious belief systems. Yet as Pettman (*ibid.*: 62) argues, whether nationalism is understood to be progressive or reactionary, liberal or illiberal, racist or multi-cultural, democratic or undemocratic:

> [N]ationality and citizenship, like race and ethnicity, are unstable categories and contested identities. They are all gendered identities and the construction of 'women', inside and outside their borders, are part of the processes of identity formation.

However, it is the very contestability and instability of these categories that create the scope for change. Armed with a feminist consciousness and enjoying access to political power women can mobilize in favour of the legitimation of their own *identities of nationality*. This bespeaks genuine cultural pluralism not uniformity, a clear alternative to the adherence to *a nationalist identity*, the form and content of which they have played little part in constituting (Yuval-Davis 1994). Such a strategy describes a culture of resistance. Freed from the snares of nationalism set by past male-formed imaginings, it implies that plural identities of nationality can take wing and begin to forge a post-nationalist citizenship (Geoghegan 1994) that validates differences of *inter alia* ethnicity, class and gender.

LAYOUT OF THE BOOK

The latter remark may seem unduly sanguine in the light of the experiences confronting women which are recounted by the contributors to this book. In her revision of an earlier article Nira Yuval-Davis surveys and interrogates the different dimensions of ethnic and nationalist projects and their interaction with various aspects of gender relations. In so doing she critically examines the notion of a 'universal citizenship' and the ways in which women in differing cultural contexts have been excluded from what has been loosely termed 'the community of citizens'.

Such exclusion rests, as she observes, on the dualistic nature of women's citizenship: on the one hand seemingly sharing in the more general rights of citizenship while simultaneously being the subject of particularistic laws and customs which constrain their freedoms. Indeed, as she carefully explains, within ethnically diverse or multi-cultural societies those constraints are acutely felt by women from various communities who are pressurized to embody 'the true "essence" of their collectivity's culture and religion'. But, as she also points out, women are themselves complicit in recycling the symbolic, biological and political roles allocated to them and are not simply the hapless victims of nationalist and ethnic projects. Though Nira essays a still existing gulf of understanding among women both within and between the more and less developed worlds, she also sounds an optimistic note. She observes that feminists and activists in each 'world' are beginning to bridge that rift through new networks of solidarity and, perhaps ironically, by pursuit of a military career, thereby demystifying and effectively emasculating the conduct of fighting nationalist wars.

The influence of Nira's ideas and those of her sometime collaborator Floya Anthias, are evident in Elisabeth Porter's discussion of diversity and commonality in Northern Ireland. Sparked by the emergence and impact of the 'Women's Coalition' in 1996, she links recent political developments in the province to current concerns within feminist discourse with identity politics. The uncertainties and instability of Northern Ireland's deeply divided society are perceived by Elisabeth to be no bar to – indeed provide the spur for – cross-community action by women seeking to reconcile difference with a wider unity through the pursuit of a pluralist and inclusive agenda. While the pull of the past is apparent in the primordialism of Northern Ireland's contending nationalisms, her discussion exemplifies that the task of feminist re-imagining can be effective, even within the stubborn context of an armed patriarchy mired in ethnic conflict.

Northern Ireland's constitutional future is, as yet, undecided. At times it seems poised on the brink of change, at others immutable. Yet, as in South Africa (as Sheila Meintjes shows) many women are determined to ensure that the process of transition is fully inclusive. The role of coalition politics among women in South Africa and their determined efforts to influence the terms of the political settlement are recounted by Sheila in her discussion of the campaign for the 'Women's Charter for Effective Equality'. As she states, the post-apartheid coalition 'stands out as an extraordinary anomaly' in a society riven by ethnic, class and gender cleavages and within which there remains 'a patchwork quilt of patriarchies'. But she also sounds a cautionary note in documenting both the backlash against women that has occurred since the transition of the regime and the unravelling of coalescent politics among women now that the constitution-making phase of South Africa's recent past has been concluded.

Caution, and dismay, is even more apparent in Rosalind Marsh's discussion of women in the former Soviet Union and contemporary Russia. Crisis-ridden and exhibiting manifold divisions, Russia since the collapse of communism has witnessed the recrudescence of an always barely concealed patriarchy. Sensitive to the enormous differences that separate 'post-Soviet women' (itself a contestable concept), Rosalind adumbrates the limits to self-actualization by women in the midst of the revival of nationalisms and chronic economic dislocation. She also conveys a clear sense in which the proponents of feminist ideas are swimming against a tide of female essentialism that is welcomed by many, if not most, women.

Complementing Rosalind's chapter, that by Tanja Rener and Mirjana Ule on gender and nationalism in post-socialist societies offers a broader sweep of the costs to women of political transition in the former Yugoslavia and other Eastern bloc states. The 'redelegation' of women into the private sphere of home and family is perceived by Tanja and Mirjana to be the product of the failure to comprehend the meaning of democracy within the Balkans, not least within 'the left'. One result has been the attempt to 'reprivatize' women through an assault on their reproductive and employment rights. Though they catalogue a successful campaign of resistance by Slovenian feminists against state-led attempts to prohibit abortion, the common emphasis by regimes in Eastern Europe on body politics offers compelling evidence of the resilient attachment among nationalists to the primacy of women's role as biological reproducers of 'the nation'.

The limited 'space' afforded to women and feminists in Eastern Europe seems positively capacious when compared to that in the Yemen, Lebanon and Malaysia, the three remaining states included in this book. Maxine Molyneux's discussion of Yemen is an especially interesting case. Formerly two separate states, in 1990 the more religiously conservative Yemen Arab Republic (North Yemen) and the more secular People's Democratic Republic of Yemen (South Yemen) agreed to embark on a process of unification, which broke down in 1994 when a civil war erupted. The resulting enforced 'unification' process has had profound effects upon women as the *shari'a* based legal system of the north came to prevail in the field of family law. Maxine documents this process and the ensuing plight of women who have become increasingly powerless in the process of transition to the new regime.

Ethnic conflict has also been the recent fate of Lebanon, the focus of Kirsten Schulze's chapter. Like Maxine, she concludes that the experience of civil war in a society characterized by a mosaic of ethnic identities has been detrimental to women, reinforcing the already male-dominated structures of the conflicting communities. Though recognizing the mediating effects of religion and class upon women in Lebanon, Kirsten notes that both Muslim and Christian women are defined by patriarchal cultural norms that were reinforced by the hostilities of 1975–90. Despite their active involvement during the conflict, Lebanese women – irrespective of their clan loyalties or religious and ideological beliefs – have experienced continuing marginalization in the public realm, buttressed by the influence of the patriarchal Syrian regime.

The ending of the civil war has, though, witnessed the increased entry of Lebanese women into the labour market and a sustained and high level of educational attainment among them – though the levels of achievement are not matched by access to decision-making positions. In Malaysia, the focus of Norani Othman's chapter, the rapid modernization of the economy has posed singular difficulties for women given the concurrent process of Islamization. The reconciliation of the need for female labour to accomplish economic development, with the rejuvenation of Islam, creates tensions and contradictions within the country and, as Norani notes, leads to the neglect of issues affecting non-Muslim women. The latter, however, have been spared the fate of Muslim women who have become a site of contestation between the more fundamentalist exponents of Islam and the existing regime in the pursuit of Islamic modernity.

Besides exploring the terms and nature of the transitions experienced in each of the countries, the contributors also address the role of feminists and feminisms in these changed and changing contexts. Even in the more ethnically divided of these societies there is evidence of feminists and other women joining in a common cause to entrench the rights of their female populations. However, as Robert Miller explains, this is invariably a rearguard action as neo-nationalists revert to gender stereotypes, resurrecting or reinforcing the division between male-dominated public spaces and the private spaces defined as women's domain. If there is a compelling lesson from this collection it is that even if women in general, and feminists in particular, are well integrated into the institutions pressing for transition, the persistence of ethnic conflict and the primacy of nationalism tends to relegate them to the margins of change. The onus remains on women to redefine and re-imagine what nationalism can mean.

BIBLIOGRAPHY

Abdo, N. (1994) 'Nationalism and Feminism: Palestinian Women and the *Intifada* – No Going Back' in V. Moghadam (ed.) *Gender and National Identity: Women and Politics in Muslim Societies*, London: Zed Books, 148–170.

Adams, M.L. (1989) 'There's No Place Like Home: On the Place of Identity in Feminist Politics', *Feminist Review* 31, Spring 1989, 22–33.

Afshar, H. (ed.) (1993) *Women in the Middle East*, London: Macmillan.

—— (1996) *Women and Politics in the Third World*, London: Routledge.

Allen, S. (1994) 'Race, Ethnicity and Nationality: Some Questions of Identity' in H. Afshar and M. Maynard (eds) *The Dynamics of 'Race' and Gender: Some Feminist Interventions*, London: Taylor and Francis, 85–105.

Anderson, B. (1983) *Imagined Communities: Reflections on the Origin and Spread of Nationalism*, London: Verso.

Anthias, F. and Yuval-Davis, N. (1993) *Racialized Boundaries*, London: Routledge.

Azari F. (1986), 'Islam's Appeal to Women in Iran: Illusion and Reality' in F. Azari (ed.) *Women of Iran: The Conflict with Fundamentalist Islam*, London: Ithaca Press, 1–71.

Bridger, S., Kay R., and Pinnick K. (1996) *No More Heroines? Russia, Women and the Market*, London: Routledge.

Bystydzienski, J. M. (ed.) (1992) *Women Transforming Politics: Worldwide Strategies for Empowerment*, Bloomington: Indiana University Press.

Chazan, N. (1989), 'Gender Equality? Not in a War Zone!', *Israeli Democracy* Summer 1989, 4–7.

Cherifati-Merabtine, D. (1994), 'Algeria at a Crossroads: National Liberation, Islamization and Women' translated by Farida Madjoub in V. Moghadam (ed.) *Gender and National Identity: Women and Politics in Muslim Societies*, London: Zed Books, 40–62.

Comaroff, J. L. (1995) 'Ethnicity, Nationalism and the Politics of Difference in an Age of Revolution' in J. L. Comaroff and P. C. Stern (eds) *Perspectives on Nationalism and War*, London: Gordon and Breach, 243–276.

Drakulic, S. (1993) 'Women and the New Democracy in the Former Yugoslavia' in N. Funk and M. Mueller (eds) *Gender Politics and Post-Communism: Reflections from Eastern Europe and the Former Soviet Union*, London: Routledge, 123–130.

Enloe, C. (1989) *Bananas, Beaches and Bases: Making Feminist Sense of International Politics*, London: Pandora.

—— (1993) *The Morning After: Sexual Politics at the End of the Cold War*, London: University of California Press.

Evans, K. (1996) 'Feminists Challenge the Mullahs', *The Guardian* 20 May.

Funk, N. and Mueller M. (eds) (1993) *Gender Politics and Post-Communism: Reflections from Eastern Europe and the Former Soviet Union*, London: Routledge.

Geoghegan, V. (1994) 'Socialism, National Identities and Post-Nationalist Citizenship', *Irish Political Studies* 9: 61–80.

Glavanis-Grantham, K. (1996) 'The Women's Movement, Feminism and the National Struggle in Palestine: Unresolved Contradictions' in H. Afshar (ed.) *Women and Politics in the Third World*, London: Routledge, 171–185.

Gorbachev, M. (1988) *Perestroika*, London: Fontana.

Hall, C. (1993a) 'Gender, Nationalisms and National Identities', *Feminist Review* 44: 97–103.

Hall, C., Lewis J., McClelland K., and Rendall J. (1993b) 'Introduction', *Gender and History* 5, 2: 159–164.

Helie-Lucas, M.-H. (1993) 'Women's Struggles and Strategies in the Rise of Fundamentalism in the Muslim World: From Entryism to Internationalism' in H. Afshar (ed.) *Women in the Middle East*, London: Macmillan, 206–241.

—— (1994) 'The Preferential Symbol for Islamic Identity: Women in Muslim Personal Laws', in V. Moghadam (ed.) *Identity Politics and Women: Cultural Reassertions and Feminisms in International Perspective*, Oxford: Westview Press, 391–407.

Holt, M. (1996) 'Palestinian Women and the Intifada: an Exploration of Images and Realities' in H. Afshar (ed.) *Women and Politics in the Third World*, London: Routledge, 186–203.

Horowitz, D. L. (1985) *Ethnic Groups in Conflict*, London: University of California Press.

—— (1994) 'Democracy in Divided Societies' in L. Diamond and M. F. Plattner (eds) *Nationalism, Ethnic Conflict and Democracy*, London: Johns Hopkins University Press, 35–55.

Jayawardena, K. (1986) *Feminism and Nationalism in the Third World*, London: Zed Books.

Kandiyoti, D. (1988) 'Bargaining With Patriarchy', *Gender and Society* 2, 3: 274–290.

Klatch, R. (1994), 'Women of the New Right in the United States: Family, Feminism, and Politics', in V. Moghadam (ed.) *Identity Politics and Women: Cultural Reassertions and Feminisms in International Perspective*, Oxford: Westview Press, 367–388.

McClintock, A. (1993) 'Family Feuds: Gender, Nationalism and the Family', *Feminist Review* 44: 61–80.

McKinley, J. (1995) 'Eritrea's Women Fighters Long for Equality of War', *The Guardian* 6 May.

McWilliams, M. (1995) 'Struggling for Peace and Justice: Reflections on Women's Activism in Northern Ireland', *Journal of Women's History*, 6, 4, and 7, 1: 13–39.

Maynard, M. (1994) '"Race", Gender and the Concept of "Difference" in Feminist Thought' in H. Afshar and M. Maynard (eds) *The Dynamics of 'Race' and Gender: Some Feminist Interventions*, London: Taylor and Francis.

Milič, A. (1993) 'Women and Nationalism in the Former Yugoslavia' in N. Funk and M. Mueller (eds) *Gender Politics and Post-Communism: Reflections from Eastern Europe and the Former Soviet Union*, London: Routledge, 109–122.

Mir-Hosseini, Z. (1993) 'Women, Marriage and the Law in Post-Revolutionary Iran' in H. Afshar (ed.) *Women in the Middle East*, London: Macmillan, 59–84.

—— (1996) 'Women and Politics in Post-Khomeini Iran: Divorce, Veiling and Emerging Feminist Voices' in H. Afshar (ed.) *Women and Politics in the Third World*, London: Routledge, 142–170.

Moghadam, V. (1993) *Modernizing Women: Gender and Social Change in the Middle East*, London: Lynne Reiner.

—— (1994a) *Identity Politics and Women: Cultural Reassertions and Feminisms in International Perspective*, Oxford: Westview Press.

—— (1994b) *Gender and National Identity: Women and Politics in Muslim Societies*, London: Zed Books.

—— (1994c) 'Women in Societies', *International Social Science Journal*, 139: 95–115.

Mohanty, C. T. (1991) 'Introduction: Cartographies of Struggle: Third World Women and the Politics of Feminism' in C. T. Mohanty, A. Russo and L. Torres (eds) *Third World Women and the Politics of Feminism*, Bloomington: Indiana University Press, 1–47.

Molyneux, M. (1985) 'Mobilization without Emancipation? Women's Interest, the State and Revolution in Nicaragua', *Feminist Studies* 11, 2: 227–254.

Mosse, G. L. (1985) *Nationalism and Sexuality: Respectability and Abnormal Sexuality in Modern Europe*, New York: Howard Fertig.

Najjar, O. A. (1992) 'Between Nationalism and Feminism: The Palestinian Answer' in J. M. Bystydzienski (ed.) *Women Transforming Politics: Worldwide Strategies for Empowerment*, Bloomington: Indiana University Press, 143–161.

Norval, A. J. (1993) 'Minoritarian Politics and the Pluralisation of Democracy', *Filozofski Vestnik, Acta Philosophica* 2: 121–139.

Parker, A., Russo, M., Sommer D., and Yaeger, P. (eds) (1992) *Nationalisms and Sexualities*, London: Routledge.

Pettman, J. J. (1996) *Worlding Women: A Feminist International Politics*, London: Routledge.

Pridham, G. (1993) 'Political Parties and Their Strategies in the Transition from Authoritarian Rule: The Comparative Perspective' in G. Wightman (ed.) *Party Formation in East-Central Europe*, Aldershot: Edward Elgar, 1–28.

Racioppi, L. and O'Sullivan See, K. (1995), 'Nationalism Engendered: A Critique of Approaches to Nationalism', Conference Paper, Annual Meeting of the International Studies Association, Chicago.

Radcliffe, S. and Westwood S. (1996) *Remaking the Nation: Place, Identity and Politics in Latin America*, London: Routledge.

Rai, S., Pilkington H., and Phizacklea, A. (eds) (1992) *Women in the Face of Change: The Soviet Union, Eastern Europe and China*, London: Routledge.

Regulska, J. (1992), 'Women and Power in Poland: Hopes or Reality?' in J. M. Bystydzienski (ed.) *Women Transforming Politics: Worldwide Strategies for Empowerment*, Bloomington: Indiana University Press, 175–191.

Sahgal, G. and Yuval-Davis, N. (1992) 'Introduction: Fundamentalism, Multiculturalism and Women in Britain' in G. Sahgal and N. Yuval-Davis (eds) *Refusing Holy Orders: Women and Fundamentalism*, London: Virago.

Sharoni, S. (1996) 'Gender and the Israeli–Palestinian Accord: Feminist Approaches to International Politics' in D. Kandiyoti (ed.) *Gendering the Middle East*, London: I. B. Tauris, 107–126.

Smith, A. (1986) *The Ethnic Origins of Nations*, Oxford: Blackwell.

—— (1991) *National Identity*, London: Penguin.

Stacey, J. (1993), 'Untangling Feminist Theory' in D. Richardson and V. Robinson (eds) *Introducing Women's Studies*, London: Macmillan, 49–73.

Tohidi, N. (1991) 'Gender and Islamic Fundamentalism: Feminist Politics in Iran', in C. T. Mohanty, A. Russo and L. Torres (eds) *Third World Women and the Politics of Feminism*, Bloomington, Indiana University Press, 251–267.

—— (1994) 'Modernity, Islamization, and women in Iran' in V. Moghadam (ed.) *Gender and National Identity: Women and Politics in Muslim Societies*, London: Zed Books, 110–147.

Ward, M. (1995) *In Their Own Voice: Women and Irish Nationalism*, Dublin: Attic Press.

Waylen, G. (1992), 'Rethinking Women's Political Participation and Protest: Chile 1970–1990', *Political Studies*, 40, 2: 299–314.

—— (1996) 'Analysing Women in the Politics of the Third World' in H. Afshar (ed.) *Women and Politics in the Third World*, London: Routledge, 7–24.

Woolf, V. (1993) [1938] *A Room of Her Own and Three Guineas*, M. Barrett (ed.), London: Penguin.

Young, I. M. (1990) *Justice and the Politics of Difference*, Princeton NJ: Princeton University Press.

Yuval-Davis, N. (1994) 'Identity Politics and Women's Ethnicity' in V. Moghadam (ed.) *Identity Politics and Women: Cultural Reassertions and Feminisms in International Perspective*, Oxford: Westview Press, 408–424.

Yuval-Davis, N. and Anthias F. (eds) (1989) *Woman-Nation-State*, London: Macmillan.

Zimmerman, B. (1985) 'The Politics of Transliteration: Lesbian Personal Narratives' in E. B. Freedman (ed.) *The Lesbian Issue: Essays from Signs*, Chicago: University of Chicago Press.

2 Gender and nation[1]

Nira Yuval-Davis

INTRODUCTION

The purpose of this chapter is to outline some of the main dimensions in which gender relations are crucial in understanding and analysing the phenomena of nations and of nationalism. Most of the hegemonic theorizations about nations and nationalism (e.g. Gellner 1983; Hobsbawm 1990; Kedourie 1993 (1960); Smith 1986, 1995), even including, sometimes, those written by women (e.g. Greenfeld 1992), have ignored gender relations as irrelevant. This is most remarkable because a major school of nationalism scholars, the 'primordialists' (Geertz 1963; Shils 1957; Van der Berghe 1979), have seen in nations a natural and universal phenomenon which is an 'automatic' extension of kinship relations.

And yet, when discussing issues of national 'production' or 'reproduction', the literature on nationalism does not usually relate to women. Instead, it relates to state bureaucrats or intellectuals. Materialist analyses, such as those by Amin (1978) and Zubaida (1989), have given primary importance to state bureaucracy and other state apparatuses in establishing and reproducing national (as well as ethnic) ideologies and boundaries. Although national and ethnic divisions also operate within the civil society, it is the differential access of different collectivities to the state which dictates the nature of the hegemonic national ethos in the society.

Other theorists of nationalism and the sociology of knowledge, such as Smith (1986) and Gellner (1983), have stressed the particular importance intellectuals have had in the creation and reproduction of nationalist ideologies, especially those of oppressed collectivities. Being excluded from the hegemonic intelligentsia and from open access to the state apparatus, these intellectuals 'rediscover' 'collective memories', transform popular oral traditions and languages into written ones, and portray a 'national golden age' in the far – mythical or historical – past, whose reconstitution becomes the basis for nationalist aspirations. However, it is women – and not (just?) the bureaucracy and intelligentsia who reproduce nations – biologically, culturally and symbolically. Why, then, are women usually 'hidden' in the various theorizations of the nationalist phenomena?

The classical theories of 'the social contract' which are widely influential and have laid the foundation for common sense understanding of western social and political order have been examined by Carol Pateman (1988). These theories divide the sphere of civil society into the public and private domains. Women (and the family) are located in the private domain, which is not seen as politically relevant. Pateman and other feminists have challenged the validity of this model and the public/private divide even within its own assumptions, and claim that the public realm cannot be fully understood in the absence of the private sphere, and, similarly, the meaning of the original contract is misinterpreted without both mutually dependent halves of the story. Civil freedom depends on patriarchal right (Pateman 1988: 4). As nationalism and nations have usually been discussed as part of the public political sphere, the exclusion of women from that arena has affected their exclusion from that discourse as well.

Following Pateman, Rebecca Grant (1991) has an interesting explanation of why women were located outside the relevant political domain. She claims that the foundation theories of both Hobbes and Rousseau portray the transition from the imagined state of nature into orderly society exclusively on what they both assume to be natural male characteristics – the aggressive nature of men in Hobbes, and the capacity for reason in men in Rousseau. Women, as women, are not part of this process and are therefore excluded from the 'social' and remain close to 'nature'. Later theories followed these assumptions as given.

A welcome exception in this respect has been the work of George L. Mosse (1985; see also the discussion in the introduction to Parker *et al.* 1992). He linked the rise of bourgeois family morality to the rise of nationalism in Europe at the end of the eighteenth century. In a sense Mosse follows the anthropological tradition of Lévi-Strauss (1968) which has been more aware of the central links between gender relations and social cohesion. Lévi-Strauss has seen the exchange of women as the original mechanism for creating social solidarity among men of different kinship units as the basis for constructing larger collectivities. It is not the exchange of women but their control (or subordination, to use Pateman's terminology) which is so often at the base of the social order – both in terms of power relations within and outside the family and in terms of property relations and the paternal genealogy of children (Yuval-Davis 1980). Nevertheless, it would have been greatly beneficial for political theory to have been more open to anthropological literature rather than continuing to count, even unintentionally, on 'man's pre-contractual natural state' which has never been more than a convenient fiction.

My general approach to the phenomena of nations and nationalism has been elaborated elsewhere (Anthias and Yuval-Davis 1992; Yuval-Davis 1987b; but especially in Yuval-Davis 1997). Basically, as both Smith (1986) and Zubaida (1989) would agree (in spite of the debate between them about cause and effect) there is an inherent connection between the ethnic and national projects. While it is important to look at the historical specificity of the construction of collectivities, there is no inherent difference (although sometimes there is a difference in scale) between ethnic and national collectivities: they are both the Andersonian 'imagined communities' (Anderson 1983).

Focusing on the myth of common ethnic origins of nations, however, is insufficient to explain the nationalist phenomenon and what Kitching (1985) has called the 'nationalist passion'. A vital complementary element is the myth of 'common destiny' which was theorized by Otto Bauer (1940; see also Nimni 1991; Yuval-Davis 1987). People construct themselves as members of national collectivities not just because they, and their forefathers (and mothers) have shared a past, but also because they believe their futures are interdependent. It can explain the subjective sense of commitment of people into collectivities and nations, such as in settler societies or in post-colonial states, in which there is no shared myth of common origin (Stasiulis and Yuval-Davis 1995) and can also explain individual and communal assimilations in other nations. At the same time it can also explain the dynamic nature of any national collectivity and the perpetual processes of reconstruction of boundaries which take place in them, via immigration, naturalization, conversion and other similar social and political processes (Bhabha 1990).

While this process of continuous reconstruction of boundaries usually takes place, it is important not to see nationalism as an inherently inclusive endeavour. Although not all nationalist ideologies are equally racist, processes of exclusion and inclusion are in operation wherever a delineation of boundaries takes place – as is the case with every ethnic and national collectivity – and many, if not most, include some elements of racist exclusions in their symbolic orders.

The specificity of the nationalist project and discourse is the claim for a separate political representation for the collectivity. This often – but not always – takes the form of a claim for a separate state. The base of this claim, however, can vary in the different historical cases. There have been many attempts to classify different types of nationalist projects, on both moral and on sociological grounds (Smith 1971; Snyder 1968). However, attempting to classify all different states and societies according to any abstract category is an ahistorical, impossible and misleading mission. Instead of attempting to 'fit' concrete historical cases into ideal-type categories of such typologies, they can be used to signify different dimensions of nationalist ideologies and projects, which would play more or less central roles in different concrete historical cases, and be promoted by different members of the same national collectivities at any given time. The dimensions I am using for this purpose have been constructed by a combination of Anthony Smith's influential typology (1971, 1986) which differentiates between the 'ethnic-genealogical' nationalist movement and the 'civic-territorial' one, and the German typology (Stolke 1987) which differentiates between *Staatnation* (civic nationalism) and *Kulturnation* (cultural nationalism). The combination is necessary, as culture and origin should not be conflated when discussing nationalist projects.

I shall differentiate, therefore, between the dimensions of *Staatnation*, *Kulturnation* and *Volknation*: in other words, between nationalist ideologies which focus on citizenship of specific states (in specific territories); those which focus on specific cultures (or religions); and those which are constructed around the specific origin of the people (or their 'race').

Different aspects of gender relations play an important role in each of these dimensions of nationalist projects and are crucial for any valid theorization of them. I shall present each of them separately, and mention some of the main issues that have to be looked at in this context.

GENDER RELATIONS, CITIZENSHIP AND MEMBERSHIP IN THE NATIONAL COLLECTIVITY

The 'universalistic' nature of citizenship which emanates from the traditional liberal and social democratic discourses is very deceptive (Balibar 1990; Yeatman 1992; Yuval-Davis 1991a, b). As mentioned above, the expression 'nation-state' camouflages the only partial overlap between the boundaries of the hegemonic national collectivity and the settled residents or even citizens of the state. But even beyond this, the integrity and viability of the 'community of citizens' thus defined is very much dependent on clear-cut definitions of who belongs and who does not belong to it – hence continuous fears and debates about immigration as well as systemic exclusions of many who are situated within the boundaries of the state, such as indigenous peoples and other minorities. The exclusions become much clearer if we take into account the three dimensions of citizenship as defined by T. H. Marshall (1950, 1975, 1981) – civil, political, and social.

For the purpose of this discussion the exclusion of women is of particular importance. As mentioned above Carol Pateman (1988) has shown that the whole social philosophy which was at the base of the rise of the notion of state citizenship was constructed in terms of the 'Rights of Man', a social contract based on the 'fraternity of men' (as one of the slogans of the French revolution states – and not incidentally). Ursula Vogel (1989) has also shown that women were not simply latecomers to citizenship rights as in Marshall's evolutionary model of the development of citizenship rights. Their exclusion was part and parcel of the construction of the entitlement of men to democratic participation which 'conferred citizen status not upon individuals as such, but upon men in their capacity as members and representatives of a family (i.e. a group of non-citizens) (Vogel 1989: 2).

Unlike in Marshall's scheme, where political rights followed civil rights, married women have still not been given full civil and legal rights. And, as Vogel points out, the image of the Thatcherite 'Active Citizen' of the late 1980s in Britain, has still been personified in the image of the man as responsible head of his family. The construction by the state of relationships in the private domain, i.e. marriage and the family, is what has determined women's status as citizens within the public domain. In some non-European countries, notably those ruled by Muslim laws, the right of women even to work and travel in the public domain is dependent on formal permission of her 'responsible' male relative (Kandiyoti 1991).

Some have attempted to formulate the recent changes in Eastern and Central Europe in terms of the reconstruction of civil society. By this they mean a presence of a social sphere which is independent of the state. Many Western feminist analyses of the relationships between women and the state have shown this 'independence' to be largely illusory, as it is the state which constructs, and often keeps surveillance of, the private domain, especially of the lower classes (Showstack Sassoon 1987; Wilson 1977). However, in 'third world' societies often there is only partial penetration of the state into civil society, especially in its rural and other peripheral sections. In these cases, gender and other social relations are determined by cultural and religious customs of the national collectivity. This may also happen in 'private domains' of ethnic and national minorities in the state.

However, it is not only in the 'private domain' that gender relations are different in the state. Often the citizenship rights and duties of women from different ethnic and racial groupings vary. They would have different legal positions and entitlements; sometimes they might be under the jurisdiction of different religious courts; they would be under different residential regulations, including rights of re-entry when leaving the country; might or might not be allowed to confer citizenship rights to their children; or – in the case of women migrant workers who had to leave their children behind – may or may not receive child and other welfare benefits as part of their social rights.

With all these differences, there is one characteristic which specifies women's citizenship: that is its dualistic nature. On the one hand women are always included, at least to some extent, in the general body of citizens of the state and its social, political and legal policies; on the other – there is always, at least to a certain extent, a separate body of legislation which relates to them specifically as women. These policies can express different ideological constructions of gender – such as allocating different age categories for women and men to retire; they can discriminate against women – such as in cases when women could be forbidden to vote or be elected for certain public posts; or they might privilege women – such as in cases when they would be granted maternity leave or accorded special 'privileges' in labour legislation.

Marshall's definition of citizenship is one of 'full membership in a community', which encompasses civil, political and social rights and responsibilities. This has led some feminists to think that the only way women could gain full equality would be if they were to share equally in all citizenship responsibilities and duties. This has been the debate especially in relation to women's participation in the military (Enloe 1983; Yuval-Davis, 1985, 1991b, 1997). In many ways this debate is similar to earlier debates on the entry of women into the waged labour market – especially in modern highly technological armies which are professional, rather than based on conscription. As in the civil labour market, the entrance of women to the military has usually resulted in introducing a new arena rather than changing the principle of the sexual division of labour and power. This can change only when men as well as women are defined in a dualistic manner as reproducers as well as producers of the nation – a project which has only begun in a few Western countries and even there generally in a purely symbolic way. Nevertheless, the participation of women in the military can erode one of the most powerful cultural constructions of national collectivities – that of 'womenandchildren' (Enloe 1990) – as the reason men go to war, and there is some evidence that, at least for a while, the active participation of women in the military and in national liberation struggles can empower them socially and economically in new ways (Addis 1994; Konogo 1987; Zerai 1994).

GENDER RELATIONS AND CULTURAL CONSTRUCTIONS OF COLLECTIVITIES

The mythical unity of national 'imagined communities' which divides the world between 'us' and 'them', is maintained and ideologically reproduced by a whole system of what Armstrong (1982) calls symbolic 'border guards', which identify people as members or non-members of a specific collectivity. They are closely linked to specific cultural codes of style of dress and behaviour as well as to more elaborate bodies of customs, literary and artistic modes of production and, of course, language. Gender symbols play a particularly significant role in this.

Women are often the ones who are given the social role of inter-generational transmitters of cultural traditions, customs, songs, cuisine, and, of course, the mother-tongue (*sic.*!). (Anthias and Yuval-Davis 1983; Yuval-Davis and Anthias 1989) The actual behaviour of women can also signify ethnic and cultural boundaries:

Often the distinction between one ethnic group and another is constituted centrally by the sexual behaviour of women. For example, a 'true' Sikh or Cypriot girl should behave in sexually appropriate ways. If she does not then neither she nor her children may be constituted part of the community (Yuval-Davis and Anthias 1989: 10).

The importance of women's culturally 'appropriate behaviour' can gain special significance in 'multi-cultural societies'. A basic problem in the construction of multi-culturalism is the assumption that all members of a specific cultural collectivity are equally committed to that culture. It tends to construct the members of minority collectivities as basically homogeneous, speaking with a unified cultural voice. These cultural voices have to be as distinguished as possible from the majority culture in order to be able to be seen as 'different'; thus, the more traditional and distanced from the majority culture the voice of the 'community representatives' is, the more 'authentic' it would be perceived to be within such a construction (Sahgal and Yuval-Davis 1992).

Therefore, such a construction would have space for neither internal power conflicts and interest difference within the minority collectivity, nor conflicts along the lines of class and gender as well as of politics and culture, for instance. As Yeatman (1992) observes:

> It becomes clear that the liberal conception of the group requires the group to assume an authoritarian character: there has to be a headship of the group which represents its homogeneity of purpose by speaking with the one, authoritative voice. For this to occur, the politics of voice and representation latent within the heterogeneity of perspectives and interests must be suppressed.
>
> (Yeatman 1992: 4)

This liberal construction of group voice, therefore, can in actuality collude with fundamentalist leaderships who claim to represent the true 'essence' of their collectivity's culture and religion, and who have high on their agenda the control of women and their behaviour – as campaigns like the forceful veiling of women by Muslim fundamentalists and the major anti-abortion campaigns by Christian fundamentalists demonstrate.

Women are often required to carry the 'burden of representation', as they are constructed as the symbolic bearers of the collectivity's identity and honour, both personally and collectively. Claudia Koontz (1986: 196) quotes the different mottoes which were given to girls and boys in the Hitler youth movement. For girls it was 'be faithful; be pure; be German'. For boys, 'live faithfully; fight bravely; die laughing'. The national duties of the boys were to live and die for the nation; girls did not need to act – they had to become the national embodiment.

A figure of a woman, often a mother, symbolizes in many cultures the spirit of the collectivity, whether it is Mother Ireland, Mother Russia or Mother India. In the French revolution its symbol was 'La Patrie', a figure of a woman giving birth to a baby; and in Cyprus, a weeping woman refugee on roadside posters was the embodiment of the pain and anger of the Greek Cypriot collectivity after the Turkish invasion. In peasant societies, the dependence of the people on the fertility of 'Mother Earth', has no doubt contributed to this close association between collective territory, collective identity and womanhood. However, women also symbolize the collectivity in other ways. As Cynthia Enloe (1990) has pointed out, it is supposedly for the sake of the 'womenandchildren' that men go to war – the embodiment of the collective 'honour'. Systematic rapes in war are aimed not just – and often not primarily – at the tortured women, but at the enemy collectivity. Women are associated in the collective imagination with children and therefore with the collective, as well as the familial future.

Collectivities are composed, as a general rule, by family units. A central link between the place of women as national reproducers and women's subjugation can be found in the different regulations – customary, religious or legal – which determine the family units within the boundaries of the collectivity, and the ways they come into existence (marriage), end (divorce and widowhood) and what children are considered legitimate members of the family.

The question of legitimacy of children relates to the ideologically constructed boundaries of families and collectivities. But a major part of the control of women as national reproducers relate to her actual biological role as bearer of children.

GENDER RELATIONS AND THE BIOLOGICAL REPRODUCTION OF 'THE NATION'

If membership in the national collectivity depends on being born into it, then those who do not share the myth of common origin are completely excluded. The only way 'outsiders' can conceivably join the national collectivity is by intermarriage. It is no coincidence that those who are preoccupied with the 'purity' of the race are preoccupied also with the sexual relationships between members of different collectivities. Typically, the first (and only) law proposal that Rabbi Kahana, the leader of the Israeli fascist party, Kach, raised in the Israeli Parliament was to forbid sexual relationships between Jews and Arabs. The legal permission of people from different 'races' to have sex and marry was one of the first significant steps that the former South African Government took in its slow but inevitable journey toward the abolition of apartheid.

In different religious and customary laws, the membership of a child in a national collectivity might depend exclusively on the father's membership, the mother's membership, or it might be open for a dual, or voluntary choice membership. The inclusion in the collectivity is far from being only a biological issue. There are always rules and regulations governing the cases in which children born to 'mixed parenthood' would be part of the collectivity and the cases when they would not; about when they would be considered a separate social category, like in South Africa; part of the 'inferior' collectivity, as during slavery; or – although this is rarer – part of the 'superior' collectivity, as was the case in marriages between Spanish settlers and aristocratic Indians in Mexico (Gutierrez 1995). When a man from Ghana a few years ago tried to claim his British origin, stating the patriality clause in the British Immigration Act, arguing that his African grandmother was legally married to his British grandfather, the judge rejected his claim, arguing that at this period no British man would genuinely marry an African woman (WING 1985).

The worry about the quality of the 'stock' has been a major concern in the British empire and its settler societies. The Royal Commission on Population declared in its 1949 report:

British traditions, manners, and ideas in the world have to be borne in mind. Immigration is thus not a desirable means of keeping the population at a replacement level as it would in effect reduce the proportion of home-bred stock in the population.

(Quoted in Riley 1981)

And it was concern for the 'British Race' which Beveridge describes in his famous report as the motivation for establishing the British welfare state system (Beveridge 1942).

The control of women as producers of 'national stocks' start with pre-natal policies. A variety of techniques and technologies, used by various social agencies, exist for controlling rates of birth. These can include allowances for maternity leave and child care facilities for working mothers; availability and encouragement of contraception as a means of family planning; availability and legality of abortions; clinics for infertility treatment and, at a more draconian level, forced usage of contraceptives and sterilization. Encouraging or discouraging women from bearing children is determined, to a great extent, by the specific historical situation of the collectivity, and by no means exists as a *laissez-faire* institution even in the most permissive societies. Notions like 'population explosion'; 'demographic balance' (or 'holocaust' or 'race'); or 'children as a national asset', are expressions of various ideologies which might lead controllers of national reproduction into different population control policies. These policies are very rarely, if at all, applied in a similar manner to all members of the civil society. While class differences often play a major role in this, membership in different racial, ethnic and national collectivities is usually the most important determinant of being subject to differential natal policies. Moreover, such membership can affect differently – but as effectively – women of both hegemonic majorities and subjugated minorities. These policies, however, are not used only by national collectivities who have control over states, but can be used also as a mode of resistance. A common Palestinian saying a few years ago, for instance, was: 'The Israelis beat us at the borders but we beat them in the bedrooms' (Yuval-Davis 1987b).

However, it would be a mistake to see women as passive victims in such 'national/biological warfare', whether pro-natal or anti-natal. Older women would often play important parts in controlling younger women, and all women might be parties to these ideologies, as the active participation of women in various religious fundamentalist and fascist movements can show.

CONCLUSION

As we have seen, women play crucial roles in biological, cultural and political reproductions of national and other collectivities. But more than that, gender relations have proved to be significant in all dimensions of national projects – whether it is the dimension of *Staatnation*, i.e. the gender dimensions of the construction of citizenship; *Kulturnation*, i.e. the gender dimension of the cultural construction of collectivities and their boundaries; or *Volknation*, in which the control of women as biological reproducers has been aimed at controlling the actual size of various majority and minority collectivities.

What is important to remember, however, is that we cannot view women as a homogenous category. Gender divisions interrelate and are intermeshed in concrete social situations with other social divisions such as ethnic, racial, class, age and sexuality. Nationalist projects would be more open to incorporating some groupings of women from certain social collectivities and categories than others, and would establish different policies, as we have seen, towards them.

The relationship between feminist and nationalist movements has been complex (Jayawardena 1986; Rowbotham 1992; Yuval-Davis 1997). Since the rise of 'second wave feminism' in the West during the 1970s and 1980s, there has been a recurrence of non-dialogue between women from the 'first' and 'third' worlds at international conferences, in which the former would call for women's liberation as the primary/only goal of the feminist movement, while the latter would respond that 'as long as our people are not free, there is no sense in discussing women's liberation'. It was a dialogue of the deaf. For Western feminists, as members of a hegemonic collectivity, their membership in the collectivity and its implications for their positionings was often rendered invisible, while 'third world' women acutely experienced being part of a subjugated collectivity and often did not see autonomous space for themselves to organize as feminists. To the extent that the Western feminists did relate to their national collectivities it was usually from an oppositional point of view. Not only did they agree with Virginia Woolf's stricture 'as a woman I have no country', but they were also often involved in anti-government political movements such as the anti-Vietnam war, civil rights and other anti-colonial and leftist movements and, later, in women's peace movements such as at Greenham Common. This created in both sides very different assumptions concerning relationships between individual women and their collectivities – and their governments at the time.

However, things have moved forwards during the last few years. Partly this has been a result of the growing sensitivity of feminist theorists as well as activists to differential positionings among women, as well as the growing recognition by mainstream international agencies of the 'impact of gender'. To a large extent, however, it was due to the growing realization of women in the liberation or post-liberation movements that 'national liberation' usually not only did not guarantee women's rights in the nation but also that women were often confronted with new oppressions in the name of 'custom and tradition'. There has been a growing accumulated body of shared experience and knowledge among women from different countries in the south – much of it came to the fore in the NGO Forum in Beijing, and a growing sense of cross national solidarity. Women, therefore, have been at the forefront of most peace movements across divided societies and national and ethnic conflicts and often organized themselves in international networks of solidarity such as 'Women In Black'. At the same time, more and more women have been entering the professional militaries in the West, in which fighting is constructed not as a citizenship duty but as a professional career.

One way and another, it seems that the old justification of nationalist wars being fought for the sake of the 'womenandchildren' might gradually lose some of its naturalized persuasive powers.

NOTE

1 An earlier version of this chapter appeared in *Ethnic and Racial Studies*, 16: 4, October 1993, and constitutes part of the introduction to my book *Gender and Nation* (Sage 1997).

BIBLIOGRAPHY

Addis, E. (1994) 'Women and the Economic Consequences of Being a Soldier' in E. Addis, V. Russo and L. Sebesta (eds) *Women Soldiers: Images and Realities*, London: Macmillan/St Martin's Press.

Amin, S. (1978) *The Arab Nation*, London: Zed Books.

Anderson, B. (1983) *Imagined Communities*, London: Verso.

Anthias, F. and Yuval-Davis, N. (1983) 'Contextualizing Feminism: Gender, Ethnic and Class Divisions', *Feminist Review* 15: 62–75.

—— (1992) *Racialized Boundaries*, London: Routledge.

Armstrong, J. (1982) *Nations before Nationalism*, Chapel Hill: University of North Carolina Press.

Balibar, E. (1990) 'The Nation Form – History and Ideology', *New Left Review* XIII, 3: 329–361.

Bauer, O. (1940) *The National Question*, Tel Aviv: Hakibutz Haartzi.

Beveridge, W. (1942) *Report on Social Insurance and Allied Services*, London: HMSO.

Bhabha, H. K. (ed.) (1990) *Nation and Narration*, London: Routledge.

Enloe, C. (1983) *Does Khaki Become You? The Militarization of Women's Lives*, London: Pluto Press.

—— (1990) 'Womenandchildren: Making Feminist Sense of the Persian Gulf Crisis', *The Village Voice* 25 September, 19: 2.

Geertz, C. (ed.) (1963) *Old Societies New States*, New York: Free Press.

Gellner, E. R. (1983) *Nations and Nationalism*, Cambridge: Blackwell.

Grant, R. (1991) 'The Sources of Gender Bias in International Relations Theory' in R. Grant and K. Newland (eds) *Gender and International Relations*, Bloomington: Indiana University Press, 8–26.

Greenfeld, L. (1992) *Nationalism: Five Roads to Modernity*, Cambridge, Mass.: Harvard University Press.

Gutierrez, N. (1995) 'Mixing Races for Nation Building: Indian and Immigrant Women in Mexico' in D. Stasiulis and N. Yuval-Davis (eds) *Ethnicity, Race and Class*, London: Sage.

Hobsbawm, E. (1990) *Nations and Nationalism since 1780*, Cambridge: Cambridge University Press.

Jayawardena, K. (1986) *Feminism and Nationalism in the Third World*, London: Zed Press.

Kandiyoti, D. (1991) 'Identity and its Discontents: Women and the Nation', *Millennium*, 20, 3: 429–444.

Kedourie, E. (1993) [1960] *Nationalism*, Cambridge: Blackwell.

Kitching, G. (1985) 'Nationalism: the Instrumental Passion', *Capital and Class*, 25: 98–116.

Konogo, T. (1987) *Squatters and the Roots of the Mau Mau (1905–1963)*, London: Currey.

Koontz, C. (1986), *Mothers of the Fatherland*, London: Jonathan Cape.

Lévi-Strauss, C. (1968) *Structural Anthropology*, London: Allen Lane.

Marshall, T. H. (1950) *Citizenship and Social Class*, Cambridge: Cambridge University Press.

—— (1975) [1965] *Social Policy in the Twentieth Century*, London: Hutchinson.

—— (1981) *The Right To Welfare and Other Essays*, London: Heinemann Educational Books.

Mosse, G. L. (1985) *Nationalism and Sexuality: Middle Class Morality and Sexual Norms in Modern Europe*, Madison: University of Wisconsin Press.

Nimni, E. (1991) *Marxism and Nationalism*, London: Pluto Press.

Parker, A., Russo, M., Sommer, D. and Yaeger, P. (eds) (1992) *Nationalisms and Sexualities*, New York: Routledge.

Pateman, C. (1988) *The Sexual Contract*, Cambridge: Polity Press.

Riley, D. (1981) 'The Free Mothers' *History Workshop Journal*, 59–119.

Rowbotham, S. (1992) *Women In Movement: Feminism and Social Action*, London: Routledge.

Sahgal, G. and Yuval-Davis, N. (eds) (1992) *Refusing Holy Orders: Women and Fundamentalism in Britain*, London: Virago.

Shils, E. (1957) 'Primordial, Personal, Sacred and Civil Ties', *British Journal of Sociology* 7: 113–145.

Showstack Sassoon, A. (ed.) (1987) *Women and the State*, London: Hutchinson.

Smith, A. (1971) *Theories of Nationalism*, London: Duckworth.

—— (1986) *The Ethnic Origins of Nations*, Oxford: Basil Blackwell.

—— (1995) *Nations and Nationalism in a Global Era*, Cambridge: Polity Press.

Snyder, L. (1968) *The New Nationalism*, Ithaca NY: Cornell University Press.

Stasiulis, D. and Yuval-Davis, N. (eds) (1995) *Unsettling Settler Societies: Articulations of Gender, Race, Ethnicity and Class*, London: Sage Publications.

Stolcke, V. (1987) 'The Nature of Nationality', paper presented at the conference on *Women and the State*, Berlin: Wissenschaftsinstitut.

Van den Berghe, P. (1979) *The Ethnic Phenomenon*, New York: Elsevier.

Vogel, U. (1989) 'Is Citizenship Gender Specific?', paper presented at the Political Science Association meeting, April.

Wilson, E. (1977) *Women and the Welfare State*, London: Tavistock.

WING (eds) (1985) *Worlds Apart: Women, Immigration and Nationality Laws*, London: Pluto Press.

Yeatman, A. (1992) 'Minorities and the politics of difference', *Political Theory Newsletter* Canberra, March: 1–11.

Yuval-Davis, N. (1980) 'The Bearers of the Collective: Women and Religious Legislation in Israel', *Feminist Review* 4: 15–27.

—— (1985) 'Front and Rear: the Sexual Division of Labour in the Israeli Army', *Feminist Studies* 11, 3: 649–676.

—— (1987a) 'Marxism and Jewish Nationalism', *History Workshop Journal* 24, Autumn: 219–225.

—— (1987b) 'The Jewish Collectivity and National Reproduction in Israel' in *Khamsin* (ed.) *Women in the Middle East*, London: Zed Books.

—— (1991a) 'The Citizenship Debate: Women, the State and Ethnic Processes, *Feminist Review* 39: 56–68.

—— (1991b) 'The Gendered Gulf War: Women's Citizenship and Modern Warfare' in H. Bresheeth and N. Yuval-Davis (eds) *The Gulf War and the New World Order*, London: Zed Books.

—— (1997) *Gender and Nation*, London: Sage.

Yuval-Davis, N. and Anthias, F. (eds) (1989) *Woman-Nation-State*, Basingstoke: Macmillan.

Zerai, W. (1994) 'Women in the Eritrean Military' an unpublished project for the course Gender and Nation ISS, The Hague.

Zubaida, S. (1989) 'Nations: Old and New; Comments on Anthony D. Smith's, *The Myth of the 'Modern Nation' and the Myths of Nations*, paper presented at the Anthropology Seminar Series, University College, London.

3   Identity, location, plurality
Women, nationalism and Northern Ireland

Elisabeth Porter

INTRODUCTION

The relationships between women, ethnicity and nationalism in Northern Ireland are complex.[1] To explore them, I examine three main themes: identity, location and plurality. First, *competing identities* dominate nationalist discourse. Northern Ireland represents a clash of nationalisms where there is a serious conflict between core sources of shared cultural identity like symbols, myths and aspirations. Cultural, class, ethnic, gender and political identities intersect and require intricate negotiation. Second, women activists in Northern Ireland respond to the *politics of location*. Women's communal activism is a situated politics of everyday life. Third, feminist analyses on ethnicity and nationalism in divided societies include a *politics of plurality*. Such a politics appreciates that common interests on issues of justice, equality and socio-economic matters will be interpreted differently. Despite women's groups in Northern Ireland agreeing over many shared goals, entrenched divisions render it difficult to formulate common political agendas. Developing plural modes of citizenship that incorporate the diverse practices of women's narratives is crucial.

COMPETING IDENTITIES

The topic of nationhood and ethnicity 'approaches the soul of our social and political organisation: that which distinguishes insiders from outsiders, that for which wars and revolutions are fought' (Lerner 1993: 1). The boundaries between insiders and outsiders define citizen and alien, member and stranger. Insiders share culture, language and religion. Outsiders do not share cultural similarities and are excluded. In Northern Ireland the basis of shared belonging or exclusion is the ethnic identity associated with being part of a Protestant or a Catholic community. It is not that all citizens are active church attenders or practise their faith, but that religion provides the basis for the cultural context in which one is raised and the distinctive mindset which that forms.

The Catholic and Protestant communities differ in their common culture, myths of collective origin, history, memory, language, religion, customs and feelings of solidarity. It is intrinsic to national ideology that political organization should represent the interests of particular ethnic groups. The nationalist political claim is that groups with historical myths of common origin, culture and destiny should rule themselves and that political boundaries be coterminous with cultural boundaries (Eriksen 1993: 6). While nationalism is a political identification, at its core lies a cultural claim, viz 'that national movements are motivated by a desire to assume the existence and flourishing of a particular community, culture . . . tradition and language' (Tamir 1995: xiii). The mindset of each community in Northern Ireland perpetuates cultural, political and religious differences between 'Us' and 'Them' ensuring significant barriers in interaction. The conflict is driven by clashes of different identities. My view, developed progressively, is that for there to be any hope for peace and inclusivity in Northern Ireland, a plural acceptance of 'identities of nationality' (Geoghegan 1994) is imperative.

In Northern Ireland, nationalism and ethnicity, politics and culture, religion and identity are tightly meshed. These interlocking facets provide the basis for the conflict which revolves around the 'national question', state boundaries and cultural identity. The conflict is viewed as a clash between Irish nationalists and British unionists but it is multi-layered. Nationalists who view Northern Ireland as a spurious political entity with contested government, control and law enforcement, aspire towards some type of united Ireland, generally come from a Catholic background, and sometimes identify with the more militant republican tradition. They are in a minority position, in the same sense that we talk of women being marginalized, rather than numerically small. Indeed, Catholics make up more than 40 per cent of the population. Unionists support the union of Northern Ireland with Great Britain, generally come from a Protestant background and may be influenced by the paramilitary loyalist tradition. Viewing the conflict in Northern Ireland as one between nationalists and unionists has three main shortcomings: it oversimplifies national identity, it fails to recognize that unionism is also a form of nationalism, and it silences the extent to which nationalism is thoroughly gendered. I use the concept of national identity to explain why the Northern Ireland conflict is a clash of nationalisms, and then attempt to unravel its gendered nature.

Crude or simplistic nationalism views allegiances in narrow frameworks of state, boundary and nationalistic symbols. Narrow frameworks no longer reflect the complex reality of multi-ethnic societies and of citizens whose identification is founded neither on a state nor the elitism of nation-building. Like Sarah Radcliffe and Sallie Westwood (1996) I argue that a sense of *national identity* is more multi-faceted than the doctrine of nationalism, since it 'can exist within subjects (collectively or individually) without there being a process of mobilization around a specific goal' (1996: 16). Furthermore, the struggles to define nationhood and identity, claim an identity individually and express collective sentiments through political projects, are constitutive and constituting of identity.

A survey on national identity showed that 70 per cent of Protestants identified themselves as 'British', while 11 per cent identified as 'Ulster', 15 per cent as 'Northern Irish' and 3 per cent as 'Irish'. In the Catholic community 62 per cent identified as 'Irish', 28 per cent as 'Northern Irish' and 9 per cent as 'British' (Gallagher 1996: 179). Of the 27 per cent of Northern/Irish citizens who identify as 'Irish', and who see the borders established in 1922 as artificial, and would prefer a reunited Ireland,[2] 60 per cent are Catholics (Breen 1996: 34). National identity and ideological allegiance is not clear-cut. A quarter of those who identify as 'British' and 40 per cent who identify as 'Irish' are not willing to describe themselves as either unionists or nationalists (Trew 1996: 145).

National identity is much more than a simplistic clash between the Irish and the British, or between Catholics and Protestants or between nationalists and unionists. Indeed it does not merely reflect diverse ethnicities based on immigration as in most multi-cultural societies. Rather, it is rooted in the colonization of Ulster by Protestants, conflicting views on the legitimacy of the state and its boundaries (Moxon-Browne 1991: 23) and the complex nature of identity.

CLASH OF NATIONALISMS

Hence my focus is on *national identity as a narrative* of what individuals in communities attach meaning to, rather than on the ideology of nationalism. This perspective finds support in Alan Finlayson's argument, *viz* large areas of nationalist activity are depoliticized if we assume only that to be a nationalist means struggling for an independent state. As Finlayson maintains, we need 'a more flexible understanding of nationalism that recognizes it as a way of orienting oneself in the world and of inferring political attitudes from that orientation' (1996: 92). Generally, loyalism, the paramilitary unionist movement, is not regarded as a nationalist movement and its advocates definitely do not call themselves nationalists. Irish republicans desirous of a united Ireland monopolize the term 'nationalist'. To see Irish unification nationalism as the only representation of nationalism fails to recognize that unionism also is a form of nationalism. Indeed a mural in Protestant East Belfast reads, 'The Ulster Conflict Is About Nationality'. Broadening the definition of nationalism allows us to see that communities are made up of different combinations of identification of Irishness, Catholicism, republicanism, and nationalism; Britishness, Protestantism, loyalism, and unionism; as well as cross-overs across the 'traditional' communities; and individuals whose identity is not easily categorized. Viewing the conflict as a clash of nationalisms allows us to examine the multiple constitutive intersections of narrative, gender, identification, belonging and exclusion. Hence I distinguish between *Irish nationalism* and *Unionist nationalism*.[3]

To appreciate contemporary Northern/Irish women's identities and voices, some understanding of history is needed. In the early 1900s, three strands emerge. First, there was a unionist pro-empire position. Second, there was a nationalist anti-imperialist position struggling for an independent Irish state. Third, pacifist feminists from both unionist and Irish nationalist backgrounds challenged state militaristic powers that exploited and excluded women. In putting suffrage first, these women were not merely saying that the vote was more important than national freedom or resolving a European conflict: they articulated a vision of new political and social arrangements opposed to the sexism of nationalist movements north and south and attempted to minimize any divisiveness between unionist and Irish nationalism (Hearne 1992: 2–3).

Such a vision was not shared by unionist women whose first commitment was to the Empire or by Irish nationalists whose revolutionary fervour was directed against the suppression of social, cultural and racial identity. Margaret Ward (1995) argues that in Irish nationalist movements women were drawn in during moments of exceptional political crisis, but were never accepted as equals. The one nationalist organization that was completely independent was *Inghinidhe na hEireann* (Daughters of Erin), formed in 1900 because of women's exclusion from all other groups. It became part of Sinn Féin in 1908, fostering a conscious nationalist culture that built on Ireland's Celtic past, peopled with its goddesses, queens and legendary women. This movement rejected the parliamentary and the suffragette routes, maintaining that with independence from the British the self-reliance gained would ensure that women would be granted full political rights. Hanna Sheehy-Skeffington, co-founder of the Irishwomen's Franchise League in 1908, criticized Sinn Féin for not freeing women as individual citizens, but keeping them in their roles as mothers and housewives (Rowbotham 1992: 111). For example, women's citizenship rights alone were never part of the programme: even a school meals campaign was justified on nationalist grounds, *viz*, a healthy nation needs healthy children.

Women in the Ladies' Land League grasped opportunities of directing a militant resistance to landlord power. The League and *Inghinidhe* were to synthesize in *Cumann na mBan* (Irishwomen's Council) of 1914: 'While *Cumann na mBan* would be an integral part of the military challenge to British rule in Ireland, its status was deliberately circumscribed by its constitutional requirement to "assist" the men in their fight for freedom' (Ward 1995: 88). Sheehy-Skeffington, who attempted to incorporate feminism into a nationalist framework, did not join *Cumann na mBan*, whose history reflects tensions between women's subordination and autonomy. Ward argues that its inability to lead Irish women 'was a failure that originated in their narrow conception of their role as guardians of the Republican conscience, rather than as representatives of the interests of women' (1995: 250).

De Valera's 1937 Constitution reinforced women's family roles. Article 41 2–1 reads, 'In particular, the State recognises that by her life within the home, woman gives to the State a support without which the common good cannot be achieved.' Article 40 2–2 reads, 'The State shall, therefore, endeavour to ensure that mothers shall not be obliged by economic necessity to engage in labour to the neglect of their duties in the home' (in Ward 1995: 238). The Irish Housewives' Association, formed in 1941 by Protestant women, sought to ameliorate the impoverished conditions of the unemployed and poor. Veterans of the suffrage movement joined them to work on issues of price control of food, proper rationing, school meals and salvaging waste. Throughout Northern/Irish history women are family nurturers, but do all women negotiate with gendered identities similarly, or what differences do the differences really make?

INTERACTING INCLUSIONS AND DIVISIONS

Understanding national divides is simplistic when expressed through binary oppositional identities such as Catholic nationalist and Protestant unionist, or men and women. Also, such oppositions assume negative antagonisms rather than positive differences, and ignore the complex nature of identity formed through overlapping relationships of race, ethnicity, class, gender, religion, family and national identifications, each of which radically affects the 'collective ideologies which different segments of a population hold and the ways in which they construct their boundaries' (Wekker 1995: 72).

Overlapping relationships, intersections between divisions and modes of belonging, and identifications with national identity are not static, they shift, as do our attachments to different communities. Boundaries exclude or include and are conditional on the pressures exerted on them. Inter-ethnic marriages, cross-community relationships or economic, political and even general morale factors alter boundaries. Boundaries are contextual, defining the shared basis of belonging, and who or what is excluded from membership. In Northern Ireland, belonging or exclusion hinges on the interaction between religion, class, area of residence, schooling and national identity. Working-class areas are segregated into Catholic or Protestant estates. The majority of schools for all classes are segregated. Segregation excludes, prevents or minimizes interaction, and often objectifies, exploits or inferiorizes 'the Other'. Misunderstanding, distrust, fear and ignorance obstructs positive interaction.

Religion provides the core for community identity. For example, loyalists stress liberty as a religious fundamental, a tenet used to defend their Orange marches. It is not that all loyalists are practising Christians or regular church attenders, but any suggestion that they should reroute marches from a traditional route to one where Catholics do not reside is perceived as an attack on religious freedom and thus on national identity. Such a perception supplies loyalists with another pretext for representing Catholics as 'the

Other', the suppressors of their civil and religious liberties. While it is mainly men who march, women within the loyalist community also defend their alleged rights. So Protestantism posits itself in opposition to Catholicism, a sectarianism that is reflected in its graffiti, whereas in Irish nationalist areas, the wall murals depict political messages, even if it is somewhat strained to accept that nationalist political designs are always free from religious connotations. Oppositional identities marked by religious differences are concerned with the defence of community and politics (Finlayson 1996: 104).

When identity is perceived to be under threat, as currently is the case with the Protestant/unionist identity, its importance becomes more conspicuous, and public displays psychologically reassuring. The threat is perceived to be an encroachment on the unionist way of life, whereas Irish nationalists view their attempt to influence politics as the need to reflect their particularity and to be self-determining. For this to occur, they must be active participants in political processes. Currently there is an estrangement for Irish nationalists, a political asymmetry among territory, action and membership (Connolly 1993: 50). While the ceasefires held, there was a 'pan-nationalist front', constituted by Sinn Féin, the Social Democratic Labour Party and the Irish Government. The 'front' supported the urgency for all-party talks leading to substantive negotiations. It was the British Government's role to instigate these negotiations. Whether the IRA ceasefire was a 'totally unarmed strategy' or a 'tactical use of the armed strategy' is debatable. Anyway, given the procrastination of the British Government over acting prudently when the IRA and loyalist ceasefires held, the IRA broke the ceasefire on 9 February 1996. Consequently, Sinn Féin was excluded from the formal peace talks. Debate on the decommissioning of weapons, argued by mainstream unionist parties as a precondition for entry to the talks, is currently unresolved, and may stymie substantive negotiations.

It is a mistake to treat violence in the name of a nation 'as something separate from the discourses which keep the idea of the nation alive in times that are supposedly peaceful' (Lerner 1993: 1). There is an industry of media, journalism and academic interest built around 'the troubles'. Consequently, 'the troubles' become 'normalized' as if they accurately reflect the lives of most people. They do not. Certainly the conflict has a daily all-pervasive shadow, and if one lives in certain areas it is impossible to avoid the visible signs of conflict like the presence of the armed forces, barbed wire, burnt-out cars and political graffiti; but most people have lives that are not defined entirely by the conflict. Sensationalist reporting in a divided society minimalizes the everyday practices of gender, sexuality, family, work and friendship that also inform us about how the nation is sustained. The nation-state exists as a physical space and it is grounded in ordinary practices 'that reproduce national identities in a variety of sites' (Radcliffe and Westwood 1996: 23). This grounding allows us to theorize the contextual interrelationships of historically contingent categories and to understand how these categories encourage inclusivity or exacerbate social divisions. Nationalism occurs in complex interaction with all aspects of identity.

NEGOTIATING WITH GENDERED IDENTITY

How are women's lives reflected in the gendered nation and how do women negotiate everyday life with gendered identities? Nira Yuval-Davis and Floya Anthias (1989: 7) suggest five major means by which women participate in ethnic and national processes. It is interesting to note that in Northern Ireland women of *all nationalist persuasions* participate in each of the five ways, though sometimes differently. They include: as biological reproducers of members of ethnic collectivities; as reproducers of the boundaries of ethnic and national groups; as actors in the ideological reproduction of the collectivity and as transmitters of its culture; as signifiers of ethnic and national differences; and as participants in national, economic, political and military struggles. There is also a gendered and racialized labour market (Anthias and Yuval-Davis 1992; Yuval-Davis 1996: 17). Women's reproductive roles extend beyond the biological in influencing ethnic and national discourses. Notions of 'common origin' are central. Generally, birth signifies joining the collectivity. Endogamy and the social separation that occurs because of segregated areas and schooling ensures that intra-group marriage maintains boundaries. Mixed marriages between Protestants and Catholics are numerically small and difficult to measure precisely because of a hesitancy about being identified. Mixed marriages are about 4 per cent of all marriages but more than 16 per cent in the greater Belfast area (Lee 1994: 23–24). Many couples in mixed marriages leave the province because of the fear of ostracism, sectarian harassment, and having their homes burnt.

Women are 'caught physically and symbolically in the angry crossfires produced by ethnic, nationalist and racist conflicts. Women are also at cross-purposes in these fires, positioned on different sides and thereby divided' (Lutz, Phoenix and Yuval-Davis 1995: 17). Women are caught differently in nationalist crossfires. Some are warriors, fighting. Some fire rhetoric through the war machinery of the media, others physically and psychologically support their male partner-warriors. Many are silent 'watchers' observing cautiously, keeping quiet in the attempt not to offend. This is the position many middle-class women (and men) take. These women enjoy a comfortable materialism, live in areas where an army presence, bombs, paramilitary community surveillance or police harassment is rare, and therefore do not have to confront the harsher realities to which those in working-class communities are subjected. While women are active participants in ethnic and national struggles, organizing, campaigning, attending to others' needs and sometimes participating in armed struggle, generally men act as agents and women as symbols, reinforcing existing gender oppressions. How does this occur?

On a *cultural level*, traditions, myths, stories, memories and communal symbols are part of each generation's socialization into a nation's history, carrying the past into the present. Women, as prime socializers of children, impart much of the national heritage, including perpetuating sectarianism and glorifying men as national heroes. A significant study found that women tend to predominate as moral arbiters and that men tend to predominate as transmitters of partisan identity (Miller, Wilford and Donoghue 1996) but morality and restrictive expectations often coincide and so women's arbitration may reinforce divisiveness. Children identify readily with a nation's name, flag, anthem, currency, slogans, myths, music and political life. Traditional ceremonies draw citizens into the national sphere. In divided societies, it is rare for any national emblems to sit side-by-side. Even the flying of the British Union Jack or the Irish Tricolour often is perceived as a provocative act.

At a *political level*, masculine agency and feminine symbolic representation reinforce cultural influences. Despite its language of freedom, equality and consent of the individual, liberal theory's conception of the universal individual as a public rights-bearing, autonomous rational citizen is conceptualized in masculine imagery in contrast to the feminized private realm of family, nature and the emotions (Pateman 1989). Rather than admitting that war is fought over masculinized spaces, the nationalistic rhetoric is that citizens fight for their 'mother country' and women provide the 'mother's milk of citizenship' (Sylvester 1993: 81). Consequently, 'we are all marked, deeply and permanently, by the way political life gets embodied in images of motherland and fatherland: so much so that the human body itself is politicized' (Elshtain 1993: 168). The sovereign and the warriors have masculinized faces, but the nation is feminized, usually as a mother, sometimes as a sweetheart or lover.

The frequent image is of a mother who has given up her sons in battle for the 'higher' cause of the nation. It is an easy slide from seeing nature-as-female to nation-as-woman. The idea of motherland as embodied femaleness speaks of the land and her women's fecundity that needs protecting by defending women's bodies and nation's boundaries. 'Men who cannot defend their woman/nation against rape/invasion have lost their proprietary claim to that body, that land' (Peterson 1996: 7). In Irish literature Yeats offers

the myth of Mother Ireland as symbolic compensation for the colonial calamities of history. The mythological motherland served as a goddess of sovereignty who, at least at the imaginary level, might restore a lost national identity by summoning her sons to the sacred rite of renewal through sacrifice.

(Kearney 1997: 113)

At a profound symbolic level, 'men have finally found ways to give birth: through sacrificial death' (Condren 1989: 208). Men's sacrifice in death parallels women's self-sacrifice in life (Condren 1995).

The theme of the nation as female implies the gendering of the citizen as male, limiting the forms of national belonging available to women (Hall 1993: 100). By deconstructing the image of the citizen who inhabits the state, feminists get a clearer picture of the political discourse of citizenship (Curthoys 1993: 34). The relationship between feminism and nationalism is mediated by militarism, since men and women often have different perceptions of war: 'This may mean that women are simultaneously both less militaristic and less nationalistic because militarism is often seen as an integral facet of a national project' (Walby 1996: 252). This does not imply that women are intrinsically peaceful or apolitical, but it does suggest that, given women's prime caretaking roles, many are not prepared to jeopardize their safety or their family's safety in a nationalistic cause that is militaristic.

There are more women active in Irish republican paramilitary groups than in loyalist groups. I suggest that the nominal claim to socialist credentials in republicanism provides an ideological space for egalitarianism. The conservative leanings in much loyalism stultify gender equality. Some women from all paramilitary groups provide 'safe-houses', others relay information, drive on terrorist assignments or carry weapons. The public face of paramilitaries of all types is male, as is that of the 'punishment beating gangs' that increased in frequency in the short span of relative peace from August 1994–February 1996, and since. Nationalized behaviours depend on gendered subjects with gendered bodies who are offered distinct means and images through which to identify with the national community. Gendered identities are fundamental to nation-building, state ideologies and political decision-making.

SAME DIFFERENCE

A clear link between gender and ethnic divisions is the assumption of naturalness, the belief that one group is naturally superior to another or biologically suited to separate functions, and hence that inequalities are understandable and differential discriminatory treatment is justified. Gendered identities for women reflect the social construction of a nation's expectations of sexual difference, biological reproduction and nurture. This construction influences dominant notions of mothering, family life, bread-winning, and the suitability or non-suitability of certain types of waged labour. Curiously, despite the claims to significant differences from the cultural, political and religious groupings in Northern Ireland, there is ample evidence to demonstrate that in relationship to women's position *as gendered identities*, there is more *in common* with women than in difference.

Comprehending the commonalities and differences between expressions of nationalism is complex. While the divisiveness of Northern Ireland is beamed across global television screens, pictures of commonalities across national and gendered divisions are largely ignored. The noticeable exception to this is the apparent ubiquity of women in peace movements, north and south of the border, seized upon by the media as a means of reproducing the cultural roles of women, couched in naive essentialist assumptions about women's 'naturally peaceful natures'. This exposure hides the men who are active peace-makers. Generally, gender relations differ according to ethnicity, with culturally specific practices of mothering and sex roles, but 'commonalities in the nature of gender relations sometimes transcend national frontiers and ethnic and "radical" specificity' (Walby 1996: 252). In Northern Ireland, many commonalities pivot around the extensive levels of socio-economic deprivation that are the highest in the United Kingdom. The three strong common factors are the importance of the family to Northern/Irish people; the influence of the church in reinforcing religious fundamentalist conservative theology and practices; and the conspicuous absence of women from public life.

First, family and kin ties are very strong. This is evident particularly in working-class estates where extended families live in close proximity and mother and daughter with children have daily contact (McLaughlin 1993: 561), and in rural communities where families live alongside each other. In a study in Derry, more than three-quarters of the respondents in both communities have a half or more of their relatives in immediate proximity (Smyth 1996: 44). In this study, more than 70 per cent saw their area as a segregated community and therefore a target for sectarian attacks, but agreed the greater benefits were the freedom to express culture and confirm a sense of identity. As one person states, 'Here it's close-knit communities. They, the nationalist people, are a close-knit community and we, the Protestants, are a close-knit community. Where I live, it's like a family – that's how the Ulster people are' (in Miller, Wilford and Donoghue 1996: 117). Part of this protectiveness of families is women's role as transmitters of values and traditions and this includes the conveying of stereotypically divisive attitudes, beliefs, loyalties and practices, teaching children about the bogeys of 'Fenians' and 'Orangemen', entrenching a 'them' and 'us' mentality. Even when there is an emphasis on mutual understanding in segregated schools, school yard biases prevail, and it seems reasonable to deduce that women contribute as well as men to teaching children sectarian values.

The perception of many women is that feminism's analysis of the family as a prime site of women's oppression does not reflect their personal, positive experiences of family life, and this makes them reluctant to identify with feminism. Yet it is the family role that prompted women to become politically active in the early 1970s as a response to housing and job discrimination, arrests and internment, houses being ransacked during British army raids and children being harassed. Women, particularly in nationalist communities, experienced frequent disruptions as their traditional maternal role as guardian of the family was invaded by aliens who had no right to trespass on their territory. While women consistently have protested against military and paramilitary violence, principally their activity has been 'as the guardians of family life and in the interests of the community rather than as fighters for women's benefits alone' (Roulston 1989: 222). This guardian role increased in communities where husbands, sons, fathers and brothers were in prison. While women's community involvement emerged from their concern with families it did not alter their perceptions about their own social positions (Edgerton 1986: 67). Community activists were called 'family feminists' (Mitchison 1988). This term is not equated with weakness in women for whom domesticity, marriage and motherhood is a priority.

Second, religious conservatism within both the Protestant and Catholic traditions is antagonistic to changes in gender roles and stresses women's special responsibility for the home and the upbringing of children (Morgan and Fraser 1994: 5). Fundamentalist Protestantism and traditional Catholicism share conservative views on pre-marital and extra-marital sex, contraception, family size, abortion, divorce, single mothers, male headship, female submission, and complementary sex roles based on men's instrumental wage-earning and women's expressive nurturance. When these views are socially sanctioned and reinforced through religious teachings, it is unsurprising that women's involvement in government agencies, political parties and socio-economic businesses is limited. Indeed, deviations from accepted tenets of social and moral behaviour are regarded as betraying communal or national norms. As 'handmaidens of the Lord' many women feel that the church leaves them with a crippling sense of guilt about being female (Fairweather, McDonough and McFadyean 1985: 111), particularly if women make choices on sexuality and reproductive rights, or on career or waged labour, that conflict with standard religious teachings or men's desires.

Fundamentalism, religious and political, is founded on the absolute, unquestionable correctness of the cause or beliefs and is resistant to critique or change. It is not difficult to find examples of fundamentalist views. In interviews people were asked to respond to the statement 'women are by nature happiest when making a home and caring for children', and 51 per cent of males and 41 per cent of females across all party divisions agree. The majority of men 'believe women are naturally disposed to find happiness within the private realm', a view that finds greatest favour in the Protestant Democratic Unionist Party (71 per cent) and the nationalist Sinn Féin party (64 per cent) (Miller, Wilford and Donoghue 1996: 166). The authors of this study are right to conclude that such results supply a pro-familism rationalization for parties 'to concentrate their policy proposals for women on the basis that they belong within the narrow confines of home and family' (1996: 167).

History reminds us of the entrenchment of these beliefs. The Ladies' Land League was formed in 1881 to assist tenant farmers fight against rack rents and landlord power, given that the male leaders of the fight were in jail. Women supported the evicted, prevented land-grabbing and erected wooden huts for displaced families. When the men were released from jail, the League was shunted aside and this led to a profound rift between the brother and sister Parnell. In the *Belfast Newsletter* of 18 March 1881, the editor wrote, 'Sensible people in the North of Ireland dislike to see women out of the place she is gifted to occupy, and at no time is woman further from her natural position than when she appears upon a political platform' (in Ward 1995: 23). Change is very slow.

Third, in terms of public life, women's absence from elected office runs across political divides. Since 1920 when Northern Ireland began sending MPs to Westminster, only three women have served. During the existence of Stormont, the quasi-federal institution that had extensive powers which were abused by the unionists, women were never more than 6 per cent of candidates out of a 52-seat parliament. Women make up 12 per cent of local councillors (Miller, Wilford and Donoghue 1996: 8–9). These authors draw attention to the fact that the historic influence of both Catholic and Protestant fundamentalism acts in concert with the traditional hostility of both Irish nationalism and unionism to feminism, yet women are advancing steadily in political representation in other culturally conservative political systems like the Republic of Ireland and Germany. In the Republic of Ireland, while 40 per cent agree that 'a woman's *proper* place is in the home', 64 per cent agree that the feminist movement is very necessary (Mac Gréil 1996: 294) and women constitute 12 per cent of national politicians.

Reasons for hostility to feminism and women in prominent public positions in Northern Ireland must be sought beyond merely a prevailing religious fundamentalism. In a divided society where schools and residential estates are segregated and the majority of the population is rural, there are few meaningful contacts across community differences. The churches strongly sanction women's family roles and conservatism reinforces traditional gender barriers. Strategies to support women's electoral representation and public status appear to most men, and many women, as unnecessary diversions to constitutional issues and achieving peace. Family, religion and public standing affect women's identity across national divisions. How then do identity and political locality interact?

POLITICS OF LOCATION

Women and community activism

Conventional views of nationalism are narrowly aligned with territory as fixed physical boundaries, whereas place, position and location, as fluid markers of national experience, refer us more directly to the lived experiences of national identity as they occur in the political, economic, cultural and social dynamics of people's narratives (Radcliffe and Westwood 1996: 3). These markers respond to immediate contexts. My focus on *location* opens the political space to where women's activism lies. Yet much of the vibrancy of Northern Irish civil society occurs in territorially defined communities where, if not known, one is open to suspicion. Many of these communities are divided by tall walls and wire barricades. Within these communities women's activism extends to charity, church, voluntary and community activities and includes groups focused on mothers and toddlers, refuges, advice, rape crisis, support, and education; and groups responding to pressures of poverty, housing, welfare rights, fuel debt, youth alienation, unemployment and sectarian strife. These are local, immediate, practical activities suggesting that women's typical communal activity is on a different spatial scale from men's.

Unlike most Western nations, the women's movement in Northern Ireland has been generated more by working-class women. Monica McWilliams (1995) documents five major stages of women's activism. First, there was the 'civil rights activism' of the late 1960s and 1970s, prompted initially by housing discrimination and by internment of mainly Irish nationalists without legal charge or trial, which heightened the level of conflict. It was primarily women from working-class Catholic areas of Belfast, Derry and Newry who were the most active in these civil rights campaigns. Women were prominent in the formation of the Campaign for Social Justice, formed in 1964, the Northern Ireland Civil Rights Association of 1967 and the radical student group, the People's Democracy of 1968, within which Bernadette Devlin rose to political prominence. McWilliams calls the second stage the 'accidental activists', women who unwittingly found themselves engaged in political organization as the wives of prisoners, or as the mothers of sons imprisoned. Third, 'conflictual activism' refers to the central role of conflict that arises inevitably in a divided society around contested nationalist questions. Activists form a tactical alliance to achieve resources but the alliance dissipates once the goal is achieved and the constraints of competing nationalist views resurface. Fourth, the 'peace activists' led by women who had suffered personal loss of children through terrorist violence briefly united women, then were disrupted partly by internal discord. The fifth stage is that of 'feminist activism as an agent of change'. Women in trade unions, community development and umbrella and single-issue women's groups of the voluntary sector 'have become the unofficial agents of change making representation to the various government departments and demanding resources' (McWilliams 1995: 29). Increasing numbers of feminist groups organize through the Women's Support Network which is non-sectarian and deals with controversial issues in culturally sensitive ways.

The community basis to these groups raises significant conflicts of interpretation. Carol Coulter, in discussing the popular appeal of the former

President of Ireland, Mary Robinson, highlights her interest in the decentralized, communalist, locally responsive politics that have had a profound relationship with the Irish nationalist tradition. Coulter argues that in the nationalist areas of the north, local groups 'form a network of organisations that offer an implicit alternative to state structures, and as such have a literally subversive content' (1993: 4). While these groups see the state as hostile in a way that unionist groups do not, and while Irish nationalist women's groups are more thoroughly incorporated into republican causes, women's activism also is important in unionist areas where their involvement similarly is local, women or family-based, but is not as integrated into unionist politics. The unionist tradition embodies a social conservatism and belief in the constitutional *status quo* and hence the status of women in its tradition is historical subordination. Official debates in unionism concerning women's role in the party did not begin until the early 1990s (Rooney and Woods 1995: 26). For many unionists, feminism's focus on justice and equality is closely associated with socialism which is more aligned with nationalism. Thus, the dominant feminist voice is an Irish nationalist one, with experience gained through civil rights activism. Consequently, many Protestant unionist women regard feminism suspiciously and admit to feeling alienated from the women's movement because of their lack of a tradition of struggle and their different political allegiance from the more vocal Nationalist/Catholic voice (McWilliams 1995: 27).

Whatever identities locally-based women's groups embrace, their distinctiveness of organization is evident, including user-participation in management, disdain for formalized hierarchy, and a tendency for women who have been recipients of services to become involved in service provision (McDonough 1996: 29). There is a preparedness by most women to cooperate, connect, care and act with interdependence on practical issues that have neither religious nor constitutional ramifications.

There are two further aspects to the uniqueness of women's politics of location. First, 'often women involved in "the politics of everyday life" do not see their activities as political' (Waylen 1996: 17). The response to community issues on the basis of the needs of others occurs irrespective of religious or national identity. The situated politics that emerges when 'marginalized groups develop political and knowledge-seeking projects that originate explicitly from their own socially devalued lives' attempts to encourage and energize the democratic tendencies of everyday social life (Harding 1993: 143–144).

The places in which women typically locate their actions are different from the orthodox public political territory more typical of men's involvement. While male activists tend to engage in intra-communal activities, women activists tend to occupy a civic space that hovers between the formal political and the informal domestic (Wilford 1996: 49). If feminism's motivation is to integrate women as actors into conventional politics, then women's absence from elected representation is the sole struggle. However, clearly women are engaged in activities outside of male dominated institutional politics and these must be included in an assessment of citizenship. Such activities reveal something of what it means *to be a woman* as well as what it means *to do politics*. Given the family responsibilities that women adopt, whether voluntarily or through social pressures, being a woman often means being caught between the demands of domesticity and public life in ways that, with the exception of single fathers, are not experienced by most men.

Yet the basis of women's identity and politics cannot be accepted uncritically. Many women from both 'Orange' and 'Green' forms of nationalism cleave to traditional family roles as their only sanctioned roles. Hence, much of women's unique political activity is a response to restrictive gender roles. Unless we see the boundary shift from exclusive views of citizenship as a relationship between the state and its subjects towards the inclusion of political spaces such as women's community activism, much of women's political activity goes theoretically unrecognized and practically undervalued. Talk of 'citizenship' must encapsulate the distribution of power and the relations of control and negotiation that occur in different arenas of social, economic and political life (Waylen 1994: 332; Yuval-Davis and Anthias 1989: 6) and produce traditional gendered responses as well as feminist challenges.

However, I contend that there are advantages and disadvantages to be gained from reconceptualizing political spaces to extend beyond representative government and the male public realms. It is desirable because expanded notions of political engagement capture women's traditional community involvement and are more inclusive. Yet there are problems in concentrating solely on the informal political arena – the location of local development, networking, protest, demonstration and informal coalition building – when there are no women from Northern Ireland in elected representative government in the British or European parliaments, limited numbers of women in the elected Forum and only two women from the Northern Ireland Woman's Coalition (NIWC) at the multi-party peace talks. A situated politics of everyday life does not automatically translate to electoral representation and decision-making. Certainly the women's movement in Northern Ireland with its grassroots activism, critique of authority and commitment to non-hierarchical collective decision-making is a form of participatory democracy, but community activism is not political representation (Porter 1998). Without such representation, the efficacy of activism and of feminism is not maximized.

Second, regarding a politics of location, Georgina Waylen (1996) extends a distinction made earlier by Maxine Molyneux (1985) that women's political activity can be divided into 'practical' and 'strategic' gender interests. *Practical gender interests* arise from actual situations in response to immediate needs such as the civil and welfare rights movements described earlier. Waylen maintains that practical movements are generally working-class and populist, revolving around women's roles as mothers and household managers, and politicize women's social roles without reducing gender inequality. In contrast, *strategic gender interests* are 'derived deductively from an analysis of women's subordination and from the formulation of a more satisfactory set of arrangements' (Waylen 1996: 20). Strategic-based movements require a specific feminist level of consciousness. There is no simplistic rigid dichotomy between practical and strategic interests, and overlaps are considerable. In Northern Ireland local, practical interests prevail. There are over a thousand women's groups, but few of these are concerned explicitly with changing policies and structures. Indeed, many groups reinforce women's traditional family roles without encouraging the sharing of responsibilities with men that is necessary for parenting and nurture to be valued. Middle-class women support working-class women in practical politics, but strategic orientations require the skills of negotiation, debate, policy-making, report writing and grant applications that educated women of all classes typically possess. Class intersects with nationalism, and education, rightly, is seen as the tool to translate practical gender interests into strategic changes.

Position, locality and the 'national question' continue to haunt feminists north and south of the border. There are a range of views. Some see no contradiction between simultaneously struggling for the liberation of a nation and for women. Others believe that women's issues need to be priori-tized because if women themselves do not raise their needs, their oppression will be ignored. Some women are hostile, or indifferent, or confused as to the struggle for national freedom. In the late 1960s some of the younger women who joined *Cumann na mBan* expressed their disillusionment with women's continued subordinate role, and argued forcefully for their integra-tion into the IRA, and some were given military training (Ward 1995: 258). For these women, the struggle for a united Ireland is such a priority that all other issues must be subsumed under this central issue. The contradiction between Irish nationalism and feminism was stark with the campaign for the political status waged by women prisoners in Armagh jail. Some women who were appalled at their suffering were reluctant to be involved for fear that this may be interpreted as support for the IRA. Similarly, with the campaign to extend the British 1967 Abortion Act to Northern Ireland, some women who would support women's reproductive choices did not want to be seen to be supporting the extension of British influence (Porter 1996a). Yet since the proroguing of the Northern Ireland Parliament in 1972, progressive legislation which the unionist majority previously thwarted has been extended from Britain, including the Equal Pay Act, the Sex Discrimination Order, improved contraception facilities, divorce law reforms and domestic violence legislation (Fairweather, McDonough, McFadyean 1985: 259), as well as the extension of European conventions and policies as part of membership of the European Union.

Interestingly, Ailbhe Smyth writes that 'almost imperceptibly, the National Question has ceased to be a major dividing issue within the Women's Movement in the Republic' (1995: 204). She explains three major reasons for this: the urgency of the economic situation and unemployment; the need to resist the assault of the extreme right; and the fact that the younger generation have grown up with a national identity influenced by processes of modernization and Europeanization. Smyth argues that feminism has shifted 'the centre of political debate in the Republic from an obsessive concern with nationhood and nationalism on to a much broader social and political basis' (1995: 205). She explains that it is not that feminist challenges to state institutions and practices are expressed explicitly as protests against nationalism, but their effect undermines the ideological bases of the state as expressed through the Constitution. In defiance of state and church, many Irish women make autonomous choices, declining to be merely symbols or reproducers of the nation. Through these changes, they 'are dislodging the cornerstone of control of the patriarchal state: women's privatized place in the sacrosanct family, and foundation of the nation' (1995: 205). In so doing, they redefine politics, Irishness and, specifically, what it means to be an Irish woman. The Irish Catholic nation-state is being redefined, and feminism plays a revitalizing role. In contrast, the contested and violent nature of Northern Ireland dominates the political landscape, diminishing the radical effectiveness of feminism's role.

CITIZENSHIP AND PLURALITY

Common political identity and pluralism

Given the identities and locations of women in Northern Ireland, is there political scope for plurality? Or does the nature of divided societies render it difficult for feminists to formulate a common political identity, even though they agree on many shared desired goals? Tamir argues that the liberal tradition's emphasis on personal autonomy, reflection and choice and the nationalist tradition's emphasis on belonging, loyalty and solidarity can accommodate each other (1995: xviii). This might be true in a multi-national state that wishes to bridge differences and nourish cross-communal understanding and thus fosters those shared values that provide a basis for social and political cooperation. Northern Ireland is not one of these states. All sides of the political divide seem reluctant to acknowledge common allegiances. Yet it is the web of shared understandings, identities, debates and traditions that makes a common moral life possible (Connolly 1993: 50). To emphasize ethnic diversity above shared social vision leaves little room for coalition. Compromise necessary for coalition does not come easily. The polity and society of Northern Ireland is ingrained with either/or dualities that frustrate fine nuance: 'The resulting zero-sum nature of its politics – if "we" win, "they" lose – marginalizes those concerned with aspects of citizenship, including its gendered character, that are expressed in terms other than those of either "Irishness" or "Britishness"' (Miller, Wilford and Donoghue 1996: 12). Deciding how to include different versions of national identity that truly capture the multiplicity of its multifarious subjects is vital. Indeed, some individuals identify with both British and Irish cultural affiliations. 'Parity of esteem' is the term 'used by the British and Irish governments to signal the even-handedness of their approach to Northern Irish politics, to indicate that the North's two major traditional identities are equally deserving of accommodation or equally undeserving of privileged treatment' (N. Porter 1996: 187). Norman Porter advocates the stronger notion of 'due recognition' which he argues 'implies an absence of relations of domination and subservience and the presence, rather, of relations of reciprocity' (1996: 191). Due recognition requires cultural groups to respect the rights of others to express themselves differently. A reciprocal recognition affirms differences contingent on their implications on others not to undermine, humiliate or destroy another's integrity.

The problem of how to grant due recognition to culturally different groups and to the multiple identities within such groups sits uncomfortably with political divisions and the need for common political solutions. It is a problem that urgently requires a solution, for the refusal to acknowledge group differences often explodes into violence. The idea of 'group representation' generally refers to marginalized cultural groups, including the representation of women. Judith Squires suggests that there are three distinct conceptions of what is being represented: interests, like economic status and regional location; ideologies and statements of belief; and identities of social or ethnic group membership (1996: 78). The liberal tradition extols virtues of representing individuals not social groupings. Squires asks how desirable is the shift 'from the liberal transcendence of identity difference to the radical democratic recognition of cultural difference' (1996: 82). She is responding to Iris Marion Young's (1990) argument that the politics of difference requires the participation and inclusion of all groups by different means in order to recognize how attachments to traditions, language and cultural practices are important aspects of identity.

Young argues that the recognition of equal value of different cultures requires the specific representation of social groups. I am sympathetic to the four problems Squires raises with Young's attempt to graft identity politics onto representative government. First, 'the assumption that people cannot empathise across lines of difference leads to factionalism and the politics of the enclave'. Second, 'the assumed sameness and cohesion within the groups merely replicates the assumption of sameness within society that group representation advocates want to criticise'. Third, 'mechanisms of accountability are hard to realise when one's constituents are self-defined identity groups with no formal membership mechanisms'. Finally, 'how are we to decide which groups should be entitled to group-based representation?' (Squires 1996: 84). These problems raise serious questions of whether the recognition of differences of identity becomes the priority, relinquishing the common striving towards just political structures.

My view, developed elsewhere (1997) is that in regard to women in Northern Ireland, there are potentially positive and divisive aspects of group representation that is based on identity politics. First, it can be empowering to women who have been marginalized and it provides scope for alliances across overlapping identities. Second, it is potentially divisive when its exclusionary nature privileges a republican, loyalist or a woman-centred identity and is narrow-minded, dogmatically defining politics as a single issue like a united Ireland, union with Britain or overcoming patriarchy. Hence I argue in support of a *middle ground*[4] between commonality and diversity, where democratic institutional structures encourage the striving towards the common good in political community, yet provide space to work through the conflicts, divisions and antagonisms of groups' divergent interests without privileging or denying differences. This middle ground is a principled space – there are limits to pluralism – not all interests are legitimate. Group interests that are violent, destructive, oppressive, or deny the integrity of others are not deserving of political space. Furthermore, while identity and difference is important, so too is the need sometimes to transcend the constraints of specificity. What is desperately needed in Northern Ireland 'is a set of institutions and practices which constitute the framework of a consensus within which pluralism can exist' (Mouffe 1992: 14).

Coalitions in dialogue

Dialogue is the key to finding acceptable paths in this middle ground between common political aspiration and pluralism. One positive sign of hope for feminism is the role of the Northern Ireland Women's Coalition, formed in 1996 to ensure that women will no longer be ignored in political processes (Porter 1996b). Two women were elected to the peace talks, Monica McWilliams from a Catholic background and Pearl Sagar from a Protestant one. While alliances between Irish and unionist nationalist women's groups have struggled for improved socio-economic rights, electoral coalitions were non-existent prior to the Women's Coalition. The Coalition stresses the need for a common denominator, namely its feminist principles and goals of openness to possible solutions, inclusivity, equity, listening to women and striving to incorporate cross-community concerns. Advocates of feminist coalition politics maintain that women's differences should be recognized without fixing boundaries 'in terms of "who" we are but in terms of what we want to achieve' (Yuval-Davis 1994: 189). Yet often political agendas depend on the constitutive aspects of self-identity, including different meanings attached to divergent national experiences.

The NIWC is practising a 'transversal politics' based on dialogue and coalition politics which recognizes the specific positionings of its members as well as the 'unfinished knowledge' that each such situated positioning offers (Yuval-Davis 1996: 23). Instead of presupposing unity or consensus, mutual understanding and solidarity have to be worked at through dialogue;

between women's groups, within differing political viewpoints in the Coalition, and between other parties in order to listen to the meanings and justifications of each other on state, nation, decommissioning of weapons, the roles of the Irish and British governments, policing, political prisoners, and national identity. This willingness to listen and strive towards mutually agreeable solutions is lacking in most mainstream politicians. In the reflective processes of dialogue, a new reformulation of taken-for-granted assumptions aims to transcend the rigidities of nationalistic boundaries without denying their tensions and lived differences. The middle ground is precarious – it repudiates the safe dogmatism of one's own position or being ignorant of another's views.

The key to workable political solutions is reasonable, albeit untidy, compromises, a common sense acceptance of the social reality of incompatible, incommensurable values (Tamir 1995: xv). The disposition to seek consensus or compromise is regarded by both sexes within the general population to be characteristic of female, not male, politicians. A study of community activists shows that 'the "ruthlessness" and "ambition" of male politicians frustrates compromise' (Wilford 1996: 52–53). In Norway, one of the few countries where there is a relatively high participation of women in government structures, strong coalitions formed in the 1960s and 1970s between establishment women who fought for equality within the system and feminists who worked through alternative institutions.[5] By the 1980s a feminist agenda was being incorporated into the platforms of political parties. It is 'increasingly common for Norwegian women activists to argue for the necessity of bringing female values and discourse into the public arena' (Bystydzienski 1992: 18).

Women can make a difference if their numbers are substantial enough and if they have an alternative agenda to offer. The attempts of the Northern Ireland Women's Coalition to alter intransigent political discourse is evident by their disposition to work towards reasonable compromise and by their focus on socio-economic realities and improving everyday life. They are demonstrating the positive role that what William Connolly terms 'a *democratic politics of disturbance*' (1993: 61) can play in exposing violence and exclusions, and in projecting new challenges to old views on identity and difference, thereby disrupting the dogmatism of long-held understandings of democratic rule.

Feminist visions of citizenship

In conclusion, I suggest that there are two central aspects to any viable feminist visions of citizenship that incorporate the identity, location and plurality of women in Northern Ireland – that of taking seriously *women's narratives* and their *care*. Narratives focus on women's actual life stories that reflect their sense of belonging, attachments, political engagement and situatedness. Care is the thread that weaves through the disjunctions of a divided society.

First, it is a central notion of Anderson's 'imagined communities' that the reader imagines that s/he is written into the narrative. Telling the story about the nation is itself part of the nation's creation, but who is telling the story of Northern Ireland and whose story is it? In 'reimagining the nation' Lerner writes that the nation is never imagined on its own, because no text is solely a nationalist text, and 'the nation is always forging liaisons with *other boundary-marking constructs*' (1993: 3). We have noted how nationality interacts with gendered bodies, economics and democratic theory. We need to tell personal stories and listen to each other's stories. Dialogue and openness are crucial in explicating our narratives. There seems evidence that women listen and learn from each other. Yuval-Davis (1994) writes of Italian feminists who, in working with feminists of conflicting national groups like the Serbs and Croats or Palestinian and Israeli Jewish women, use key words like 'rooting' and 'shifting'. The idea is that each woman brings her rooting in her national identity but simultaneously tries to shift in order to empathize and exchange with women from different backgrounds. The process of shifting does not involve 'losing one's own rooting and set of values' (1994: 193) but accepts that, as there is diversity amongst those similarly rooted, one cannot homogenize the Other. Identities constituted by sectarianism do not recognize the validity of other identities. A narrative understanding of identity as 'self-in-relations' confirms 'the social basis of our selfhood through the intermeshing of personal histories' (Porter 1991: 196). This understanding invites critical reflection on and engagement with different national narratives.

Chandra Talpade Mohanty points out that part of the advantage of the 'imagined community' is the suggestion of potential alliances across divisive boundaries, and the notion of community indicates a commitment to 'horizontal comradeship' (1991: 4). She is imagining communities of women who, despite having divergent narratives, develop interdependent relationships in opposition to pervasive and systemic forms of domination. Part of re-imagining the nation is re-thinking what transforms citizenship. Ailbhe Smyth's powerful question is pertinent: 'Who gets to do the imagining and is imagining enough?' (1995: 208–209). In moving away from the male citizen who sacrifices his life for his motherland, Elshtain (1993) shifts the political focus of loyalty and identity from sacrifice to responsibility. Her argument is that an *ethic of responsibility* requires citizens to be accountable. In Northern Ireland such an ethic requires: elected representatives to condemn acts of terrorist violence; the militarized violence of men in security, police and the army to be answerable for abusing their control in the household; the predominantly male paramilitary forces to be called to account for the physical and psychological damage inflicted on communities; and for all politicians to engage in constructive dialogue.

Second, care is central to this ethic of responsibility in feminist visions of citizenship. This argument does not imply that female essentialism is a solution to the Northern Irish problem. Rather, it affirms care as being central to women's and men's engagement with plural narratives. Building on the centrality of care, Angela Miles identifies four main features of transformative feminisms. First, they are *antidualistic*, refusing the fragmentation of patriarchal oppositions between public and private, reason and emotion, knower and known, common identity and diverse national allegiances. Second, transformative features *resist dominations* – whether by patriarchal structures, individual men or imperialist states. Third, they *adopt life-centred values* like community, sharing, nurturing and cooperation. Fourth, they practise a '*dialectical politics* in which the apparently opposed principles of women's equality and specificity, their commonality and diversity become dynamic contradictions' (Miles 1996: xii) that are mutually constitutive. For example, when equality coexists with specificity and difference it no longer implies sameness, and difference no longer implies inequality.

At the heart of transformative politics is the *middle ground* that I am defending, the commitment to deal creatively and constructively with the inevitable tensions between contradictions, conflicting views, opposing priorities and plural narratives. The transformative potential of the middle ground is neither naive nor simplistic, it acknowledges the real gaps between contrasting ideals and reality but it opens new possibilities. Working in this difficult space means questioning one's own ideas and practices as well as listening to others' explanations. While not always endorsing others' traditions, the middle ground respects the legitimacy of different identities. In valuing plurality, the concept of politics associated with the middle ground becomes more complex, less susceptible to colonization by the discourse of belonging, so that 'shared understandings no longer cover political life with a blanket: the gaps, porosities and ambivalences they contain become constitutive elements in politics' (Connolly 1993: 58).

The way we define citizenship is linked intimately to the kind of society and political community we desire. A vision of citizenship that is viable in Northern Ireland builds on an ethic of responsibility to fulfil common desires for justice, equality and socio-economic well-being, and takes into account that different national, ethnic and gender identities experience common needs differently. For the public sphere to reflect the particularities of its multi-ethnic members, political space must be made to encompass distinctive voices in public dialogue and collective decision-making. Inclusivity recognizes shared and different ethnic and national identifications, accepts that tensions and conflicts are real, and strives to deal imaginatively with these interrelationships. Pursuing the treacherous middle ground 'is a way of conceptualizing our identities and our political existence as individuals and as citizens, as embodying particularity and universality, diversity and commonality so that neither is sacrificed to the other' (Porter 1997: 94). In such a pursuit, empathetic dialogue, reciprocal recognition and contextual judgement is crucial. In such a polity, care is situated at the centre of political lives and practices of nurturance are constitutive ingredients of our definitions of a good society. Until the disputing political traditions in Northern Ireland no longer fear pluralism, there will be no embrace of cultural and gender differences.

NOTES

1   As an 'inside-outsider', an Australian living and working in Northern Ireland, the task of understanding has necessary limitations. Hopefully, it also has certain advantages, like its critical distancing.
2   A recent national survey of attitudes in the Republic of Ireland shows that 75 per cent desire a united Ireland with a central government and 30 per cent would accept a central and provincial government (Mac Gréil 1996: 244).
3   Where I do not distinguish between various types of nationalism, I adopt the common usage of the term 'nationalist' as representing those coming from Catholic communities.
4   In Northern Ireland, talk of the 'middle ground' often is identified with the politics of the Alliance Party or a weak position that disguises implicit privileging. The middle ground that I am defending is neither of these identifications, but is a *strong position* that respects diversity, makes space for difference and seeks grounds for commonality.
5   Norwegian parliamentarians agree that women's increased participation has contributed towards changing party viewpoints on: care-and-career politics, social welfare, family-based care, environment, bodies, labour market, representation, disarmament (Skjeie 1993: 243). Despite embracing new political agendas, 'the traditionally divergent role models of the "woman worker" and the "Mother housewife" still come to guide final party priorities' (1993: 259).

BIBLIOGRAPHY

Anderson, B. (1991) *Imagined Communities: Reflections on the Origins and Spread of Nationalism*, London: Verso.

Anthias, F. and Yuval-Davis, N. (1992) *Racialized boundaries. Race, Nation, Gender, Colour and Class and the Anti-racist Struggle*, London: Routledge.

Breen, R. (1996) 'Who wants a United Ireland? Constitutional Preferences among Catholics and Protestants' in R. Breen, P. Devine and L. Dowds (eds) *Social Attitudes in Northern Ireland*, Belfast: Appletree Press, 33–48.

Bystydzienski, J. M. (ed.) (1992) *Women Transforming Politics. Worldwide Strategies for Empowerment*, Bloomington: Indiana University Press.

Condren, M. (1989) *The Serpent and the Goddess. Women, Religion, and Power in Celtic Ireland*, San Francisco: Harper.

—— (1995) 'Work-In-Progress. Sacrifice and Political Legitimation: The Production of a Gendered Social Order', *Journal of Women's History* 6, 4/7, 1: 160–189.

Connolly, W. E. (1993) 'Democracy and Territoriality' in M. Ringrose and A. J. Lerner (eds) *Reimagining the Nation*, Buckingham: Open University Press, 49–75.

Coulter, C. (1993) *The Hidden Tradition: Feminism, Women and Nationalism in Ireland*, Cork: Cork University Press.

Curthoys, A. (1993) 'Feminism, Citizenship and National Identity', *Feminist Review* 44: 19–38.

Edgerton, L. (1986) 'Public Protest, Domestic Acquiescence: Women in Northern Ireland' in R. Ridd and H. Calloway (eds) *Caught Up in Conflict. Women's Responses to Political Strife*, London: Macmillan Educational, 61–83.

Elshtain, J. B. (1993) 'Sovereignty, Identity, Sacrifice' in M. Ringrose and A. J.

Lerner (eds) *Reimagining the Nation*, Buckingham: Open University Press, 159–175.

Eriksen, T. H. (1993) *Ethnicity and Nationalism: Anthropological Perspectives*, London: Pluto Press.

Fairweather, E., McDonough, R. and McFadyean, M. (1985) *Only the Rivers Run Free. Northern Ireland: the Women's War*, London: Pluto Press.

Finlayson, A. (1996) 'Nationalism as Ideological Interpellation: the Case of Ulster Loyalism', *Ethnic and Racial Studies* 19,1: 88–112.

Gallagher, A. M. (1996) 'Community Relations, Equality and the Future' in R. Breen, P. Devine and L. Dowds (eds) *Social Attitudes in Northern Ireland*, Belfast: Appletree Press, 178–192.

Geoghegan, V. (1994) 'Socialism, National Identities and Post-Nationalist Citizenship', *Irish Political Studies* 9: 61–80.

Hall, C. (1993) 'Gender, Nationalism and National Identities', *Feminist Review* 44: 97–103.

Harding, S. (1993) 'Reinventing Ourselves as Other: More New Agents of History and Knowledge' in L. S. Kauffman (ed.) *American Feminist Thought At Century's End: A Reader*, Cambridge, Mass.: Blackwell Publishers, 140–164.

Hearne, D. (1992) 'The Irish Citizen 1914–16: Nationalism, Feminism, and Militarism', *The Canadian Journal of Irish Studies* 18, 1: 1–14.

Hobsbawm, E. (1990) *Nations and Nationalism Since 1780: Programmes, Myth and Reality*, Cambridge: Cambridge University Press.

Kearney, R. (1997) *Postnationalist Ireland. Politics, Culture, Philosophy*, London and New York: Routledge.

Lee, R. M. (1994) *Mixed and Matched. Interreligious Courtship and Marriage in Northern Ireland*, New York: University Press of America.

Lerner, A. (1993) 'Introduction' in M. Ringrose and A. J. Lerner (eds) *Reimagining the Nation*, Buckingham: Open University Press, 1–5.

Lutz, H., Phoenix, A. and Yuval-Davis, N. (1995) 'Introduction: Nationalism, Racism and Gender – European Crossfires' in H. Lutz, A. Phoenix and N. Yuval-Davis (eds) *Crossfires: Nationalism, Racism and Gender in Europe*, London: Pluto Press, 1–25.

Mac Gréil, M. (1996) *Prejudice in Ireland Revisited*, Maynooth: Survey and Research Unit.

McDonough, R. (1996) 'Independence or Integration?' in *Power, Politics, Positioning. Women in Northern Ireland*, Belfast: Democratic Dialogue, 25–32.

McLaughlin, E. (1993) 'Women and the Family in Northern Ireland: A Review', *Women's Studies International Forum* 16, 6: 553–568.

McWilliams, M. (1995) 'Struggling for Peace and Justice: Reflections on Women's Activism in Northern Ireland', *Journal of Women's History* 6, 4/7, 1: 13–39.

Miles, A. (1996) *Integrative Feminisms. Building Global Visions, 1960s–1990s*, New York and London: Routledge.

Miller, R. L., Wilford, R. and Donoghue, F. (1996) *Women and Political Participation in Northern Ireland*, Aldershot: Avebury.

Mohanty, C. T. (1991) 'Cartographies of Struggle. Third World Women and the Politics of Feminism' in C. T. Mohanty, A. Russo and L. Torres (eds) *Third World Women and the Politics of Feminism*, Bloomington: Indiana University Press, 1–47.

Molyneux, M. (1985) 'Mobilization without Emancipation? Women's Interest, the State and Revolution in Nicaragua', *Feminist Studies* 11, 2: 227–254.

Morgan, V. and Fraser, G. (1994) *The Company We Keep: Women, Community and Organisations*, University of Ulster: Centre for the Study of Conflict.

Moxon-Browne, E. (1991) 'National Identity in Northern Ireland' in P. Stringer and

G. Robinson (eds) *Social Attitudes in Northern Ireland*, Belfast: The Blackstaff Press, 23–38.

Mouffe, C. (1992) 'Democratic Politics Today' in C. Mouffe (ed.) *Dimensions of Radical Democracy. Pluralism, Citizenship, Community*, London: Verso, 1–14.

Pateman, C. (1989) *The Disorder of Women. Democracy, Feminism and Political Theory*, Cambridge: Polity Press.

Peterson, V. S. (1996) 'The Politics of Identification in the Context of Globalization', *Women's Studies International Forum* 19, 1/2: 5–15.

Phillips, A. (1991) *Engendering Democracy*, Cambridge: Polity Press.

—— (1993) *Democracy and Difference*, Cambridge: Polity Press.

Porter, E. (1991) *Women and Moral Identity*, Sydney: Allen & Unwin.

—— (1996a) 'Culture, Community, and Responsibilities: Abortion in Ireland', *Sociology* 30, 1: 279–298.

—— (1996b) 'Report: Northern Ireland Women's Coalition', *Australian Feminist Studies* 11, 24: 317–320.

—— (1997) 'Diversity and Commonality: Women, Politics, and Northern Ireland', *The European Journal of Women's Studies* 4, 1: 83–100.

—— (1998) 'Political Representation of Women in Northern Ireland', *Politics* 18, 1: 25–32.

Porter, N. (1996) *Rethinking Unionism. An Alternative Vision for Northern Ireland*, Belfast: Blackstaff Press.

Radcliffe, S. and Westwood, S. (1996) *ReMaking the Nation. Place, Identity and Politics in Latin America*, London: Routledge.

Rooney, E. and Woods, M. (1995) *Women, Community and Politics in Northern Ireland: A Belfast Study*, Coleraine: University of Ulster.

Roulston, C. (1989) 'Women on the Margins: The Women's Movement in Northern Ireland 1973–1988', *Science and Society* 53, 2: 219–236.

Rowbotham, S. (1992) *Women in Movement. Feminism and Social Action*, New York and London: Routledge.

Skjeie, H. (1993) 'Ending the Male Political Hegemony: the Norwegian Experience' in J. Lovenduski and P. Norris (eds) *Gender and Party Politics*, London: Sage, 231–262.

Smyth, A. (1995) 'International Trends. Paying Our Disrespects to the Bloody States We're In: Women, Violence, Culture, and the State', *Journal of Women's History* 6, 4/7, 1: 190–215.

Smyth, M. (1996) *Life in Two Enclave Areas in Northern Ireland*, Derry: Templegrove Action Research Ltd.

Squires, J. (1996) 'Quotas for Women: Fair Representation?' *Parliamentary Affairs* 49, 1: 71–88.

Sylvester, C. (1993) 'Homeless in International Relations? Women's Place in Canonical Texts and Feminist Reimaginings' in M. Ringrose and A. J. Lerner (eds) *Reimagining the Nation*, Buckingham: Open University Press, 76–97.

Tamir, Y. (1995) *Liberal Nationalism*, Princeton, NJ: Princeton University Press.

Trew, K. (1996) 'National Identity' in R. Breen, P. Devine and L. Dowds (eds) *Social Attitudes in Northern Ireland*, Belfast: Appletree Press, 140–152.

Walby, S. (1996) 'Woman and Nation' in Balakrishnan, G. (ed.) *Mapping the Nation*, London and New York: Verso, 235–254.

Ward, M. (1995) *Unmanageable Revolutionaries. Women and Irish Nationalism*, London: Pluto Press.

Waylen, G. (1994) 'Women and Democratization: Conceptualising Gender Relations in Transition Politics', *World Politics* 46, 3: 327–354.

—— (1996) 'Analysing Women in the Politics of the Third World' in H. Afshar (ed.) *Women and Politics in the Third World*, London and New York: Routledge, 7–24.

Wekker, G. (1995) 'After the Last Sky, Where do the Birds Fly?' in H. Lutz, A.

Phoenix and N. Yuval-Davis (eds) *Crossfires. Nationalism, Racism and Gender in Europe*, London: Pluto Press, 65–87.

Wilford, R. (1996) 'Women and Politics in Northern Ireland', *Parliamentary Affairs* 49, 1: 41–54.

Young, I. M. (1990) *Justice and the Politics of Difference*, Princeton, NJ: Princeton University Press.

Yuval-Davis, N. (1994) 'Women, Ethnicity and Empowerment' in K.-K. Bhavnani and A. Phoenix (eds) *Shifting Identities. Shifting Racisms. A Feminism and Psychology Reader*, London: Sage, 179–197.

—— (1996) 'Women and the Biological Reproduction of "the Nation"', *Women's Studies International Forum* 1, 2: 17–24.

Yuval-Davis, N. and Anthias, F. (eds) (1989) *Woman-Nation-State*, London: Macmillan.

4 Gender, nationalism and transformation

Difference and commonality in South Africa's past and present

Sheila Meintjes

INTRODUCTION

Race and class have held pride of place in explaining the specific form and process of the South African political economy. Explanations have ranged from simplistic notions of primordial racial identities and capacities to a richer understanding that race, as well as class, ethnicity and regional identities, has shaped South African politics and society since the advent of settlers in the southern tip of Africa in the seventeenth century. There is a wide and textured historiography for those who wish to understand the history of colonialism, segregation and apartheid in South Africa. Whilst pre-colonial societies, colonial history, the history of industrialization and labour history have been the focus of scholarship, it is significant that gender relations have not received the same close analytical attention from scholars in general. None the less, a small corpus of literature addressing gender relations and women's struggles does exist, although gender remains a 'bit on the side' in most academic disciplines.[1] The existing work shows that women have been at the centre of shaping the nature of South African society and its political economy.

Belinda Bozzoli (1983) suggested that feminist theoretical concerns would considerably alter our understanding of race and class relations in South Africa. In particular she showed how the concept of patriarchy deployed in a variety of historical and social contexts revealed what she called a 'patchwork quilt of patriarchies'. She argued that the particularity of gender relations amongst different cultural and ethnic groups determined the different nature and timing of male and female migrancy and proletarianization. She did not take this analysis further to explore the multiple dynamics of women's social position and political participation. But her analysis pointed to the vital importance of recognizing what has become commonplace in the writings of the 1990s, the significance of difference – in terms of class, race and ethnic location – as well as the significance of geographic location, in understanding the nature of South African society and of women's economic and political status.

Since the early 1980s there has been considerable debate amongst women political activists in South Africa involved in the political struggle against apartheid about their positioning in relation to feminism. Some have eschewed any association with the concept, claiming that it is Western in origin, and that, in the context of the South African struggle, it had divisive effects. It divided women from each other, for there were many women who could not identify with the idea of women's liberation. It also divided men and women from one another. Others have embraced the term, attempting to give it a meaning germane to the national struggle in which South Africans were engaged. Thus in the 1980s women in the African National Congress Women's Section fought for recognition of a simultaneous struggle against apartheid oppression and gender oppression as the only way for true national liberation to be achieved. But it is only in the 1990s, since the demise of formal apartheid, that the debate has begun to probe more searchingly the implications of race in the construction of a South African feminist politics.

A recent account of women's organizations in South Africa has suggested that they are part of 'a women's movement' because they reflect the fact that 'women organize around issues that affect them in ways that challenge patriarchal assumptions' (Kemp *et al.* 1995). This suggests a feminist project in intent, a project which presupposes a challenge to the systemic aspects of women's subordination and oppression. It is true that women from different locations have not been passive bystanders in the making of South African history. Black[2] women, and African women in particular, have belligerently asserted their specific needs in the context of state actions curtailing their mobility and opportunities. Less understood, because not explored, are the reasons women have not directed their struggles against the various types of patriarchies which have limited their actions within tradition and customary laws. Rather, women's struggles have targeted the state. It was against attempts to contain their freedom of movement, and the pass laws in particular, that African women mobilized their oppositional energies at different times. In the 1980s, women's organizations articulated a new consciousness about the relationship between women's emancipation and national liberation. The context of national oppression has not easily embraced feminist objectives. But women's organization and struggles from at least the 1950s did pose a challenge to aspects of patriarchal domination, even if they did not offer an overt feminist agenda.

This chapter is an attempt to evaluate the political organization of women in their diverse locations in South Africa in the past and in the present. It attempts, first, to locate the enormous social divisions between women, and how these have been expressed politically over time. In so doing it provides a profile of the divisions between women in the twentieth century, and especially since the Second World War. It then analyses the diverse ways in which nationalist discourses have shaped the manner in which women have organized and been incorporated into political movements.

It considers some of the debates amongst women involved in those organizations. The final section focuses on developments in the post-1990 period, during the transition to democracy. In this period a coalition, known as the Women's National Coalition (WNC), was formed in an attempt to bridge the divisions between women across the ideological, racial and class divides during the crucial years of negotiation between 1991 and 1994. In the conclusion the impact of the WNC on the political and constitutional process is assessed.

WOMEN DIVIDED: STATE POLICY, TRADITION AND GENDER

The key divisions within the political economy have rested not merely upon race, but also upon the rural–urban divide. In 1988 it was estimated that some 75 per cent of the population was African, 14 per cent White, 9 per cent Coloured and 3 per cent Indian; 30 per cent of the black African population live in the former 'Bantustans' (Budlender 1991: 4). Although there is a more or less even division between men and women, their geographic location is very unevenly dispersed. The urban industrial heartland of South Africa, Johannesburg, became a great melting pot of races, cultures and ethnicities from the moment gold was discovered in vast quantities in the 1890s. By the 1920s at least 42 per cent of the black population was living on white owned farms and in towns (Walker 1982: 12). Because of its history of pre-colonial settlement patterns, state formations, and the processes of settler colonial domination, South Africa has also been geographically divided into relatively discrete regions with distinctive ethnic majorities. Colonial policies of divide-and-rule maintained traditional authorities and areas reserved for African settlement. These were entrenched during the first years of Union with the 1913 Land Act, which delimited 13 per cent of the land for African usufruct. White farmers enjoyed access to the rest of the agriculturally rich areas of South Africa. They, too, were differentiated by class and culture, encompassing Afrikaner and English-speaking traditions. Segregation was further entrenched during the period of greatest proletarianization of all races under the 'Pact' (1924–1933) and Fusion (1934–1939) governments.[3] The period of apartheid under National Party rule built on these pre-existing foundations to institutionalize the segregation of black and white, urban and rural, South Africa. Apartheid introduced ethnic homelands and tightened up urban influx controls.

Gender was a key variable in the reproduction of all forms of economic and political relations in South Africa. For whites and blacks the experience was different. It was not simply that the initial form taken by the migrant labour system rested specifically on the needs and capacity of the rural African homesteads to produce their own means of subsistence, although this was an important element in explaining the periodization of the migrant labour system (Wolpe 1972). The key element in the maintenance of the rural homesteads was the labour and status of women. They did most of the agricultural work, planting, weeding and harvesting of crops for exchange, as well as maintaining kitchen gardens for home consumption. White women were less involved in agricultural production, although their domestic responsibilities included running kitchen gardens as well. Women of all groups, however, were subordinated within strictly hierarchical gendered relations of power and authority embedded within custom and tradition, albeit very different ones.

Under customary law all African women, from both urban and rural areas, were denied adult status, and were subject to male control. The migrant labour system had given women in rural areas greater responsibility for ensuring the maintenance of subsistence production and for the upbringing and welfare of children. This placed a much greater burden on women. Yet women in rural areas were in many ways more disadvantaged than their counterparts in urban areas. They were directly affected by the authority of chiefs and customary law. As minors in law, women could not own or inherit land or moveable property nor could they gain credit. Their access to means of subsistence depended upon their subservience to a chief and attachment to a male relative or spouse. Also significant was that whilst motherhood gave women great responsibilities, it did not provide women with rights over their children. Instead, custody and guardianship over children rested, in theory, solely with men. In practice, however, women found multiple ways of asserting their independence, and of protecting themselves within the parameters of tradition and custom. But this did not take any organized form of resistance. Rather one might argue that the high rate of urban influx of women reflected a desire to evade controls. Educated women in particular were able to escape the worst aspects of male control. Where organized opposition did emerge, it was to resist official controls, such as the pass laws.

Controls over white women were very different. A substantial rural class of tenant farmers, *bywoners*, had emerged in the early part of the century. As agriculture became more commercialized, so their security of tenure was eroded, and many of them were driven to join the white working class. Poor and unskilled, it was this stratum which became the object of class action by the state in the 1920s. Women were amongst the first of the *bywoner* class to migrate to the cities, where they were incorporated into the earliest textile manufacturing industries in the late 1920s and 1930s. Some of these women joined trade unions which introduced them to a new, more inclusive, cultural discourse. Afrikaner social welfare organizations linked to the Afrikaner cultural movement and the *Broederbond* (a secret Afrikaner nationalist political movement formed in 1918) were concerned to pre-empt the cultural 'degeneration' they saw in the industrial environment. Women in particular were the target of improvement programmes. Afrikaner trade unions were encouraged and supported by these movements. Worker organizations began to reflect the racial and gender diversity of the workforce.

There had been a steady increase in the numbers of people, including women, moving to Johannesburg during the 1920s and 1930s. The city provided a range of options for women unavailable in rural areas, including the possibilities of independence from male control. Schooling, especially by missionary societies, was widely available, as were jobs in white homes, shops and factories. The 1930s and 1940s saw a widening of opportunities for men and women alike as the industrial sector began to grow. A small, largely male, professional class of African lawyers, teachers, ministers and journalists began to flourish. Educated African women found opportunities in nursing, midwifery, and social work, whilst those with less education found jobs as waitresses, working in shops or as domestic workers in white homes. Where no formal jobs existed, a burgeoning informal service sector was monopolized by women as hawkers, beer brewers, dressmakers or washer-women (Wells 1993: 93). But township life was hard, and most people were very poor.

Welfare organizations were set up towards the end of the 1930s, concerned to improve conditions in the townships, often spearheaded by middle-class African women like Charlotte Maxeke, a social worker and first President of the Bantu Women's League which was formed in 1919. In the 1940s Madie Hall Xuma, American wife of Dr A. B. Xuma, President of the ANC during those years, organized a home improvement course through the Young Women's Christian Association (YWCA). These organizations were somewhat elitist in approach, emphasizing domestic duty, improving family life, and Western refinement. A fee-paying system tended to exclude the poor. But significant self-help organizations also emerged in the form of the *manyanos*, women's church groups, and *stokvels*, which were rather like cooperative savings clubs (Wells 1993: 96). These created very broad networks between women from a range of class backgrounds, but they were not obviously political in nature.

White liberals linked into these organizational networks as well. Perhaps the best known philanthropist during this period was Margaret Ballinger who in 1936 formed the Association of European and African Women. This organization encouraged cooperation between white and black women, but was based more on paternalistic white dominance than on equality. However, the association did establish the Bantu Children's Holiday Fund and the Margaret Ballinger Home for convalescent children before the Second World War (*ibid.*).

The National Party victory in 1948 substantially altered the political context for black people. Predicated on a belief in segregation, policy was directed towards tightening up control over individual migrancy and family urbanization. However, in 1951 the Tomlinson Commission Report pointed to the incapacity of rural reserves to maintain levels of consumption without considerable investment in infrastructure and agricultural extension. During the 1950s, the economics of commercial agriculture and urban industry determined rural policies. Economics and politics were closely intertwined in the restructuring of rural society. The role of 'Bantu Authorities' were redefined in the 1953 Bantu Authorities Act. This was followed in 1959 and 1967 with the Promotion of Bantu Self-Government Act and the Physical Planning and Utilisation of Resources Act. A key aspect of these policies was the effort to canalize labour to white farms rather than to urban areas. Linked to this was a programme to 'rehabilitate' production in the reserves. This involved stock culling as well as villagization programmes known as 'betterment schemes' (Lodge 1983: Chapter 11). They gave rise to widespread opposition and rural rebellion.

In tandem, the Nationalist government also established 'group areas' for people of different colour and Coloureds and Indians became subject to removal under the Group Areas Act. The outcome of these policies was to lead to the creation of distinctive 'political communities' based on ethnic, racial and cultural identities. But these racist policies at the same time created conditions for broad political alliances to be formed between organizations representing a more inclusive vision for South Africa's political future. This was the basis of the 1950s 'Congress Movement', which included the African National Congress (ANC), the South African Indian Congress (SAIC), the African People's Organization (APO) (a mainly Coloured organization based in the Western Cape), as well as the Congress of Democrats (COD) (an organization of white opponents to the Nationalist regime). The Federation of South African Women (FSAW) formed an important component of this movement.

After 1964 African women were barred from entering the urban areas to join their husbands. This created a huge potential army of labour in the reserves, where few opportunities for employment existed outside the white agricultural sector. The effect of this legislation created a twilight world of illegality for desperately poor women from rural areas who sought to find work in urban areas. Tens of thousands of women experienced arrest and endorsement back to rural homes. This intensified during the early 1980s, as the state attempted to curb growing urbanization (in 1982, for instance, 16,532 women were arrested for influx control offences) (Cock *et al.* 1982: 282).

The demographics of employment by the 1980s had changed markedly since the war. Women's proportional share of the labour market was 36 per cent, with white women in preponderance in higher paid jobs. This reflected educational and material advantage. African women dominated the service sector, especially domestic labour, but a small proportion had entered professions as well. Women tended to cluster in certain sectors, like textiles, food and canning, and in the service industry. In the popular upsurge of the 1980s, women's organizations gave an impetus to women trade unionists to become more militant in making demands to fulfil their own needs.

Apart from the opposition movements discussed above, white women were notably absent from national politics. However, women were active in voluntary associations concerned with welfare, health and education. This emphasis on welfare planning and provision can be seen as an extension of the 'domestic' focus of women's private functions. This included working for charities such as child welfare or nursing homes for unmarried mothers. The Church was a key institution in promoting a public role for women from all sections of the population. Women's Church Unions played a significant part in providing the voluntary staff for the Church's social welfare role. Indeed it was in this latter arena that much of the creative energy and dynamism came from women in all sections of the population. South Africa was, and remains, a highly religious society. It has been estimated that 70 per cent of all women in South Africa belong to a church.

Whilst these activities provide a social profile of women, they do not give one a sense of the structural aspects of subordination and exploitation which has given the notion of oppression real substance in South Africa. The segregation of the workplace by race at the same time segregated the workplace by sex. The canalization of labour from homeland to agricultural or urban employment affected the gender division of labour in specific ways. It established the notion that black women in towns, for instance, were part of an urban family unit. In reality, since the Second World War divorce rates have risen, and women were increasingly left to fend for themselves and their families without the assistance of what the authorities recognized as a 'primary bread winner'. During the height of the apartheid period, black housing in the urban areas was reserved for a male household head and his family. This led to appalling exploitation of women if their husbands left them or died. Women were expelled from their family homes and forced to depend on close male relatives for access to housing or else became shack-dwellers in the overcrowded backyards of rack-renting 'landlords'.

It was the specific differences in their life chances and life experiences which gave rise to very different ideological and political concerns of women from different cultural and ethnic groups. It is to these differences that we now turn.

IDEOLOGY AND POLITICS: THE INVENTION OF NATIONAL DISCOURSES

Women's involvement in politics, often described as an extension of their private roles as nurturers, service providers, and as wives and mothers, has been both passionate and militant. In South Africa women have been identified as the 'mothers of the nation'. In this way, black and white women have been able to influence the substance of politics within their specific communities. Women have been central to the process of inventing a national identity for their group. However, the ideological discourse employed in defining the sphere of women's actions was predominantly around motherhood, responsibility for children, and the protection of 'the family'. It was a national discourse which existed within the bounds of different patriarchies.

The relationship between national identity, race, gender and class is very complex in South Africa. The boundaries and meanings associated with different identities have had a changing dynamic, and have depended very crucially on situational factors. In particular, ideology and political affiliation have played a significant role in determining how people have identified themselves. Apartheid foregrounded race and ethnicity in its policies. By so doing, it often created divisions and conflict where none had existed before. For instance, the creation of Bantustan boundaries based on ethnic affiliation belied the melting-pot nature of South African society. Racial and ethnic intermingling had been a feature of its history. There were also strong cultural and religious affiliations which became embryonic nationalisms. The emergence of an Afrikaner identity, for instance, was both cultural, associated with an evolving language, and political, associated with an anti-imperialist stance. African nationalism, on the other hand, was an identity which embraced different ethnicities in order to create a single political movement for assimilation into the broader social and political framework.

For the success of the national project, whether it was Afrikaner or African nationalism, it was crucial that women be drawn into the process. This reflected the significance given to their mothering role as nurturers of the nation. It was imperative that women be the purveyors of this nationalism, to keep them within the 'patrimony'. This gave women a special and revered place, but also allowed for their continued subordination to the broader nationalist project. Recognizing and revering mothers was to deny them autonomy and authority beyond the domestic realm.

As early as 1913 African women engaged in striking and bold militant protest against attempts by the Bloemfontein municipality to impose passes. This protest was translated into an abiding portrayal of African women as 'mothers of the nation' in their struggle for the unity and sanctity of family life. In the most comprehensive study of women's anti-pass struggles yet conducted, Julia Wells (1993) argued that the resistance of women 'far exceeded the actions of their male counterparts in militancy' (Wells 1993: 1). But this militancy did not emanate from any innate or superior political instinct. Rather it was inspired by a more conservative concern for their roles as mothers and homemakers in the context of permanent urbanization. The 1913 women's protest was one of the earliest campaigns led by politically organized urban-based black women. Passes limited and regulated the independence of African and coloured women. Although they petitioned and complained to the authorities, including the Minister of Finance (who also held the portfolio of Native Affairs), of abuse by police and municipal officials, women were still arrested for contravening the pass laws. This led to on-going passive resistance from women all over the Orange Free State. It also led to the formation of one of the earliest politically motivated women's organizations, the Orange Free State Native and Coloured Women's Association. But these actions did not confront the underlying, more systemic, aspects of women's subordination.

At much the same time Afrikaner women were also prompted to protest as *volksmoeders* (mothers of the people) in a huge demonstration at the Union Buildings in 1914, when one of the heroes of the Boer war, General Christiaan de Wet was imprisoned for treasonous activities at the outbreak of the First World War (Brink 1990: 280). Women's passage into the public realms on these occasions were applauded.

White women in South Africa began organizing politically for the franchise as early as 1894 with the Franchise Department of the Women's Christian Temperance Union (WCTU), and more systematically with the formation of the Women's Enfranchisement Association of the Union (WEAU) in 1911 (Walker 1979). Its members, all white, never questioned the racial exclusiveness of the franchise, and indeed accepted the differential qualifications which existed between the northern provinces and the Cape Province (Walker 1990: 314). These gave the vote on the basis of education and property, excluding women and all but a tiny minority of Coloured and African men in the Cape. There was little support for the women's franchise from white men, despite the fact that the WEAU's politics provided further support for white supremacy.

Afrikaner women had kept out of the franchise debate, and the National Party had been vociferously opposed to it. However, in 1923, afraid that the issue might leave them behind, leading Nationalist women endorsed the inauguration of the Women's National Party, a grouping within the National Party. Their position was captured in the words of Mrs E. G. Malan: 'With regard to women's suffrage, they must ensure that if they get it the best men come to the head of affairs. Nationalist women must be organized. They must know on election day for whom they must vote' (Walker 1990: 333). The campaign for the vote for women then became tied to excluding black women. *'Die vrou wil nie saam met die kaffer stem nie'*,[4] announced the Transvaal region of the Women's National Party (*ibid.*: 335). The final acquisition of the vote for women in May 1930 constituted a paternal triumph, as well as a racist one, for it was a nail in the coffin of the African vote in the Cape, and of course it excluded all black women.

A small but vociferous group of liberal white women reacted to government attempts to disenfranchise the African and Coloured voters in the Cape. They formed an organization called the Defence of the Constitution League in 1955. The 'Black Sash', as it came to be called, remained small and middle-class. Their protests comprised silent vigils outside Parliament or in other public places of prominence, holding placards and wearing the distinctive black sash, symbols of mourning for the death of constitutional government. Few black women were induced to join. However, Black Sash Advice Offices served an important support function for people facing the consequences of apartheid laws and repression.

During the 1980s, the Black Sash also turned its attention to assisting communities under threat of removal when it formed the Transvaal Action Committee (TRAC). In 1985 TRAC joined up with similar organizations from other regions to form the National Land Committee. During the late 1980s and early 1990s women's issues became an issue in the organization as a new generation of younger women informed by feminist concerns became active members. The Black Sash, through its field workers in TRAC, in particular Mam' Lydia Kompe, became a moving force in assisting rural women to organize themselves into a Rural Women's Movement (RWM). Though small in numbers, the RWM has been important in giving voice to the problems and needs of rural black women. Since the late 1980s the RWM has called for a review of customary law and practices, and in particular has advocated the right of black women to inheritance and to land ownership. The Black Sash played a vital role during the dark days of apartheid both in monitoring the effects of apartheid legislation and in providing a vital service to people affected by repressive laws

More radical opposition came from the Congress Alliance during the 1950s. The 1950s were a time of determined popular struggles, during which protest was vociferous, defiant, but non-violent. The FSAW played a key role in the civic struggles and political opposition to apartheid. National Women's Day celebrated on 9 August commemorates the campaigns organized during 1955–1957 by the FSAW against the imposition of passes on women (Walker 1982).[5] The FSAW, formed in 1952 and 1953, brought together a broad front of women's organizations and included the African National Congress Women's League (ANCWL), the SAIC, South African Coloured People's Organization (SACPO) and members of COD. Signatures of thousands of women from all over South Africa were collected by indefatigable organizers for presentation to the Prime Minister, J. G. Strydom. The historic march of 20,000 women to Pretoria in 1956 became a symbol of women's determination and strength.

Membership of the FSAW was based on organizational rather than individual membership (Walker 1982). This had proved a sticking point in discussions, and the ANCWL, somewhat wary of the FSAW, had insisted on organizational rather than individual membership. The Federation's objectives were to improve the conditions under which women lived in South Africa. The opening conference in 1954 drafted the 'Women's Charter' which established the principle of full equality with men and challenged gender stereotypes. Walker (1982: 159) suggests that the aims of the new organization were 'far more sweeping in its proposals than any put forward by other contemporary women's organizations'. The delegates were quite explicit that their task was not merely to mobilize women in support of the programmes of the Congress organizations. They 'wanted to expand the scope of women's work within the national liberation movement' (*ibid.*).

By the mid-1950s the state was determined to limit further urbanization, and to halt the influx of women. So from the moment of its inception, the FSAW directed its energies almost entirely to anti-pass campaigns. Its organizational capacity was constantly threatened by coercive state action against its leaders, many of whom were banned. This period was decisive for resistance politics in general. The Congress of the People held at Kliptown in June 1955 drew up the 'Freedom Charter'. The FSAW participated equally in collecting demands nation-wide and ensured that issues of concern to women were reflected in the Charter. These revolved around living conditions, but extended to education and health facilities as well as emphasizing the issue of equality with men in social, political, legal and economic matters. As state repression grew in the late 1950s and early 1960s, many of the Federation's member organizations were banned. By the early 1960s it was effectively moribund, although it was never actually banned. Individuals found political work increasingly difficult as the state arrested and detained people suspected of working for the underground. Suspected activists were also banned and many were banished, like Frances Baard, a trade unionist, who was exiled to an area hundreds of miles from her home in the Eastern Cape. Helen Joseph spent nearly twenty years under banning orders and house arrest for her part in organizing women.

The 1970s saw a resurgence of popular anti-apartheid organization, led by a nascent trade union movement. Although focused initially on the shop-floor, the conditions in urban proletarian townships affected the nature of trade union concerns. But it was the struggles of the youth which dramatically altered the political terrain in the 1970s, sparked by resistance to the imposition of Afrikaans as the language of instruction in Transvaal schools. The protests began in Soweto, and after the police shootings of 16 June 1976, spread throughout the country. This proved to be a catalyst for wider opposition to emerge. Black parents organized themselves and linked up with civic organizations. It was during this period that Winnie Mandela, wife of Nelson Mandela, who was incarcerated for life on Robben Island for his role in organizing *Umkhonto we Sizwe* in the early 1960s, was banished to Brandfort, a remote town in the Orange Free State, for her participation in the new political organizations of the 1970s.

Towards the latter part of the 1970s, urban communities became increasingly involved in labour struggles. Consumer boycotts, for instance, linked civic and youth organizations with the shop-floor. Debates within the union movement about the relationship between shop-floor concerns and wider political struggles were a key aspect in attempts to forge unity in the early 1980s between progressive but independent trade unions. Unity stalled on the differences in approach to trade union organization (general or industry-based), to questions about whether to register as trade unions under existing racially discriminatory legislation or not, and the relationship between workers and popular struggles. Because of the nature of apartheid controls, trade union demands were inevitably linked to broader political demands for the dismantling of apartheid measures.

Gender was not an issue in these debates in the 1970s. In spite of growing industrial employment of women, trade unions reflected the dominance of men in the industrial sector. But in the early 1980s, along with the emergence of civic organizations, women's organizations with a political agenda linked to liberation emerged in the Western Cape, Natal and the Transvaal. Many of the women who joined these organizations were also members of trade unions and civic organizations. Indeed the interaction of working class shop-floor and community concerns was a significant aspect of the concerns of women's organizations. There was considerable cross-fertilization of strategies and demands, for instance in organizing effective consumer boycotts against specific companies like Fattis and Monis in the western Cape and Rowntree in the Eastern Cape in the early 1980s. It took somewhat longer for debates on sexual harassment in the workplace to surface, and it was not until the 1990s that this became a real issue of contention within trade unions.

In the 1980s, the tide began to turn against the apartheid regime. The emergence of the United Democratic Front (UDF) in 1983 was a crucial moment in the development of popular organization across a very broad front. Resistance during the 1980s favoured the anti-apartheid forces, in spite of brutal and unrelenting oppression, which included the regime imposing a 'state of emergency' and arrogating to itself extraordinary extra-legal powers. The UDF espoused an ideology of 'non-racialism' and included the whites-only End Conscription Campaign (ECC), as well as civic and women's organizations. These organizations in effect reflected the racial divisions embedded within the structures of apartheid society. Even non-racial organizations like the United Women's Organization (UWO) in the Western Cape reflected these racial divides in the branch structures. What held the multiple organizations together was commitment to the struggle for democracy and the principles and aspirations of the 1955 Freedom Charter.

During the 1980s, as youth and civic movements grew in numbers, so women too began to articulate specific needs. Non-racial regional women's organizations sprang up from 1981 onwards. The United Women's Organization (UWO) in the Western Cape was one of the first of a new generation of organizations to espouse and practice a systematic non-racial and cross-class perspective.[6] A number of its members were former FSAW and ANCWL members, like Dorothy Nyembe, Mildred Lesia and Amy Thornton. Nyembe had been a member of the banned ANCWL. Lesia had cut her political teeth in the trade unions and the ANC in the 1950s, and Amy Thornton had been a white activist in the 1950s. But the driving force in the organization were younger women, who drew inspiration from the past traditions of the FSAW, but who were very conscious of the different political conditions pertaining in the 1980s. For instance, the issue of membership was clear, it was to be on an individual basis, which would allow for all progressive women to join. However, there was also an understanding of the difficulties such a broad-based membership could have. Thus a principle of the organization was that members should not belong to other women's organizations. This stricture did not affect union membership or membership of civic structures, but it posed dilemmas for women who belonged to the Black Sash, for instance.

The branch structure of the UWO was the subject of considerable debate. There was concern that residential area branch organization would simply reproduce the separation imposed by the group areas act. This was overcome by the inclusive council structure, to which the executive was accountable. Each branch became an arena for the empowerment of women: there they built confidence and learned about conducting meetings, taking minutes, engaging in discussion and establishing their own area programmes based on their specific needs and interests. Each member had the opportunity to chair meetings and take responsibility for minutes and organizing meetings. Every member had the opportunity to represent her branch at the fortnightly council meetings. Thus, branch initiatives were balanced with the issues raised in the executive, and the regional programmes which emerged from the council discussions and decisions. The UWO had built a close-knit, efficient and effective organization by the time the UDF emerged in 1983, and was able to take up issues and act upon them quickly. Meetings were frequent and well attended. The objectives of the UWO were to mobilize women in the struggle against apartheid, and to bring women's interests to bear on the wider movement.

With the establishment of the UDF, the UWO was faced with a dilemma: it had built up a strong leadership cadre, but it was not so strong that it could do without them. Yet it was imperative that its leadership be part of the UDF leadership core. Indeed the departure of leaders like Cheryl Carolus to the UDF, and the involvement of women in UDF branch structures, did in fact weaken the effectiveness of the UWO. An 'Organising Group' was set up to try and counter these problems, but it became very difficult for women to attend branch meetings of both. In the later 1980s, as both resistance and repression intensified, members of the UWO and other UDF affiliated organizations were increasingly detained for long periods.

Women's organizations in the other provinces took somewhat longer to establish themselves, and neither the Natal Organization of Women (NOW) nor the Federation of Transvaal Women (FEDTRAW) achieved the effective organizational strength of the UWO. This was partly a reflection of the different political conditions pertaining in the different regions, and partly to do with the strength of other organizations, like civic and youth organizations, which attracted the support of politically motivated women.[7] It reflected, too, a limited concern and understanding of gender relations and the subordination of women in the anti-apartheid struggle.

During the 1980s, women played a very prominent role in organizations and in the struggles against repression. Women had by that time been considerably influenced by the experiences of women's organizations and the women's movements in many parts of the world. This had sparked a debate about the necessity of organizing *as women*. There was some caution in the way in which the debate about the relationship of women to liberation politics was articulated. Although many individual feminists joined these organizations, discussion of feminism was actively discouraged by the leadership as potentially divisive. Feminism was seen to be both Eurocentric and a particularly white middle-class concern, which did not resonate with the needs of black working-class women. The discourse of 'national struggle' overrode all other forms of debate. This was central to the strategies adopted by the UDF, to which these organizations were affiliated. Whilst prioritizing women's needs, and recognizing a need to organize separately, mobilization was crucially tied to 'national liberation', which meant the dismantling of apartheid.

In practice women's specific concerns were subordinated to the more general programmes which emerged out of UDF politics. However, the influence of women's organizations was evident in the acknowledgement of women's subordination in the adoption of an added principle of political behaviour, that encapsulated in the concept of 'non-sexism'. Women's organizations during the period of the 1980s participated equally with other organizations in the structures of the UDF.

Whilst this non-racial, non-sexist trend gained widespread support throughout South Africa, the more separatist ethno-nationalism of the Zulu Inkatha Movement found itself ideologically opposed to the UDF in Natal and KwaZulu. Fearful of mass support for the UDF, the Inkatha movement, with support from the KwaZulu Administration under Chief Mangosuthu (Gatsha) Buthelezi, began to persecute UDF members. This led to conflict which in the late 1980s and 1990s developed into full-scale civil war on the ground. The rivalry was enflamed by the intervention of a 'Third Force', which had the support of very senior members of the Nationalist Government, implicating even cabinet ministers. The death toll in this civil war is difficult to estimate with confidence, though numbers have been put at 20,000 for the decade from 1984.

In the 1950s and 1980s significant women's organizations had emerged dedicated to ending apartheid and oppression. The 1950s FSAW, though its affiliates comprised racially exclusive members, was linked to the Congress Movement: the objective of both was to create a non-racial society. In the 1980s, the organizations which emerged were themselves explicitly non-racial. In both periods, these were not feminist movements in the sense that their concerns were merely the ending of women's subordination. Their objective was to mobilize women for the general struggle against apartheid, whilst also introducing a women's perspective into that struggle. Their strategies included public and militant protest. There existed also a host of women's organizations, like the Housewives League (Women's Institutes), the National Council of Women, and welfare organizations whose concerns were more limited to promoting domesticity, or improving the legal and social position of women. They eschewed, and opposed, public displays of protest.

WOMEN'S RESPONSE TO POLITICAL CHANGE: NATIONALISM AND TRANSFORMATION IN THE 1990s

The unbanning of the liberation movements transformed the whole texture of politics in South Africa. Instead of clandestine meetings, covert membership, and armed struggle, the ANC, Pan Africanist Congress and other political organizations were able to enunciate their political principles and recruit members openly. An area of tension did arise in respect of what would happen to the UDF and its affiliate organizations. What was the relationship of the ANC, still a movement rather than a political party, to the internal movements? Would dissolution not demobilize civil society in the long run? This dilemma also faced the women's organizations around the country. There was particular concern about the need for women's organizations to remain autonomous. One of the lessons learned from Mozambique and Zimbabwe was how the incorporation of women's organizations in the state had demobilized women's initiatives. Would dissolving into the ANCWL fetter that independence? The re-launch of the ANCWL in 1990 as an autonomous organization aligned with the ANC seemed to put these concerns to rest, for the regional organizations did in fact dissolve and join the League. However, in the post-1994 period it has become clear that some of these concerns have been justified, for, as the ANC has transformed itself from a social movement to become a political party, so the branch structures of the ANC as well as the ANCWL have become weaker. There have also been considerable tensions between the ANC and the ANCWL.

However bitter were the divisions between different organizations and political traditions, the changed political environment after 1990 presented women with particular challenges which forced them to address the question of commonality around the 'woman question'. It was the ANCWL which first addressed the need to present a 'woman's perspective' to those deciding South Africa's future. It called a consultative 'workshop' to discuss the question of women's common interests. This led to the formation of a broad 'Women's National Coalition' in 1992 whose object was to put women's issues on the constitutional agenda. Members included national organizations and regional coalitions, amongst whom were the Inkatha Women's Brigade, the African National Congress and women from the National Party.

The debate about the relationship between nationalism and gender oppression was not part of the discourse during the 1980s. Where the issue was raised discussion did not go beyond the divisive effects which such a problematic subject might introduce into opposition politics. This only became an issue in the 1990s once a feminist perspective began to be articulated by women within the ANC itself. Even before the unbanning of the ANC in 1990, women in the Women's Section of the ANC had been concerned to place women's position and status on the political agenda for national liberation.

In January 1990 the Malibongwe Conference held in Amsterdam had brought internal women activists and exiles together, along with women from other countries, to evaluate and debate the 'woman question' in a future South Africa. The theme of the conference was 'Women United for a Unitary, Non-racial, Democratic South Africa' (Malibongwe 1990). The subsequent programme of action gave the notion of a struggle for 'non-sexism' greater prominence, and recognized that national liberation did 'not automatically guarantee the emancipation of women'.[8] Resolutions singled out problems faced by women in the rural areas, in the workplace and the 'double shift'. Patriarchy, in combination with racial oppression and class exploitation, was seen as the principal cause of these problems. Thus, women needed to organize themselves within trade unions, in civic and youth movements, to wage a struggle for emancipation. Leila Patel, a member of FEDTRAW, said in her opening address, 'The struggle must be waged simultaneously at all three levels. The question of the emancipation of women is therefore integral to our national democratic struggle'. The perspective outlined in her address suggests a much more self-conscious understanding that in order to emancipate women, a starting point had to be the material conditions within which women lived their lives: 'The point of departure is to start with women's needs and their level of understanding of their reality and to move at their pace' (Malibongwe 1990).

The ANCWL was relaunched in August 1990 in Durban, an event criticized for the pre-eminence given to male 'comrades', and questioning the movement's commitment to women's emancipation. This contrasted rather uneasily with the ANC's commitment to full equality between men and women. In May 1990 the ANC national executive committee had issued a statement, 'Emancipation of women in South Africa' (ANC 1990) which committed the ANC to the elimination of oppression and exploitation of all, but especially of women: 'The liberation of women is central to our people's struggle for freedom'. Within the ANC a small but politically astute group of feminist women in exile had, since the very early 1980s, been pushing for the issue to be debated in the wider movement. In 1981 Oliver Tambo had commented at an ANC Women's Conference:

> The struggle to conquer oppression in our country is the weaker for the traditionalist, conservative and primitive restraints imposed on women by man-dominated structures within our Movement, as also because of equally traditionalist attitudes of surrender and submission on the part of women.
>
> (ANC 1990)

Frene Ginwala, a senior member of the ANC in exile, deputy head of the ANC's Emancipation Commission and head of the ANC Research Department before she was elected to parliament in 1994 and made Speaker of the House of Assembly, also a strong feminist, saw the 2 May statement as a further means to 'help push open doors'. Ginwala is widely believed to have drafted the statement. Ginwala rather optimistically suggested that there was a growing understanding within the ANC of 'gender oppression' as a structural condition, and that radical change was required (Beall 1990: 7–8). In the past, although women's oppression was recognized in agreement about women's triple oppression, class, race, and sex, dealing with the latter was to wait until the first two had been solved by the dissolution of apartheid. This last perspective is reflected, for instance, in the pages of the *African Communist*, mouthpiece of the South African Communist Party, which argued that women's oppression was a 'subordinate, less antagonistic contradiction' than that of race or class oppression (Clara 1989: 118). However, the 1990 statement committed the ANC to including women's oppression as an integral part of the struggle for liberation. That a fundamental restructuring was in order was reflected in the commitment to tackling 'the material base, the legal system, the political and other institutions and the ideological and cultural underpinning of gender oppression now and in the future'. It acknowledged that affirmative action would have to rectify 'patterns of discrimination' (ANC 1990). For the ANCWL, a major issue was to translate the commitment of the ANC to women's emancipation into a reality reflected in leadership positions and treating women as equals.

Whilst the NEC statement may have reflected the sophisticated understanding of some in the leadership of the ANC, there was little discussion of the statement in the newly established branches of the movement. Thus at the ANC July 1991 conference, the ANCWL pushed for a women's quota system in the NEC. Although the majority of the 2,000 delegates did not support the proposal for a quota, the debate was conducted with intensity. Not a single member of the NEC spoke in favour of the quota. The ANCWL had underestimated the conservatism of the broad membership of the ANC, including many women, who also voted against the quota (Horn 1991: 37). Nelson Mandela was quoted after the conference: 'I can say with all confidence after that debate, and after the women had demonstrated their intensity of feeling on this issue, the ANC will never be the same' (Turok 1991: 9). The ANCWL conference in Kimberley in 1991 was more sober in its understanding of how great was the task of raising the consciousness of, and educating, the ANC about the oppression of women. The conference elected Baleka Kgositsile to the key post of Secretary General. She recognized that women's liberation was 'not an automatic thing, but it has to be fought for by women' (Daniels 1991: 35).

Meanwhile, discussion between the ANC and government during 1990 and 1991 had progressed beyond 'talks about talks' to agreement about formal negotiations. In this process women felt side-lined, and it was feared that, as in other transitional situations, women's particular social needs would be ignored. Women in the ANC then felt that an independent woman's voice was needed to ensure that women's issues were addressed in the negotiations process. They decided to work through the ANCWL and the newly established Emancipation Commission.

THE WOMEN'S NATIONAL COALITION AND THE CHARTER CAMPAIGN

The experience of segregation and apartheid had created yawning gulfs between women from different race, class and ethnic backgrounds. Even working-class women from different race groups had little in common in a society which had been predicated on racial identity. The migrant labour system and influx control, the labour preference system, and job segregation by race and sex, had created a differentiated labour market and a social system entirely geared to maintain it (see Posel 1991). The launch of the WNC in April 1992, after widespread consultations and preparations, was an historic moment. It saw women from different class backgrounds, race groups, political parties, from different kinds of women's organizations including the Church, welfare and the health sectors, rub shoulders with one another. They found much to agree upon in the search for common experiences. But their commonalities were based upon a recognition of the diversity of culture, race and class. It is to these differences that we must look to understand the incredible achievement of the WNC. That National Party women and the ANCWL sat together and debated the need for a coalition of women's interests was little short of a miracle.

On 27 September 1991 the first of a great number of conferences, workshops, seminars and consultations was held with thirty women's organizations to discuss the aim of drawing up a 'Women's Charter' of equality. At this meeting the delegates found common interests and concerns in a number of key areas. They agreed on the fact of gender oppression and that in diverse ways it affected all women in South Africa. They agreed, too, that fundamental changes must eliminate not only racism, but sexism also. Frene Ginwala's opening address pin-pointed the objectives of the Coalition: 'Women will have to make sure that the constitution goes beyond a ritualistic commitment to equality and actually lays the basis for effective gender equality'. When the WNC was launched at a conference in April 1992, it had sixty national organizations and four regional coalitions affiliated to it. By February 1994, when it presented the 'Women's Charter for Effective Equality' to a Women's Convention, ninety national organizations and fourteen regional coalitions were members.

The WNC approached the matter of diversity with sensitivity. Whilst recognizing that women shared subordination and oppression, their experiences in everyday life differed according to their material circumstances. Middle-class women and working-class women, black and white, Christian, Hindu, and Islamic women saw and experienced life very differently. This recognition of difference was what in fact made possible the coalition of women across such a broad ideological and political range. It moved away from the essentialism which had dogged many feminist initiatives elsewhere in the world.

But there were problems in coming to agreement about the structure of the Coalition and its relationship to member organizations. Fears were expressed that the WNC might impinge on the autonomy of organizations, whilst a number feared the dominance of political parties. The number of voting delegates also created tensions, with smaller organizations resisting being swamped by more numerous, politically aligned groups. Once these problems were resolved, the objectives of the Coalition were hammered out. The WNC was mandated by delegates at the launching conference to organize a campaign to consult with women throughout South Africa about their problems, needs and hopes for the future. It took many months for a programme, funding and an office to conduct the campaign, to be established.

During this whole process, the country was in crisis. Violence had escalated to unprecedented proportions, and the high profile media campaign envisaged by the WNC to highlight its objectives was somewhat side-lined. At the same time, members of the executive and the steering committee were also involved in the negotiations of the Conference for a Democratic South Africa (CODESA) as advisers and lobbyists. The ANCWL, for instance, engaged in a critique of the terms of reference of the working groups set up at CODESA. Women's caucuses of the different political parties were also angry at the paucity of women on the various delegations. The combined pressure of the women led to the establishment of a Gender Advisory Committee (GAC) at CODESA. But the violence of Third Force activities led to the breakdown of CODESA just as the GAC was getting off the ground. When the second round of talks began in March 1993, known as the 'Multi-Party Talks', the WNC had established its national office and campaign strategy, and was sufficiently organized to set up a monitoring process which worked very effectively.

The Negotiations Monitoring Team provided reports and information to the WNC member organizations (Albertyn 1994). Its work made possible the most significant intervention of the WNC in the constitutional process. This was over the question of the equality provisions in the Bill of Rights, to which traditional leaders objected. Chief Nonkonyana, a key spokesman in the Eastern Cape for the 'progressive' chiefs which formed themselves into the Congress of Traditional Leaders of South Africa (CONTRALESA), led the assault on equality for women by seeking the exclusion of customary law from the purview of the Bill of Rights. He also sought recognition of the powers and status of chiefs. There was an outcry from the women's caucus and members of the WNC at the compromise. The ANCWL felt that its own party was compromising the position of women, and also compromising the notion of equality. The debate was aired on radio and television, and gave the WNC much needed publicity. The final outcome was the removal of the offending compromise clause.

Meanwhile, the WNC launched its programme to educate and elicit women's demands for the charter. This process went hand in hand with a nation-wide participatory research project.[9] Research conducted by WNC researchers mapped the regional, racial, cultural and linguistic demography of women in South Africa. Research attempted to interview women on a sample based on this distribution. It is estimated that the campaign and the research reached more than two million women in the country. The findings of the research formed the basis of the 'Women's Charter for Effective Equality' which was presented to the February 1994 Women's Convention, and finally ratified in June of the same year.

The Charter redefined the notion of equality in terms of women's differentiated needs, claiming full and effective equality for women. It included points of general principle, such as the need for affirmative action and differential treatment for men and women, as well as suggesting specific policy prescriptions to redress imbalances. Its twelve articles cover every aspect of women's lives, including the law and administration of justice; the economy, specifically pointing to the implications of excluding women's informal economic activities from the national accounts; and the spheres of education and training, arguing for a view which accepts lifelong learning as its starting point. The articles on development, infrastructure, the environment and social services point to the need for the integration of a gender perspective in all programmes. The charter also calls for mechanisms to enable women's participation in political and civic life, a change in narrow definitions of family life and partnerships, and the end to subordination in custom, culture and religion. The issue of abortion proved to be very contentious in the coalition in general, but all women agreed that they 'should have the right to control over their own bodies, which includes the right to make reproductive decisions'. Articles also focus on health and on violence against women, which emerged as one of the most widespread and endemic aspects of the experience of all women in South Africa (Charter 1994: 7). The final clause dealt with the question of media representation.

It was envisaged that the charter would perform a dual function. First, it would reflect the diversity of demands of South African women, and thus be a political document around which women's organizations could mobilize and act in their own chosen ways. Some hoped that the charter could become the focus for the mobilization and organization of a strong and effective women's movement in South Africa. Since the release of the charter, this hope has not been realized. Part of the reason for this lies in the very diversity of interests involved in the WNC: there has been little to hold a sustained movement together since the election of a democratic government, apart from the recognition of diversity. Women's capacity to work together depends upon mobilizing around unifying issues, and since the elections, these have not emerged in a way to engage the WNC. The WNC elected to continue its existence in order to popularize and take forward the aims expressed in the charter, but it has been characterized by leadership problems and lack of money. The leaders capable of taking forward the aims of the charter were, on the whole, elected to parliament, where energies have been dispersed in national politics and the tasks of the moment, rather than in fighting the gender struggle.

Second, the charter was envisaged as influencing the shape of the new Constitution, law and public policy. In this area, the charter and the WNC has played an important role. The acceptance of the notion of effective equality, which points to the areas of women's experience of civil society which prevents their enjoyment of equal rights with men, was acknowledged by President Mandela when the completed charter was presented to him in August 1994.

WOMEN'S INTERESTS IN THE FIRST DEMOCRATIC ERA

How effective have these organizational realignments been for women's concerns? The effect of the campaign dramatically altered the visibility of women during its height, between June 1993 to February 1994. This had significant effects on the negotiations for a new constitution, particularly with regard to women's representation and in ensuring that women's interests would be protected by the Bill of Rights. The campaign involved mobilizing the media, initiating education workshops around the country on the themes of women's legal status, access to rural and urban land and resources, violence against women, and health and work, as well as conducting the research.

The campaign transformed the profile and discourse around women and gender relations. It gave substance to the shadowy notion of 'non-sexism' and asserted the importance of women's particular disabilities in the debate about human rights in South Africa. Changes in the law have subsequently outlawed rape in marriage, offered protection from domestic violence for women, and made illegal any discrimination against women. These changes signalled the success of women's campaigns for their rights, even in the private sphere. The WNC campaign engaged the whole of South African society in questioning its norms about women's status and women's citizenship.

The charter has been used as a touchstone for the needs and demands of women in South Africa in policy prescriptions and in legislation. An Office on the Status of Women was established towards the end of 1996 in the office of the Deputy President, Thabo Mbeki. However, its effectiveness will be determined by how seriously it is taken, and whether it will be given more than a consultative role. The office has very few resources at its command, and so far has not been given a budget of its own. A Commission for Gender Equality (CGE) was set up early in 1997, and has already begun a process of widespread consultation with women's organizations and government departments in order to find a role for itself. At the provincial level, Gender Commissions have also been set up. Within government departments, too, gender 'desks' or gender 'offices' are in the process of being set up. The question that needs to be posed is whether these will be more than mere tokenism, or whether this government machinery will be able to make a difference in promoting full gender equality.

As far as the WNC is concerned, it has not turned out to be the catalyst for the long-hoped-for women's movement which could sustain the struggle for women's emancipation.. The coalition of organizations does not seem to have produced the collective will to take on the implementation of the charter. Instead, what has transpired is a series of campaigns around burning issues which have *not* been led by the WNC. The most crucial area of concern for women has been that of violence, both against themselves and in the country at large. Yet the WNC has been unable to provide any lead as to how to prioritize this, or any other issue of immediate concern to women.

The fact that women's organizations in South Africa have managed to achieve so much in terms of a constitutional dispensation which reflects substantive equality, and spells out in particular the object of 'non-sexism' is quite remarkable. In no other constitution in the world have such progressive ideas been articulated. The problem, though, is that women will only achieve effective equality once they are able to claim their rights. This is not something individual women are going to be able to do in a society which has not reconstructed its gender power relations. The patriarchies remain substantially unchanged.

At the same time, whenever the problems of women's subordination or oppression are raised, there is a general recognition that without a women's movement in civil society to press for change, the future for women looks bleak. The ANCWL, linked to the ANC, has lost the leadership role it played in the early 1990s and has, since 1995, been beset by leadership and financial problems. The post-election period has left the ANCWL without a sense of direction in terms of a programme of action or of the needs of its very diverse membership. It includes within its ranks those who are now in parliament and in government, as well as those who live in abject poverty in the urban and rural areas. Winnie Madikizela Mandela received overwhelming support from most of the regions in her bid for the presidency, in spite of a number of scandals and the walkout of eleven National Executive Members in 1994. The ANC has tried very hard to prevent her acquiring a leadership role, but they have been unable to silence her. Mandela commands enormous popular support amongst the poor, for she amongst all the ANC leaders fearlessly expresses their basic demands for houses and jobs in her criticisms of the ANC. But Mandela seems unable to gather a strong visionary leadership around her, and she articulates a strong Africanist position somewhat at odds with the inclusive principles of the ANC. A major problem has been for the ANCWL to define a role for itself which resonates with the diverse membership of the ANC, and which would draw ANC women into its structures.

CONCLUSIONS

Apartheid created a society which was divided along a multiplicity of lines: race, class, ethnicity and gender. It created an extraordinary gap between rich and poor, white and black. Bitter divisions along lines of race and ethnicity found expression in quite distinctive African and Afrikaner nationalist ideologies. Ethnic nationalist ideologies also emerged. Women were as much part of this fracturing as men were. They were also militant and passionate actors in resistance and in oppression. Thus the post-apartheid coalition which emerged in 1992 stands out as an extraordinary anomaly.

The transition to democracy provided the setting for women across these divides to come together to seek the commonalities of their subordination under patriarchy. The process was fragile, it was fraught with undebated tensions about the past, about the uncertainties of the future. The charter reflects the remarkable areas of consensus that emerged in establishing principles for substantive equality. It reflects the common experiences of women across all the divisions. When the WNC faced crises which threatened fragmentation, these were overcome by the overriding recognition of the vital need for women to define the terms for a citizenship based on substantive equality. This concern kept the differences within manageable proportions. However, in the post-election period, the commonalities of the constitution-making period have fallen away. Women in the WNC and the ANCWL have been unable to sustain the vision which held diverse organizations together. This has meant that the emancipatory and transformatory project embedded within the charter has lost its vigour.

The story is not yet concluded, because these organizations exist within a dynamic and fast-changing environment. Challenges are being thrown up by the difficulties which South Africa faces in its democratizing process. The best example of this rests in the reaction of women to growing abuse and violence as the political struggle against apartheid was replaced by negotiation and compromise. There are clear signs that women became the target of the anger of different groups at the nature of the changes in South Africa. As women have begun to acquire more confidence and to play a more public role, so individual women have come under physical attack in the form of sexual assault. Rape and sexual assault appear to have taken on a coordinated aspect, as evidence of 'rape gangs' is beginning to emerge. Organizations dealing with this abuse have formed a network in order to coordinate campaigns and develop a common understanding. It is too early to tell how successful this coalition will be. What is clear is that the experience of violence is shared across the diversity of South African womanhood. Whilst not attempting to assert any kind of essentialism, this specifically gendered experience suggests that we still need to question the systemic nature, and consequences, of the power and authority wielded by South Africa's diverse patriarchies.

NOTES

1 This phrase comes from the title of an article by S. Hassim, J. Metelerkamp and A. Todes (1985), 'A Bit on the Side: Gender Struggles in the Politics of Transformation', *Transformation*, 5: 3–32.
2 The terms Coloured, Indian, African and White, in capital letters, refer to the terminology imposed by the Population Registration Act which established the racial classification upon which apartheid policy was predicated. In opposition to these terms, the term 'Black' was espoused by the Black Consciousness Movement during the 1970s, and included Indian and Coloured participants. Lower case was used by opponents to the regime in referring to these categories. I use the term black to refer to African, Coloured and Indian people, and when wishing to identify specific categories, I use the upper case.
3 The 1924–1933 'Pact' government was an alliance between Barry Hertzog's National Party and the Labour Party led by Colonel F. H. P. Creswell. The 1933–1939 'Fusion' government was born out of a coalition between the National Party and the South African Party led by General Jan Smuts. The outcome was the United South African Nationalist Party, known as the United Party.
4 This translates as 'The woman does not want to vote with kaffirs'.
5 Walker's book (1982) provides the most comprehensive history of women's political involvement during the first part of the twentieth century, although some of her conclusions about the failure of these organizations have been questioned.
6 The following section is based upon my own experience in the UWO, to which I belonged from its inception in 1981 until 1984, when I left Cape Town to live in Natal. There I joined the Natal Organization of Women in 1985.
7 The history of women's organization during the 1980s remains to be researched and written.
8 'Programme of Action' Malibongwe Conference Resolution, January 1990.
9 The author was a member of the Research Supervisory Group and coordinator of the overall research process.

BIBLIOGRAPHY

Albertyn, C. (1994) 'Women and the Transition to Democracy in South Africa' in C. Murray (ed.) *Gender and the new South African Legal Order*, Johannesburg: Juta.

ANC (1990) 'Statement of the National Executive Committee of the African National Congress on the Emancipation of Women in South Africa, May 2nd 1990'.

Beall, J. (1990) 'Picking up the Gauntlet': Women Discuss ANC Statement', *Agenda* 8: 5–18.

Bozzoli, B. (1983) 'Marxism, Feminism and South African Studies' *Journal of Southern African Studies*, 9, 2: 139–171.

Brink, E. (1990) 'Man-made Women: Gender, Class and the Ideology of the *volksmoeder*' in C. Walker (ed.) *Women and Gender in Southern Africa to 1945*, Cape Town: David Philip.

Budlender, D. (1991) *Women and the Economy*, Johannesburg: CASE.

Clara (1989) 'Feminism and the Struggle for National Liberation', *African Communist* 118: 38–43.

Cock, J., Favis, M., Joffe, A., Miller, S., Satchwell, K., Schreiner, J., Volbrecht, G. and Yawitch, J. (1982) 'Women and Changing Relations of Control', *South African Review, One*, Johannesburg: Ravan Press.

Daniels, G. (1991) 'ANC Women's League: Breaking out of the Mould?' *Work In Progress* 75: 34–36.

Hassim, S., Metelerkamp, J. and Todes, A. (1985) 'A Bit on the Side: Gender Struggles in the Politics of Transformation', *Transformation*, 5: 3–32.

Horn, P. (1991) 'ANC Women's Quota: the Debate Continues', *Work in Progress*, 77: 37.

Kemp, A., Madlala, N., Moodley, A. and Salo, E. (1995) 'The dawn of a new day: redefining South African feminism', in A. Basu (ed.) *The Challenge of Local Feminisms: Women's Movements in Global Perspective*, Boulder, CO: Westview, 131–162.

Lodge, T. (1983) *Black Politics in South Africa since 1945*, Johannesburg: Ravan Press.

Malibongwe Conference (Amsterdam) (1990) Malibongwe Conference Papers, Centre for Applied Legal Studies, University of the Witwatersrand.

Posel, D. (1991) *The Making of Apartheid, 1948–1961: Conflict and Compromise*, Oxford: Clarendon Press.

Turok, M. (1991) 'The Women's Quota Debate: Building Non-sexism', *Work in Progress* 76: 9.

Union of South Africa, (1951) *Commission for the Socio-Economic Development of the Bantu Areas within the Union of South Africa*, Pretoria: Government Printer.

Walker, C. (1979) 'The Women's Suffrage Movement in South Africa', *Communications*, No 2, Cape Town: University of Cape Town.

—— (1982) *Women and Resistance in South Africa*, London: Onyx.

—— (1990) 'The Women's Suffrage Movement: the Politics of Gender, Race and Class', in C. Walker (ed.) *Women and Gender in Southern Africa to 1945*, Cape Town: David Philip.

Wells, J. (1993) *We now Demand! The History of Women's Resistance to the Pass Laws in South Africa*, Johannesburg: Witwatersrand University Press.

Wolpe, H. (1972) 'Capitalism and Cheap Labour-Power in South Africa: From Segregation to Apartheid', *Economy and Society*, 1(4): 425–456.

5 Women in contemporary Russia and the former Soviet Union

Rosalind Marsh

INTRODUCTION

It would be difficult to overemphasize the depth of the crisis which has afflicted the Russian Federation and the former Soviet republics from 1985 onwards, intensifying in the early post-Soviet era. This period, which has witnessed the disintegration of the Soviet Union, the fall of communism, and a troubled transition to a more pluralistic political system and a market economy akin to early capitalism, has been interpreted as nothing short of a 'second Russian revolution'. This chapter will provide an overview of the main implications for women of the deep divisions in the societies of Russia and the Soviet successor states during the perestroika and post-perestroika periods, concentrating on certain key issues such as women and nationalism, women's role in politics and the economy, the social position and cultural representation of women, and the influence of the women's movement. Although this has been a traumatic period for men as well as women in Russia and the post-Soviet states, many social divisions have had a disproportionately harsh impact on women (a fact rarely admitted in these societies themselves). The discussion will focus primarily on the Russian Federation, although occasional reference will also be made to similar problems affecting women in other post-Soviet states. This chapter makes no claim to be comprehensive, but simply to complement and update previous research (Buckley 1992: Corrin 1992; Marsh 1996; Posadskaya 1994; Rule and Noonan 1996), and to stimulate debate on some vital questions.

THE NATURE OF THE CRISIS

Gender divisions represent only one aspect of the crisis in Russia and the former Soviet states since 1985, which have also been profoundly divided by national strife, ethnic violence, political conflict, rapid economic and social change, cultural dislocation, moral trauma and psychological instability. Even if at the beginning of perestroika the discourse of 'crisis' was to some extent artificially whipped up by Gorbachev and other politicians in order to promote reform (Klimenkova 1994: 15), by the late 1980s it was still possible to celebrate the growing democratization and pluralism in Russian society (Buckley 1993: 248). In contrast, by 1990 the crisis had become palpable and inescapable. In 1990 Gorbachev frankly admitted that a crisis existed (*Materialy* 1990: 3), and the economist Gavriil Popov, who was briefly mayor of Moscow, referred to three crises resulting from perestroika: the crisis of the state system; the national crisis; and economic crisis (G. Popov 1990).

In the political sphere, by 1990 Russia demonstrated 'not just a society divided, but a heterogeneity of political preferences' (Buckley 1993: 249). Political leaders such as Gorbachev, Popov, Yeltsin, Zhirinovsky, Chernomyrdin and Lebed have been deeply divided in their interpretations of the political situation; and Russia has experienced an ever-growing diversity of political parties, groups and social movements, including democrats, Leninists, patriots, monarchists, Christians, greens, feminists and monarchists, all of whom possess widely divergent political views and strategies. By 1990 there was a growing lack of confidence in the president and the legitimacy of the system; never before in Russian history since the period immediately before 1917 had so many political leaders, parties, movements and groups agreed that a crisis existed. Particularly dramatic moments when political conflict erupted into violence were the attempted coup of August 1991, and Yeltsin's shelling of parliament in October 1993.

The nationalities question was an old problem in Russia, pre-dating the Bolshevik Revolution, but one which had been artificially suppressed during the Soviet period. In December 1990 the historian and people's deputy Yuri Afanasyev defined the origin of the re-emerging nationalities conflict as the 'rivers of blood' created by such 'Stalinist horrors' as the deportations of entire nationalities in the 1940s. He argued that the component nations of the USSR 'reject the idea of fraternal friendship and a unified Soviet Union: the very idea of a treaty establishing a new union has lost or is rapidly losing its attraction to them' (Afanasyev 1991: 37). The processes documented by Afanasyev led in the late 1980s to the military conflicts in Nagorno-Karabakh, Moldova and Tadzhikistan, and to widespread disaffection from the Soviet Union which erupted in unrest in the Baltic states, Ukraine and other republics, culminating in the break-up of the Soviet Union in 1991. Subsequently, during the post-communist period, ethnic conflict broke out within the Russian Federation itself, most notably in Chechnia in the years 1994–1996.

By 1990 the Russian economy was suffering from growing inflation, deficits of consumer goods, a massive foreign currency debt, a lack of investment and a fiscal crisis. The words *krizis* (crisis), *krakh* (crash, failure), *razval* (breakdown) and *otchaianie* (despair) had come to permeate public and private discourse. In turn, the discourse about *krizis*, arguably the most frequently used term in Russian political life, itself contributed to and intensified the processes of division and disintegration.

The crisis of the early 1990s affected everyday life in more immediate ways than the pluralism and democratization of the late 1980s, and therefore had more impact on women, who were more closely involved in the daily struggle for existence than men. A sense of crisis has persisted in the post-communist period, and is particularly widespread among Russian women, as has been suggested by recent interviews in which women have expressed their feelings about the sharp reduction in the quality of their lives in such terms as 'catastrophe', 'fear', 'disaster', 'demolition', 'anarchy', and so on (Eremicheva 1996: 153–163). Women's sense of catastrophe in the post-communist period is linked to a multitude of factors: the decrease in the quality of life, the threat of unemployment, rising criminality in the cities, the lack of opportunity to solve housing problems, the substitution of paid medical care and education for formerly free services, and fear for the future of their families.

GENDER DIVISIONS IN RUSSIAN AND SOVIET SOCIETY

Gender has never been recognized by Soviet or Russian politicians as a particularly important cause of conflict in their society. It is, however, important to note that the divisions related to gender which have surfaced in Russia since the mid-1980s pre-date by far the crisis of the perestroika and post-perestroika periods, and are rooted in long-standing patriarchal Russian and Soviet attitudes towards women (Clements, Engel and Worobec 1991; Stites 1978). Pre-revolutionary Russia displayed many features which have been defined as characteristic of patriarchal society: 'From its inception in slavery, class dominance took different forms for enslaved men and women: men were primarily exploited as workers; women were always exploited as workers, as providers of sexual services, and as reproducers' (Lerner 1986: 89). Twentieth-century history has demonstrated that communist societies (and their post-communist successors) have tended to perpetuate the deformations which they have inherited and were formally pledged to eliminate, but which are deeply embedded in their tradition and culture (Miliband 1989: 112).

In the former Soviet Union, there was a persistent discrepancy between the official lip service paid to women's equality and emancipation, and the social and political discrimination which women endured: the absence of women in decision-making bodies; the segregation of women into low-paid jobs and professions; women's 'double burden' of paid work and domestic responsibilities (Buckley 1989; Lapidus 1978). Women's own interests and desires were always subordinated to the economic and demographic policies of the Soviet state. The claim by Stalin and his successors that the 'woman question' had been definitively resolved meant that there was little need for further action on women's behalf, since they were allegedly emancipated and equal with men. More immediately, the current 'backlash' against women's emancipation can be traced back to demographic factors in the mid-1970s, when Brezhnev's government introduced a pro-natalist propaganda campaign to persuade women to place the family at the centre of their lives; and an educational policy aimed at ensuring that the next generation of adults adopted more traditional gender roles (Attwood 1991). The media emphasized the importance of the family, and motherhood was seen as women's true vocation, although the reality of Russian society was that there were very high levels of divorce, and that many Russian women chose to resort to abortion as their main method of contraception after having their first and only child.

When Gorbachev came to power in 1985, he took a more active interest in women's issues than any leader since Lenin, and many commentators took an optimistic view that Soviet women's lives would be improved (Walker 1986: 186). However, the inception of glasnost initially led to no serious discussion of gender issues, while in the years 1987–1989, with the exception of a few rare articles by Russian feminists (Voronina 1988; Zakharova, Posadskaia and Rimashevskaia 1989), the media renewed the essentialist propaganda of the 1970s, regularly representing women not as the victims of social evils in Russian society, but as their cause. Social problems such as juvenile delinquency, drug-taking, alcoholism, not to mention the general spiritual malaise of Russian society, were frequently ascribed to family break-up and working women's neglect of their children (Waters 1992). One particularly notorious article claimed: 'Women working outside the home means the disintegration of the family and a low birth-rate' (Rash 1989). Thus, when propaganda claims about the Soviet regime's 'emancipation' of women came to be challenged in the late 1980s, it was the validity of the goal itself which was called into question, rather than the illusory nature of Soviet-style 'emancipation'.

Despite his apparently benign intentions, Gorbachev's views on women proved to be reactionary, similar to those which had been voiced in Russia by political leaders since the mid-1970s. In *Perestroika* he made the now infamous statement about the need for women to return to their 'purely womanly mission' involving 'housework, the upbringing of children and the creation of a good family atmosphere', which, he felt, had suffered on account of 'the sincere and politically justified desire to make women equal with men in everything' (Gorbachev 1987: 116–118). During the perestroika period, the two opposing camps which had formed within the predominantly male Russian intelligentsia – 'democrats', who believed in Western pluralism and the market economy, and 'patriots', who advocated a return to traditional nationalist and Orthodox values (Toporov 1991) – both agreed that women should be encouraged to devote more time to home and family. It should, however, be noted that such values were also espoused by many Russian women themselves.

It is also important to bear in mind that the 'Soviet model' of gender relations, if such a general definition can be used, has been experienced in many different ways by women in the former USSR, depending on their ethnic origin and their social and economic background and position (Pilkington 1992: 188). Soviet demographic policy, for example, was differentiated on ethnic grounds: whereas there was an emphasis on the reproductive role of Russian women, there was a concurrent campaign for Central Asian women to have fewer children. Although the term 'class' is problematic in the Soviet and Russian context, the constituent parts of class identity (level of education, rural or urban background, residence in the centre or the provinces, the socio-economic status of parents, and position in the labour market), have also contributed to the stratification of Soviet society, and thus have played both a unifying and a divisive role in the post-Soviet states.

It is very difficult to generalize about women's experience in the former Soviet Union, which is an area of tremendous disparity, chaos and dislocation. After the breakdown of the unitary state and the monolithic vision of the Communist Party, a range of differences now exists in women's experience, both between the multi-national post-Soviet states and within the Russian Federation itself. Contrary to the simplistic view frequently propounded by the Soviet Communist Party, there is no single collective entity which can be labelled 'Soviet women' (still less, 'post-Soviet women'). There are enormous differences between the lives and opinions of young women and old women, urban women and rural women, professional women and uneducated women, lesbians and heterosexuals, women of different ethnic groups, refugees and migrants, prostitutes, religious women, overt feminists and women of all ages and nationalities who wish to return to the traditional values of home and family.

Nevertheless, for all their diversity, the post-Soviet states do share two common features: the revival of nationalism and a situation of economic crisis during the period of transition to a market system. Both these factors – nationalism and economic crisis – seem historically to have been conducive to a conservative approach to the position of women. A developing nationalism – whether German Nazism, Italian fascism, Islamic fundamentalism or the national revivals in contemporary East-Central Europe – has tended to be hostile to the idea of women's liberation. Emphasis is placed on women's reproductive and nurturing roles, rather than their role in the workforce; they are expected to stay at home and look after the children. If a period of national revival coincides with a serious economic crisis, women are the first to be driven out of the labour market; and the number of women in top professional positions and representative bodies decreases. Sometimes the issue of abortion is revisited, with some sections of society seeking a total ban in order to increase the indigenous population and prevent it from being overwhelmed by 'alien' immigrants. All these elements are present in the national revivals in contemporary Russia and the Soviet successor states.

WOMEN AND NATIONALISM

The identity crisis caused by the collapse of socialism and the desire to rewrite history has led to the discovery of nationalism as a convenient legitimizing factor: it defines the USSR as 'the other', which all the people of the former Soviet republics can now be presented as having opposed. The following discussion will focus on four distinctive aspects of the question of women and nationalism defined by current political theory: woman as the biological regenerator of the nation; woman as ideological symbol of the nation; woman as a participant in national-political discourse; and woman as a participant in national-military conflict (Anthias and Yuval-Davis 1989: 7; Milič 1993).

Woman as the biological regenerator of the nation

The nationalist revival in Russia and the post-Soviet states has led to a resurgence of pro-natalist propaganda and policies, and debates about the legitimacy of abortion and contraception. The post-Soviet governments have inherited the Soviet view that only women, and not men, are associated with families, children and reproduction (Pavlychko 1996: 307; Sargeant 1996). The policies of Gorbachev and Yeltsin towards women have been largely determined by a nationalist concern for population growth, rather than the interests of women themselves. Considerable publicity has been given to the demographic situation in the country, which has been steadily deteriorating since 1988. In the 1990s, for the first time in post-war Russia, the death rate came to exceed the birth rate (Baiduzhii 1994; Khudiakova 1994a), and in 1992 a natural population decrease was noted in the country for the first time in Russia's recorded history (a reduction of almost 220,000 people) (Brui 1993). An official report of May 1994 stated that a decline in population was observable in forty-nine of the country's eighty-nine regions (in 1992 this figure was forty-one, and in 1991 it was thirty-three) ('V Rossii zhivet 148.4 milliona chelovek. Chislennost' naseleniia prodolzhaet umen'shat'sia' 1994).

Nationalist discourse has encouraged women to have babies for the nation, which, it is hoped, will inculcate in them a love of their ethnic and national heritage. The prominent Russian feminist Olga Lipovskaia has claimed that many women are prepared to accept such nationalist propaganda:

> So the new role for women is already defined: they are supposed to be mothers; wombs to produce more children for their nation. Women themselves accept this responsibility to the state, as their gender identity is not recognized as being important in comparison with the growing national one.
>
> (Lipovskaia 1992: 24)

In Russia, the population decline in the 1990s, along with the diminishing proportion of ethnic Russians in the population, has helped to reinforce this nationalistic message (Pervyshin 1993).[1] In Russian culture and the media, the childless or infertile woman is generally seen in negative terms, as a defective being, far inferior to the single mother.

The national revival has been linked with the rise in the influence of national religions – the Russian Orthodox Church, the Catholic Church in Lithuania, and Islamic fundamentalism in Central Asia – which provide further support for conservative attitudes towards women. In Russia, the Orthodox Church has expressed hostility to abortion and contraception; in Lithuania, Catholic publications have promoted virginity and purity among young women, and warned them not to place too much emphasis on a career, or they will be in danger of not getting married (N. White 1997). The gender roles implicit in the arguments of a number of current thinkers in the post-Soviet states – whether they derive inspiration from an idealization of the market, Orthodox or Catholic religion, or nationalism – have in common an attack on women's reproductive rights, especially on abortion.[2] Gender issues are defined as a political luxury which the new democracies can ill afford.

In March 1994 Yeltsin's government issued an ill-thought-out bureaucratic directive to remove most abortions from medical insurance cover, thereby introducing fees for them, in an attempt to increase the birth rate. Fears were expressed that such fees would be unlikely to make women bear children, but would most probably lead to a greater number of illegal back-street abortions (Frolov 1994), which already caused the death of many women, especially teenagers and rural women (Grebesheva 1992). By 1996, the cost of an abortion had rapidly risen to 300,000 roubles in the provinces and 800,000 in Moscow (approximately US$60 and US$160 respectively) (Lebedeva 1996). (In August 1996 the average minimum living standard in Russia was calculated as 432,000 roubles per month, although it was admitted that 40 million people fell below this level (Golovachov 1996: 19).) However, this limitation on the availability of free abortions did not force Russian women to opt for giving birth: although the number of abortions began to fall, the ratio of 3:1 between abortions and births remained static (Shishina 1994). This suggests that many Russian women may have started avoiding both childbirth and abortion, and were making greater use of contraceptives.

Thus, in the case of abortion, the nationalist agenda succeeded in modifying the situation, but not in changing it significantly (in contrast to Poland, where abortion was banned under Walesa's presidency), and Russian women were to some extent able to reassert their own needs. However, the backlash is still continuing. In 1996 a government resolution spelt out the social indications for abortion more clearly, partially limiting its availability (Lebedeva 1996; Morozov 1996). The dissemination of contraceptive advice is also being challenged: by 1997, the Russian Planned

Parenthood Association, which since 1991 had achieved some success in reducing the high rate of abortion and in promoting sexual knowledge and a contraceptive culture, was being increasingly subjected to criticism from nationalist and religious bodies (Kon 1997). The growing desire to control and regulate women's bodies in contemporary Russia provides disturbing evidence of increasing male hostility to women's sexuality and the desire for women's submission, as well as functioning as a means of implementing the socio-economic transformation.

Woman as mother and symbol of the nation

Woman as mother symbol represents a means of homogenizing the otherwise differentiated national consciousness in the post-Soviet states, and has proved to be a useful instrument in nationalist conflicts. Women's reproductive and nurturing roles are presented as crucial to survival – not of a specific social system (as under state socialism), but of the nation, or ethnic community. 'Mother Russia' is an ancient image in Russia, and is currently experiencing another revival (Heldt 1992). The return to the pre-communist role of women symbolized by this image represents a reappropriation of national identity and culture, as with the rediscovery of the Slavophile tradition in Russia.

Similarly, post-independence Ukraine has witnessed the reassertion or invention of traditions about the allegedly pure, maternal, self-sacrificial features of the traditional Ukrainian woman. The central Ukrainian myth which has been propagated is that of 'Berehynia', the Hearth-mother, the perfect Ukrainian woman and spirit of the nation who allegedly existed in some prehistoric matriarchal past (Pavlychko 1996; Ruban 1992; Rubchak 1996). At first sight, the emphasis on women's role as hearth mother and saviour of the nation might seem to be an exalted image of women, but in the former Soviet Union nationalist movements have frequently made use of the symbol of woman as mother during the struggle for independence, only to ignore women's interests once they have achieved their principal aims.

Public discourse in Russia and other post-Soviet states, dominated by nationalist ideology and often sanctified by religion, defines the family as the smallest unit of the new ethnic or wider national group, and gives it, and especially women as mothers, a mission in the name of that community. The overburdened worker-mother of state socialism has been transformed into the revered mother of the newly nationalist post-Soviet states. The family is now perceived as a crucial element in the claim to national identity and self-determination – an ironic development, in view of the fact that Mill, Bebel and Engels, whose ideas on women's issues were formerly propagated in the Soviet Union, identify the family as the key source of women's subjection and social isolation. Another source of irony is the uneasy contradiction between current reverence for the ethnically-based national community and the propagation of 'masculinized' (Attwood 1996) values of individual enterprise, initiative and self-reliance required for survival in the new market system (Bridger, Kay and Pinnick: 1996; Einhorn 1993: 40–41).

Of course, the reality of motherhood and family life in Russia falls far below a romantic ideal. Family conflict is widespread, and has become one of the most common themes in Russian films, such as *Little Vera* (1988), and women's fiction, such as Petrushevskaia's *Night Time* (1992). Another somewhat paradoxical omission in contemporary propaganda about the family, in view of the reassertion of masculinist values in the post-Soviet states, is the role of the husband or male partner. It is simply assumed that he is available and supportive, eager to help his wife to return to the home; but this is a highly misleading assumption to make (Bridger 1992: 197; Kuznetsova 1988). Many men in the post-Soviet states are unemployed or poorly paid, disillusioned, demoralized, and unlikely to be either cooperative or even sober, so many married women cannot afford to become full-time mothers. Domestic violence is also rife: every year, about 14,000 women die in Russia at the hands of their husbands (the figure in the US is 75 per cent lower) (Kharlamova 1996; Zabelina 1996: 181). Moreover, the fantasy of the perfect housewife and mother is not applicable to about 10 million Russian single mothers who have no choice but to earn their own living; and since there are 9.2 million more women than men in Russia, not every woman is able to find a man to support her (Ivanova 1992). The enhanced familial role accorded to women has also been more than offset by the shift away from the private, domestic sphere and into the public institutions of mainstream politics, which are largely a forum for men.

Women and national-political discourse

The renewed and increasingly dominant nationalist discourse in Russia and other post-Soviet states threatens in many cases to subordinate women's citizenship rights to the aims of national state-building (Einhorn 1993: 1). In the post-communist period, the former official opposition to values attached to the private sphere has simply been reversed: women are now being urged to go back to the home, rather than to go out to work (Attwood 1996; Khudiakova 1991), while the paternalistic, patronizing nature of Soviet social policy has persisted. Such views have been constantly propagated by powerful men in the post-Soviet states. The sociologist Ivan Bestuzhev-Lada, one of Yeltsin's advisers, said in 1992: 'The workplace for a woman is with her children. She is not without work – children are her work' (Levina 1992). Similarly, the new leader of Kalmykia, Kirsan Iliumzhinov, spoke for many post-Soviet men when he declared in 1993: 'Women shouldn't work at all; let them stay at home and bring up children' (Evtushenko 1993). The ideological function of the current propagation of woman's 'natural mission' is to reconcile women to redundancy, low-prestige jobs, and their isolation from politics.[3]

Patriarchal nationalist discourse sometimes takes on neo-fascist over-tones. Some of the most aggressively masculinist views have, not surprisingly, been expressed by Vladimir Zhirinovsky, who has argued that man should be the 'head of the family', deciding

> when he will marry, whether his wife will work, how many children they will have, where and how these children will study, what sort of house they will have and what will be in and around it. Then there will not be any single elderly citizens or rejected children.
>
> (*Liberal* 2–3 November 1990: 3)

An even more extreme view was voiced by the fascist party chairman (cited in *Nezavisimaia gazeta*, 14 November 1991), who declared that all the country's ills stemmed from the fact that women have too much freedom, and promised that the fascists would restore order. Echoing Hitler's words, he stated that 'Fascism is a male doctrine, and male rule must prevail'.

It would, however, be a mistake to regard nationalism as an exclusively male agenda. The relationship between women and nationalism is a two-way process: nationalism often places restrictions on women but, equally, the erosion of their rights may incite women to espouse the nationalist cause. In the late 1980s, the insensitivity of the Russian state to the needs of the non-Russian nationalities often led women in the other Soviet republics to join nationalist movements, such as 'Sajudis' in Lithuania and 'Rukh' in Ukraine, because they regarded them as a unifying force, whereas Western-style feminism was perceived as divisive. Only later (for example after independence) did some feminists realize the contradictions between femi-nism and nationalism, and decide to leave nationalist movements to safeguard their own separate identity (Pavlychko 1996). By the mid-1990s, in post-communist Russia, nationalist feelings among women from various ethnic groups may well have been fanned by the general discrimination directed against all non-Russians, particularly 'persons of Caucasian nation-ality' (Chechens, Georgians, Armenians and Azeris) ('Ethnic Georgians . . . ' 1997), and, to a lesser extent, against Jews (Hearst 1997).

Nationalists would prefer to see women in a passive, submissive, primarily domestic role – and undoubtedly there are Russian women who would them-selves subscribe to such views. It is hardly surprising that many women in Russia today do not resist their confinement to the private sphere – some embrace it as a welcome respite from the rigours of the double or even triple burden to which they were subjected by state socialism. Moreover, it could also be argued that Western feminists sometimes tend to underplay the personal costs of women's entry into the public sphere. Yet although some Russian women wish to emulate what they see as Western women's right to 'choose', they fail to realize that temporarily relinquishing the right to work may mean that in the long term they are unable to enjoy the benefits of the market as consumers. In any case, harsh economic reality imposes different constraints, such as the elimination of women's citizenship rights.

There is, however, an alternative approach to nationalism in which women envisage a very different role for themselves. A more active interpretation of the national interest has been demonstrated by the actions of businesswomen and their organizations sponsoring the development of Russian culture – both high art and traditional crafts – or in their concerns that too many men in business simply squander their money on themselves and fail to invest for the future of their communities. Recent interviews conducted with Russian women who frequently use voluntary agencies suggest that it is women rather than men who are serious both about building for the future and conserving what was good from the past. Sometimes this sentiment is expressed in openly nationalist terms: 'It's in women that I see the rebirth of Russia, both morally and spiritually' (Bridger, Kay and Pinnick 1996: 196). However, Russian women do not relate this view to notions of passivity or of providing a stable moral and spiritual background against which 'the new Russian man' would be free to act for the nation's good. On the contrary, they link this theme with the need for social and political action, and for women to take a greater part in it. Paradoxically, it is the standard prescriptions of Russian nationalism with their wilful disregard for the talents and education of a generation of women that could be seen as conflicting with Russia's true national interests. When a resurgent Russian nationalism calls for women to return to the home and foster the rebirth of the nation, one casualty may be valuable business projects established by women themselves in order to enhance their feelings of self-worth and personal achievement (Bridger and Kay 1996).

Women in national-military conflicts

Since perestroika, Russian troops have been actively involved in wars in Afghanistan, the Trans-Dniester region of Moldova, and Chechnia, and military conflicts have also occurred in other post-Soviet states (for example, the conflict between Armenia and Azerbaijan in Nagorno-Karabakh and the war in Tadzhikistan). Women have not usually been active fighters, but have become passive victims of wars caused by national and ethnic conflicts: as casualties of indiscriminate bombing; as refugees or victims of devastation; as mothers, actively opposed to war; and as initiators or supporters of peace movements.

Yet although women have suffered enormously as a result of inter-ethnic and military conflict, this subject has been characterized as 'one of the remaining taboos in the Russian press' (Zabelina 1996: 181). The Russian media have failed to inform the population about the mass violence against women in the former Yugoslavia, during the Karabakh conflict and the Armenian pogroms in Sumgait, in the course of the Georgia-Abkhazia conflict, or, more recently, in Chechnia.

Another result of national and political conflicts has been the creation of millions of refugees and migrants in Russia and the former Soviet Union. It has been estimated that by 1996 approximately 6 million former Soviet citizens had been displaced from their homes (Vladimirov 1996); and that in the years 1989–1995, 2,159,200 Russians (out of a possible total of 25,289,700) migrated from other states of the former USSR back to Russia (Grafova 1997: 12). Reasons for the mass migration of ethnic Russians back to the Russian Federation are complex: the great – and for many, insurmountable – ethnic and cultural distance between Russians and the indigenous populations of other post-Soviet states; the ethnic principles on which the new states are founded, and their corresponding ethnic policies; economic hardships, especially the loss of skilled personnel, which are caused, among other things, by mass migration; and the threat of destabilization and military conflict, particularly in Tadzhikistan (Vitkovskaia 1996).

Contrary to western theory on women's experience of migration (Buijs 1993: 4), emigration back to Russia from the former Soviet republics has not generally been emancipatory for women, since due to the housing shortage most migration has been to rural areas where there are few educational and job opportunities for women and cultural adaptation has proved difficult (Pilkington 1997). The migrants are often badly treated and live in very poor conditions: in 1996, for example, approximately 540 migrant families (about 2,000 people) were reportedly living in seven dormitories in the Tutaev Engine Plant in Yaroslavl region (Airapetova 1996). Since 1995, the experience of ethnic Russians still living in Chechnia (where the *sharia*, or Islamic law, is now in force) (Grafova 1997), and of Russian refugees and forced migrants from Chechnia to other parts of the Russian Federation, appears to have been particularly bleak (Likhanov 1996; Nadezhdina 1996; Politkovskaia 1997).

WOMEN AND POLITICS

Under Gorbachev and Yeltsin, women have possessed even less power in mainstream politics than in earlier periods of Soviet history. Some Russian feminists have called the system which has developed since 1990 'male democracy' (Lipovskaia 1992), or a 'men's club' (Semenova 1992).

Gorbachev's democratization reforms actually reduced the percentage of women at the highest level of government, which dropped to a low point of 5.4 per cent in the 1990 elections to the RSFSR Congress of People's Deputies, since seats were no longer reserved for official women's organizations (Buckley 1992: 54–71). Nevertheless, since the late 1980s women have played a prominent part in grass-roots political movements, attending demonstrations, organizing meetings, electioneering and voting. In Lithuania, for example, they were seen as particularly important in the 'singing revolution', which led to the declaration of independence in March 1990. However, a highly symbolic episode occurred during the attempted coup of August 1991, when women were requested to withdraw from the Russian parliament and leave its defence to men. Some women left, but the rest indignantly refused to go, arguing with the soldiers on their tanks and protesting that they had an equal right to participate in the political life of their country (Posadskaya 1994: 1–2).

It is a fact that when the post-communist governments and new power structures were being formed, women seemed to fade out of the picture. Of the few women in Yeltsin's government, Galina Starovoitova, his adviser on nationality issues, was dismissed in 1992, and Ella Pamfilova, the Minister of Social Protection, resigned in January 1994 because she felt unable to tackle social problems effectively, or even to gain access to the Prime Minister Chernomyrdin (Valiuzhenich 1994).[4]

The reasons why women are not more prominent in mainstream politics vary across the post-Soviet states, but two important factors are the persistent belief that politics is a 'man's world' (A. Popov 1989), and the fact that women have other priorities, not least the daily struggle to feed their families. One commonly articulated belief in Russia is that people will not vote for women (Vasil'eva 1989). Women are still much more acceptable as behind-the-scenes organizers, while men carry out frequently less demanding public duties.

Until the post-communist period there was no unanimity among women activists about whether they should form political parties, or simply act as an interest group lobbying the government. At the Second Dubna Forum of November 1992, many Russian women expressed a reluctance to participate in the patriarchal power structures, while others argued that, unless women sought power, their political influence would remain so weak that women's issues (such as female unemployment, rape, contraception and abortion) would either be kept off political agendas or, at best, be accorded low priority. After Yeltsin's suspension of parliament in September 1993, the 'Women of Russia' political movement was formed. This bloc managed to achieve relative success in the December 1993 elections, taking 8.1 per cent of the vote for the 225 seats in the Duma (parliament) awarded on the basis of proportional representation from party lists, which meant that twenty-one candidates were elected. At least two of the twenty-six women candidates were elected according to a system of first past the post in single mandate districts (and another two were sympathizers: overall there were twenty-three or twenty-five 'Women of Russia' deputies) (Slater 1994).[5] The total number of women candidates in the Duma amounted to sixty (13.5 per cent), but it was only because of the moderately good showing of the 'Women of Russia' movement that the proportion of women was greater than in the preceding parliament of 1990–1993. This achievement suggested that some Russian women at least were prepared to vote for other women, and that women's issues would have some airing in post-communist Russia. The 'Women of Russia' bloc, however, is by no means a radical feminist movement, but a descendant of the Committee of Soviet Women (the official women's organization under the communist regime), a centrist party whose main concerns are traditional feminine values of home and family[6] –

the only kind of women's politics acceptable to the majority of Russian women.

The Duma elections of December 1995

A new low in women's representation in Russian politics occurred in December 1995, in the elections to the new Duma. The 'Women of Russia' movement failed to clear the 5 per cent barrier to representation in the Duma through the list system (their final result was 4.62 per cent of the vote). The reduced fortunes of 'Women of Russia' in the 1995 elections may demonstrate some disillusionment among Russian women with the movement's marginality and ineffectiveness in Russian politics (and also, perhaps, their initial support for the intervention in Chechnia in 1994). It might also reflect the fact that by 1995 their programme had become virtually indistinguishable from that of other moderate nationalist movements.

Another factor was the considerable success achieved by other male-dominated parties in incorporating women into their movements. Several other parties (the Communist Party of the Russian Federation, 'Forward, Russia!', 'Russia's Democratic Choice', 'Power to the People', and 'Yabloko') competed with 'Women of Russia' by including a woman among their top three candidates (an important position, because the ballot papers list only the first three names for each slate). Thus, ostensibly, women were playing a larger part in these elections than they had done in the past, but this advantage was more apparent than real, since women had a low representation in most party lists, ranging from 5.8 per cent in Zhirinovsky's Liberal Democratic Party to 20.6 per cent in Ryzhkov's 'Power to the People' (a minor party which gained little support in the elections), with 13.4 per cent in Chernomyrdin's centrist party 'Our Home is Russia' (*Rossiiskaia gazeta*, 6 September–17 October 1995).

After the elections, only parties which cleared the 5 per cent barrier were allowed to chair Duma committees. As a result, in the years 1996–1997 there were only two women chairing Duma committees: Alevtina Aparina (Russian Federation Communist Party) chairs the Committee on Women's Affairs, and Tamara Zlotnikova (democratic 'Yabloko' bloc) chairs the Committee on Ecology (Iuriev 1996). By mid-1997 there was only one woman minister in Yeltsin's government: Tatiana Dmitrieva, the Minister of Health (appointed in August 1996 and reappointed in the March 1997 reshuffle).

The presidential elections of June/July 1996

A similar picture emerged in the presidential elections of 1996. Of the seventy-eight people originally nominated as 'candidate for candidate for the presidency' in January 1996, there were only four women, just one of whom, Galina Starovoitova, reached the second ballot by receiving one million signatures endorsing her candidacy. However, in May the Supreme Court upheld the Central Electoral Commission's decision not to register Starovoitova as a candidate for president, since they claimed that 283,315 signatures on her registration documents 'had been falsified' ('Verkhovnyi Sud . . .' 1996). Eventually, therefore, no woman candidate stood in the presidential election.

It is now clear that democratization in Russia has not entailed the gaining by women of a political voice, since the balance has shifted even further to male dominance of the arenas of formal politics. Russia in crisis has become even more inhospitable to the political participation of women than the former Soviet Union for a number of reasons. First, the elimination of official quotas for women has diminished both the number of women who stand for election and those who get elected into parliament. Second, the majority of women continue to have a negative attitude to mainstream politics, which they see as a 'man's world', and choose to concentrate on other, local activities which they perceive as more immediate and valuable. They doubt the efficacy of mainstream political activity, and in any case have no time for political involvement; others remain sceptical about the value of a separate women's party. Third, economic crisis and nationalist propaganda have driven many women back into the home: the overwhelming preoccupation of most women has simply been to survive and support their families. Finally, many women have become disillusioned with the marginalization and powerlessness of the small minority of women who have managed to achieve some representation in the national arena.

Yeltsin and his government have made some attempt to incorporate women's issues into their political programme. At the end of 1992, he established a fifteen-strong 'Group of Gender Expertise' within the Supreme Soviet of the Russian Federation, with the aim of helping Russian parliamentarians and legislators to create laws which would take into account the specific interests of both sexes. This objective was significant, because all Russian laws had previously been non-gender-specific.

Members of the 'Women of Russia' movement claim that they have been successful in influencing government policy, especially through Ekaterina Lakhova, a long-time associate of Yeltsin's from Sverdlovsk, who in 1992 was appointed chair of the Commission for Women, Family and Demography attached to President Yeltsin's office, and according to one Russian feminist, played a 'relatively positive' role (Posadskaya 1994: 192). However, others might take a less optimistic viewpoint. Undoubtedly, Yeltsin's female political advisers have achieved some success in obtaining the reconsideration of new labour and family laws which would have made women unprofitable employees (Sargeant 1996). Perhaps their greatest achievement to date has been to contribute to the campaign against the draft law 'For the Protection of the Family, Motherhood, Fatherhood and Children', which was re-examined and finally shelved in 1993 on the grounds that it violated the norms of the constitution of the Russian Federation, the

European Commission of Human Rights and the United Nations Convention on the Elimination of Discrimination against Women (Khudiakova 1992; Liuka 1992; Pilkington 1996b). This can be partially ascribed to the combined influence exerted by Lakhova, other members of the 'Group of Gender Expertise' who later joined the 'Women of Russia' political movement, and liberal feminists associated with the Moscow Gender Centre. A more important factor, however, may simply have been the unstable political situation of 1993.

Yeltsin's female political advisers also helped to formulate the new family code, signed by the president on 1 March 1996. This law, despite the great opposition it aroused from some male activists (Tiurin 1995), does not include many revolutionary provisions, although it does contain certain new regulations about divorce, alimony, adoption and guardianship (*Semeinyi kodeks Rossiiskoi Federatsii* 1996). It also introduces the possibility of concluding pre-nuptial agreements (Polenina 1996), which may be of significant value to housewives abandoned by their 'new Russian' husbands. In general, however, women political advisers in post-communist Russia have been obliged to play a predominantly defensive role rather than acting positively to initiate new policy on women's issues.

WOMEN AND ECONOMIC CRISIS

Since the late 1980s, women have borne the brunt of the economic crisis. During perestroika, it was they who spent most time in endless queues for food and clothes (in addition to their full-time jobs and domestic roles); and as they still do most of the shopping, they have been most affected by the deficits and hyper-inflation of the post-communist era. After the price rises of April 1991 and January 1992, poverty and unemployment initially had a disproportionate effect on women, particularly among elderly women (Gerasimova 1996; Millinship 1993: 25–29) and those in low-paid service jobs.

Unemployment

One of the proudest boasts of Soviet socialism was that over 90 per cent of women were in paid employment. Under perestroika, women were able for the first time to make choices about how to divide their working time: to do part-time work, opt for flexi-time, or even choose temporarily to give up paid work altogether. Although for many women these options appeared attractive, there was a danger that such choices might deprive them of the possibility of re-entering the full-time workforce in the future.

Under Gorbachev and Yeltsin, the state's economic needs have been conveniently defined to coincide with the aspiration to return to traditional gender roles. Whether by accident or design, recent protective legislation concerning women's employment and benefits, particularly the enforcement of the law on women's entitlement to three years' maternity leave, has had the effect of placing women in a more unfavourable competitive position with respect to men in the transition to a market economy. The economic rationale behind the powerful campaign urging women to go back to the home became abundantly clear in 1993, when the Russian Minister of Labour posed the rhetorical question: 'Why do we have to give work to women when there are men unemployed?' (*Moscow Times*, 16 February 1993). The answer seems obvious. While statistical data are variable and unreliable, the general consensus among commentators is that until the mid-1990s unemployed women outnumber men in a ratio of about 70:30 (Bridger, Kay and Pinnick 1996; Nadezhdina 1996; Pankova 1993; Rotkirch and Haavio-Manila 1996). However, the situation appears to be changing gradually: between December 1992 and March 1995 the proportion of women among the registered unemployed declined from 72.2 per cent to 62.3 per cent (Ashwin and Bowers 1997: 23).

In contemporary Russia, the market system has emphasized traditionally masculine qualities: aggression and rationality, independence, competitiveness, the willingness to take risks (Attwood 1996). On the positive side, women who exhibit such characteristics now have the opportunity to start up their own businesses – if they also have money and know-how. However, many women, particularly those with small children, are at a significant disadvantage in the post-Soviet states, because in these societies newly based on competition, women's greater domestic and parental responsibilities encourage employers to regard them as the least reliable and efficient members of the workforce, and thus as the most likely candidates for redundancy. Moreover, since creches and kindergartens have either closed or are prohibitively expensive because of the removal of state subsidies in January 1992 (Millinship 1993: 4–5), many women have little choice but to stay at home. By 1996, when the number of pre-school institutions had been almost halved, the only alternative was for working mothers to lock their children in all day (Nadezhdina 1996).

Few Russian policy-makers or journalists have bothered to discover the views of women on 'returning them to the home'. A recent study does suggest that many women are initially relieved at being able to shed their 'double burden' of paid work and domestic duties, but that subsequently it is easier for younger women (and particularly for women from the *nouveaux riches*) to adjust to their lack of employment outside the home than for older women brought up under the Soviet system (Zdravosmyslova 1996). For many women in Russia and the post-Soviet states, employment is closely linked with their sense of identity.

Poverty and hardship

Poverty has also had a differential effect on Russian women. In 1993, it was estimated that women's average real pay was one-third lower than men's, while their pensions were worth only 70 per cent of the value of men's (Pankova 1993). Although in 1996, in the run-up to the presidential election, the minimum pension was raised to 82 per cent of the minimum living standard (on 1 August 1996 the Duma passed a law raising it again), the position of elderly women is likely to remain critical in the future, especially as one out of five people in Russia is now over sixty ('Russians are Beginning to Die at a Slightly Lower Rate' 1996).

Rural women have suffered particularly badly. The encouragement of 'family farms' since 1988 has created new problems for women, including long working days, intensive non-mechanized labour, and family conflicts (Bridger 1996). Under Yeltsin's land reforms, the division of land has frequently been implemented in ways that violate women's rights, and fears have been expressed that unless the situation changes, it will be mainly men, considered to be the head of the family, who will receive land during the land reform, leaving many women landless and without social protection (Terekhov 1993).

In the late 1990s, daily life continues to be as hard, or harder than ever. Even with the introduction of the market system, many women do not have access to all the essential convenience products and services taken for granted in the West. By no means all homes yet possess labour-saving devices such as washing machines; tinned baby food is in short supply (Likhanov 1996); and tampons are very expensive and not available throughout the country. Horrific conditions still prevail in maternity hospitals (Shafran 1994; Tutorskaia 1996); modern methods of contraception are not yet in general use throughout the Russian Federation and the post-Soviet states (Millinship 1993: 23–30); and it is still true that 'given the backwardness of the country's pharmaceutical industry, the main method of terminating a pregnancy is abortion' (Baiduzhii 1994; Borzenko 1994).[7] Although by the mid-1990s both contraceptives and information on family planning had become more readily available (although the pill remains in short supply), many women and couples still find contraceptives either psychologically unacceptable, unreliable, unavailable or very expensive (Baiduzhii 1994; Kigai 1996; Remennik 1993: 56).

Women's economic activity

In Russia and the post-Soviet states the interests of many women are being sacrificed to the economic transformation. Returning women to the 'private sphere' is an important strategy for the transformation from a 'full employment' economic and political system to a quasi-capitalist system. It should, however, not be assumed that all Russian women are simply passively returning to the home in the post-communist period; many have been engaged in formal or informal economic activity (Bridger, Kay and Pinnick 1996). Since 1994, however, some previously successful women's businesses have been forced to close because of the high cost of rent and interest rates on loans from commercial banks (not to mention registration fees, taxation, and protection money), while those that remain have been concerned almost solely with survival strategies (Bridger and Kay 1996).

Nevertheless, Russian women frequently speak highly of their own potential, and complain about the general helplessness of Russian men. Although such feelings could be dismissed as an anti-male rhetoric, by the mid-1990s such protestations were being taken seriously in some quarters. Women's greater reliability, honesty and organizational skills were being increasingly valued by foreign firms (Bruno 1996: 53–54) and by commercial enterprises and banking (Skliar 1994). In October 1994, for example, Tatiana Paramonova was appointed acting head of the Central Bank. At the time it seemed possible that such appointments might mark the beginning of a shift in social and economic attitudes towards women. However, the subsequent swift rejection of Paramonova as head of the bank demonstrated that even when Russian women do attain positions of power, their jobs are far from secure.

THE SOCIAL POSITION AND CULTURAL REPRESENTATION OF WOMEN

The current status of women has also been lowered by the manner in which pornography, prostitution, rape and violence against women have been publicized, propagating an image of women as sex objects and victims of violence (Attwood 1993; 1996; Goscilo 1993). Previously, Western feminists had praised the absence of such images, which stemmed from the ban on pornography and lack of advertising in the USSR, and had favourably contrasted Soviet restraint with the widespread denigration of women as sexual playthings, victims or temptresses in the West. However, this situation changed rapidly under glasnost, demonstrating that, as in the case of national enmities, such feelings had simply been repressed, not eradicated. Yet whereas glasnost, and the limited freedom of speech which followed it (S. White 1993: 94–101) allowed the Russian press to discuss many issues affecting women's health and reproduction which could formerly only be discussed in samizdat, such as abortion, contraception, venereal disease and AIDS (Buckley 1990), issues which concern male behaviour, such as rape and domestic violence, only came to be widely discussed in the 1990s.

Hitherto the freedom brought by the 'sexual revolution' in Russia has mainly affected the male half of the population at the expense of the female half, since the society experiencing the revolution was male-dominated in the first place. In culture and the media, men are generally presented as the subjects of sexual relations; women are primarily seen as the victims of male sexuality or as sexual deviants themselves. In the mid-1990s, issues of primary concern only to women, such as lesbianism (Alenin 1994; Toktal'eva 1989) and feminism (Kravchenko 1996; Posadskaya 1994), are frequently still treated in a superficial or sensational manner.

The post-Soviet states now propagate a contradictory mixture of age-old traditional values and unprecedented, sometimes alarming, new ideas on the role and status of women. One Russian feminist has noted with dismay that the image of womanhood propagated in the contemporary Russian media is 'a model as old as the world: the dualistic image of Madonna and whore' (Lipovskaia 1992: 24). The current role models for women – the strong, suffering mother, the virtuous woman, or the sexual being – revive the typology of folk tale and traditional images in Russian culture (Einhorn 1993: 40, 226; Marsh forthcoming), but whereas the Virgin Mary and Mother Russia are ancient images in Russian culture, the representation of the seductive whore as a Cinderella figure – as in Petr Todorovsky's film *Interdevochka* (*International Girl*, 1989) – gives a new twist to an old image. Although there is currently a great diversity of women's papers and magazines in Russia, these tend to depict traditional, conformist images of women. The Barbie doll stereotype of femininity, formerly ridiculed in the USSR, is now heavily promoted.

The campaigns promoting women's traditional role and the images of violence against women can be interpreted as different facets of the same contemporary project of reasserting male dominance in the post-Soviet states after decades of concern that women were challenging male supremacy (Attwood 1996). *A fortiori* it could be argued that the attempt to establish control over women's bodies through imposing fees on abortion and the campaign to return women to the home is an expression of post-Soviet men's newly-acquired control over what they perceive as their own 'possessions', a reappropriation of male collective identity and a symbol of having won back freedom and power from the communist state.

THE RUSSIAN WOMEN'S MOVEMENT

Unofficial women's groups and organizations began to form spontaneously in the USSR in the late 1980s, because women were losing faith in the will of male politicians and media figures to consider their problems. When the reduction of quotas for women's representation in parliament halved the number of women elected to the USSR Congress of People's Deputies in March 1989, it was finally brought home to many Soviet women that they could not depend on the state to act on their behalf, but would need to work for change themselves.

Women's groups in Russia currently attract members from a variety of ethnic, social and professional backgrounds and, reflecting the cleavages in the divided society they inhabit, embrace an immense variety of goals, hopes and strategies. Attempts to classify them inevitably oversimplify their diversity (Kay 1996; Skoptsova 1993), although they can be roughly divided into four main categories (Buckley 1992: 62–66; Konstantinova 1994). The first consists of political groups, including women-only groups which formed within broader political movements during perestroika, such as 'Sajudis' in

Lithuania or 'Rukh' in Ukraine; or independent political organizations, such as the 'Women of Russia' political movement. The second type is feminist groups devoted to consciousness-raising, which try to break down traditional gender-role stereotypes in order to conduct research on women's issues and to disseminate feminist literature. The best known are the Moscow Gender Centre, the St Petersburg Centre for Gender Problems, established in April 1993, and the Moscow club 'Transfiguration' which publishes a feminist journal of the same name (*Preobrazhenie*). The third category comprises professional associations of women writers, film-makers, workers in the defence industries, lawyers, teachers in secondary and higher education, and support groups for those in business and management. The fourth and most numerous group is composed of grass-roots women's movements, particularly those associated with perceptions of women as mothers, which have protested against the infringement of their rights. The most prominent is the Committee of Soldiers' Mothers, which by June 1990 had formed an all-Union committee called 'Women's Heart'. There are also a multitude of groups in different geographical locations whose aim is to protect women and children under the new conditions of economic and social crisis, societies to help families fleeing ethnic unrest, associations of women with large families or sick children, or simply local self-help groups devoted to mutual support and survival strategies (Kay 1996). The main factor that unites all these diverse women's groups is their common belief that women had suffered ill-treatment or discrimination under the Soviet regime, but their interpretations of the legacy of socialism vary widely, as do their recommendations and solutions.

Women's groups have been theorized by Western scholars as important constituents of a 'civil society' (Miliband 1989). However, an alternative interpretation of Russian women's groups is that they could be perceived as filling a 'civil society gap' or 'civil society trap' (terms coined by Barbara Einhorn), that is, providing a voluntary, amateur substitute for the social welfare system currently being dismantled in post-Soviet society.

Feminism

The lack of influence of feminism in contemporary Russia reflects traditional gender divisions in Russian society and prevailing essentialist views of women. Feminist groups represent only one of a multitude of alternative perspectives on the current crisis, and one which finds little acceptance in Russian society and has minimal political impact.

Political theorists have generally established that the greatest obstacles to women's liberation movements are to be found under military or extreme authoritarian regimes and in predominantly Islamic political systems (Randall 1987: 141) (as has been acknowledged by some Russian women migrants to Russia from Central Asia (Pilkington 1997)). Consistent with this theory, Russian women are, as might be expected, more favourably disposed to feminism than women from Chechnia, the Caucasus, and Central Asia; yet there is a persistent reluctance among many Russian women to adopt the 'feminist' label, since it appears to conflict with their deepest traditional beliefs.

In particular, many women in Russia are highly suspicious of Western *feministki* who, in their opinion, have an easy life and cannot possibly understand their problems. There are a number of possible reasons why Russian women have so little sympathy for Western-style feminism: the general conservatism and misogyny of Soviet society inherited from the Stalin and Brezhnev eras; traditional communist hostility to 'bourgeois' feminism; the stereotypes of women presented in the media, which make Russian women feel that to be a feminist inevitably means that they will 'lose their femininity' and cease to be attractive to men; the fact that Russian women are tired of ideological slogans about 'equal rights' which meant in practice that they were obliged both to work full time for negligible pay and to shoulder the bulk of the domestic chores; and, finally, the fact that Russian women simply do not know what feminism is, since Western feminist ideas have been consistently misrepresented in the Soviet and post-Soviet media. In the post-communist period 'feminism' has been constructed as intimately linked with discredited Soviet socialism, as yet another repressive 'ideology' hostile to the individual and, increasingly, as a Western import alien to the true interests of Russian society.

In post-communist Russia feminist ideas have had to develop against a background of increasingly anti-feminist ideology. Current media discourse in Russia displays not only nationalist tendencies, but also many patriarchal sentiments released by the rejection of socialism (Goryachev 1997; Klimenkova 1994; Rasputin 1990; Tolstaya 1990), far surpassing the 'backlash' against feminism in the West (Faludi 1992). A few Russian feminists have attempted to challenge the backlash, including Olga Voronina, who frankly regards Russian propaganda in favour of selfless, self-sacrificing womanhood as 'a demagogic cover for the prevailing utilitarian, consumerist and disdainful attitude towards women' (Voronina 1994: 135). However, many post-Soviet women, in attempting to analyse the legacy of their socialist heritage, are led either to reject it completely, or to feel nostalgia for the past (Lissyutkina 1993: Pilkington 1997). Because of the experience of having their culture stripped away by the state, Russian women are often attracted by the pre-modern (by contrast with post-modernist critiques of society in the West).

Even Russian feminist groups prefer to locate their ideals in the family, and generally attempt to avoid Western-style separatism, which is totally opposed to the traditional collectivism of Russian culture. The views of many Russian women, even those active in women's organizations, are closer to pre-feminist views in the West during the 1950s or to the recent revisionist positions of Betty Friedan and Jean Bethke Elshtain (Stacey 1983). 'Family feminism' is perhaps an apt term for the majority of grass-roots women's groups in contemporary Russia (Mitchison 1988).

The emphasis on women's caring, nurturing, peace-making activities among some feminists in the West (Gilligan 1982; Pierson 1987) has been echoed, consciously or unconsciously, by many Russian women. Disturbed by the impact of rapid change on their society, they see a need for women as a whole to be central, rather than marginal, to the processes that will determine the future well-being of their communities.[8]

A positive view of women's qualities is typical of statements by the 'Women of Russia' movement which claim that women in politics will be somehow 'different', more moral and worthy of trust. They reaffirm the value of mothering and the family, seeking to transfer their caring qualities into the public domain. This message was explicitly spelt out in their electoral platform prior to the December 1993 elections, which emphasized 'feminine self-understanding' and opposition to 'the sexual objectification of women' (Pilkington 1996b: 169–171; *Predvybornaia platforma ob"edineniia 'Zhenshchiny Rossii'* 1993) (but had little chance to demonstrate these virtues when elected). The negative side of such idealization is that, as we have seen, women's mission as saviours of the nation, their important role in moral education and national survival, has frequently been emphasized in nationalist and patriarchal discourse, which has claimed to speak in the name of women. Aleksandr Rutskoi, for example, has declared 'survival of the motherland' to be the purpose of the women's movement (Buehrer 1992).

Many post-Soviet women have evinced more interest in supporting pressure groups, either on health and family problems, or on global issues, such as peace, the environment and human rights (Konstantinova 1994: 69; Waters 1993: 293–294), than in seeking to wield power in the male-dominated political structures. To a great extent, such views are linked to mothers' desire to create a better future for their children. In Ukraine, for example, members of Rukh Women's Community successfully campaigned to get the issue of Chernobyl on to the agenda of the Ukrainian parliament, to close the plant and give children holidays outside the contaminated area (Pavlychko 1992).

Some women's groups emphasize women's special role as mediators and peace activists. The idealistic manifesto of the Moscow rape crisis centre 'Sisters' proclaims: 'We are building a society free of violence' (Zabelina 1996: 183–184). The 'Soldiers' mothers' organizations, which emerged as *ad hoc* single-issue women's groups, focusing on the effect of military service on their sons, initially in Afghanistan, and subsequently in Chechnia, have played a positive role in the resolution of military conflicts. Under perestroika they succeeded in achieving benefits for Afghan veterans and in initiating an investigation into the mysterious deaths of soldiers in non-combat service, particularly from various extreme forms of bullying (*dedovshchina*); and more recently, they contributed to the climate of opinion which persuaded Yeltsin to agree to end conscription altogether. These achievements, albeit relatively modest, have been greater than those of most other Russian women's organizations.

There is some limited evidence of solidarity between women from different ethnic groups. During the war in Chechnia, for example, the St Petersburg Gender Centre issued a manifesto protesting about violence against Chechen women, particularly by Muslim fundamentalists (Zabelina 1996: 184–186). However, in Chechnia and elsewhere there are mothers on both sides of the conflict, so women's organizations can only contribute to the peace-making process when their views coincide with the relevant political leaders' perceptions of the current national interest (as in the case of Lebed's brief appointment as Secretary of the National Security Council in 1996).

Relative failure of post-Soviet women's movements

Women's movements, like other 'new social movements', generally embody a protest against the *status quo* (Miliband 1989). Women's groups in Russia and the former USSR theoretically could have cut across class, and could have mobilized masses of women around women's issues. However, they were relatively slow to form during perestroika, and have probably exerted less political impact than the 'green' movement among the new social movements of the post-communist era. On the whole, the more conservative women's groups have been the most successful, such as 'Sajudis' in Lithuania, the 'Soldiers' Mothers' Organizations' in both Russia and Ukraine, and the 'Women of Russia' political movement.

There is currently little unity between women's organizations in Russia. Since the two Independent Women's Forums held at Dubna in 1991 and 1992 (the first independent women's conferences in Russia since 1908) (Cockburn 1991; de Haan-de Vogel *et al.* 1993; Marsh 1992), the unofficial women's movement has been largely uncoordinated, although a women's information network has been established.

In the mid-1990s, feminists in Moscow and Petersburg are perceived by grass-roots provincial women's groups as 'airy-fairy' theorists alien to their far more basic concerns (Kay 1996), while both feminists and grass-roots groups are suspicious of the 'Women of Russia' movement, the former because they perceive them as conservative successors to the official women's movement propagated by the old regime, the latter because they regard them as ineffectual, remote participants in irrelevant mainstream politics.[9] In short, the Russian women's movement is as deeply divided as Russian society itself (Azhgikhina 1997). Some feminist groups (a tiny minority) try to transcend these divisions, providing powerful critiques of their society (Posadskaya 1994; Rimashevskaia 1991; Voronina 1992) and establishing links with the international feminist movement. However, most Russian feminists, themselves tired of the artificially imposed unity of the past, lay great emphasis on the value of pluralism (Marsh 1992).

Russian feminists are very concerned to discover their own paths towards feminism, and not simply to imitate the West. While grappling with the legacy of socialism in creating women's oppression and looking to capitalist theory for new insights, they also attempt to explore the dangers and difficulties, as well as the benefits, of Western feminism. As feminism has generally waxed and waned with political liberalization and repression elsewhere (Randall 1987: 161), it is probable that opportunities for the growth of feminism in Russia and the former USSR will continue to be highly dependent on broader developments within what are still politically unstable states. Feminist discourse is likely to remain a minority undertaking among a plurality of women's discourses in post-Soviet Russia.

CONCLUSION

Russia in crisis has proved more inhospitable to women's interests than the Soviet regime. Since perestroika, the gender divisions in Russian society have been accentuated, whereas previously they were largely glossed over. Women's status in Russia and the post-Soviet states has been reduced because of the nationalist revival, political instability, economic crisis and radical cultural change, notably the propagation of essentialist views of women and the proliferation of pornography, prostitution and sexual violence. Although both sexes have been seeking new identities and values to fill the ideological vacuum created by the collapse of communism, women have become even more psychologically divided than men in post-Soviet society, torn (or often reluctantly obliged to choose) between work and family responsibilities. Many women have joined the 'new poor', and for them the privations and general confusion of the post-Soviet period have been aggravated by the sexual revolution and changing propaganda about gender roles.

'Women's issues' in the post-Soviet states are still considered irrelevant or secondary to political, national and economic problems, and feminist questions are usually strongly opposed, silenced or ridiculed. Although women have generally suffered more than men from the changes in post-Soviet society, nationalism and ethnicity have surfaced as major problems, far surpassing gender as political issues. The position of Russians in the 'near-abroad' has been seen as a more important issue by the government and political activists than division by gender. Mass migration has exacerbated racial tensions, especially in conditions of economic crisis.

The multiple divisions in the societies of Russia and the Soviet successor states – political, economic, social and ethnic – are forces that can both unite and divide women in the post-communist era. In the political sphere, while women are sometimes theorized as being 'different', in practice they have been marginalized in mainstream politics, especially since December 1995, when the 'Women of Russia' movement failed to gain re-election. Yet, as the slogan of the Second Dubna Forum proclaimed, 'Democracy without women is no democracy'. Although Yeltsin has taken some notice of women advisers in formulating his policies, by the late 1990s it has become obvious that the problems of Russian women cannot be solved simply by the issuing of laws and presidential decrees, most of which are ignored (Azhgikhina 1997). The majority of Russian women will only have an opportunity to be part of the new 'democratic' culture to the extent to which they participate in the public sphere by building women's organizations.

The different forms of women's consciousness, ranging from traditionalism to feminism, reflect the diversity of the divided societies. Russian women have been undergoing a moral and cultural crisis: a desire to resist everything seen as connected with former Soviet socialism, including women's emancipation. During the Soviet period, women's liberation was regarded as an essential part of the revolution, whereas in post-communist Russia the end of women's emancipation is usually regarded as one positive result of the collapse of the USSR. However, Russian women's reluctance to problematize gender roles is constantly challenged by concrete changes in everyday life. Due tribute should be paid to the great resilience, adaptability and survival strategies of many women in Russian and post-Soviet society. Recent interviews, particularly with businesswomen and activists in the women's movement, demonstrate their ingenuity in developing new strategies in their personal and working lives to cope with the divisions in their society.

Although, as some Western scholars have pointed out, it may be futile to expect or even to hope that in present circumstances women in Russia and the post-Soviet states will unite to promote a common political agenda (Pilkington 1996b), it is nevertheless most likely that unless they do, women's issues will continue to be afforded very low priority by the post-communist governments.

NOTES

The transliteration system used is a modified version of the Library of Congress system. In the text, Russian proper names will be rendered according to conventional usage.

1 Similar sentiments have found expression in other Soviet successor states, notably Georgia, Estonia, Lithuania and Ukraine. Estonia has voiced concern that its nation is on the verge of extinction; whereas the more militaristic Georgia requires more soldiers to defend its borders and establish order within the country.
2 In both Russia and Lithuania, debates on abortion have taken place, although abortion has not yet been banned. According to Sazonov (1993), an opinion poll taken in Russia showed that 59 per cent were against a ban on abortion, and only 16 per cent for it. More women than men favoured abortion (64 per cent as opposed to 54 per cent).
3 Yeltsin's wife Naina has been perceived as the model of post-Soviet womanhood (Attwood 1996). In a rare interview, she declared: 'I am not the First Lady, I am simply the wife of the Russian president. . . . Everything is just as it was before for us. I've remained a housewife . . . I choose his ties, I take care of his shirts and suits'. She admits that, unlike Raisa Gorbacheva, she undertakes no public or

social work, but claims that this is because she has no power to effect any real change: 'All I can do is to ask the President for help. But there is an unbreakable rule in our family: I must never ask my husband about anything that relates to his work' (El'tsina 1992). Naina's long-suffering attitude, even when her husband treats her in a sexist manner in public (Hearst 1995), appears to be more acceptable to the majority of Russian women than the high political profile as 'First Lady' adopted by Raisa Gorbacheva. Naina herself was subjected to some criticism when she expressed independent views on her visit to Paris prior to the elections of December 1995 ('Mrs Yeltsin Interviewed on her Husband's Personality and Prospects' 1995). Likewise, from about February 1996, during Yeltsin's re-election campaign and his subsequent illness, he was suspected of relying too heavily on his daughter Tatiana Diachenko, who has no formal political position – a situation which has proved unacceptable to many Russians (Koshkareva 1996).

4 In May 1994 Pamfilova took up a new post as director of a Council for Social Policy under Yeltsin (Khudiakova 1994b). In December 1995 she stood as the first candidate on the slate of the small Republican Party.

5 There is some doubt about the exact figures, since the allegiance of some deputies is difficult to classify. Compare *Rossiiskaia gazeta*, 12 November 1993 and *Novaia ezhednevnaia gazeta*, 18 January 1994.

6 It was formed from the Union of Women of Russia (the renamed Committee of Soviet Women), the Association of Businesswomen of Russia, and the Union of Women in the Navy. For further discussion see Buckley (1997).

7 According to official statistics, about 4 million abortions are performed in Russia annually, although, according to experts, the real figure may be much higher (Borzenko 1994). In 1996 Russia held second place in the world, following Romania, in its number of abortions (officially quoted as 76 per 1,000 women of childbearing age) (Kokurina 1996; Morozov 1996).

8 For a similar view, see the manifesto of the newly formed 'Women for Solidarity' group (Khamrayev 1995).

9 This disunity surfaced at the 1995 UN women's conference in Beijing, where non-governmental Russian women's organizations became disillusioned with the official Russian delegation, which ignored the needs and wishes of the NGOs who were banished outside the city.

BIBLIOGRAPHY

Adamushina, M. (1995) 'Nasilie v sem'e? Net problemy', *Nezavisimaia gazeta*, 31 October: 6.

Afanasyev, Y. (1991) 'The Coming Dictatorship', *New York Review of Books*, 38, 3: 37.

Airapetova, N. (1996) 'Bespredel s pomoshch'iu zakonov', *Nezavisimaia gazeta*, 26 October: 3.

Alenin, A. (1994) ' "Muzh moi Tania" ', *Trud*, 16 February: 4.

Anthias, F. and Yuval-Davis, N. (eds) (1989) *Woman–nation–state*, Basingstoke: Macmillan.

Ashwin, S. and Bowers, E. (1997) 'Do Russian women want to work?', in M. Buckley (ed.) *Post-Soviet Women: From the Baltic to Central Asia*, Cambridge: Cambridge University Press, 21–37.

Attwood, L. (1991) *The New Soviet Man and Woman: Sex Role Socialization in the USSR*, Basingstoke: Macmillan.

—— (1993) 'Sex and the Soviet Cinema', in I. Kon and J. Riordan (eds) *Sex and Russian Society*, London: Pluto, 64–88.

—— (1996) 'The post-Soviet Woman in the Move to the Market: a Return to Domesticity and Dependence?' in R. Marsh (ed.) *Women in Russia and Ukraine*, Cambridge: Cambridge University Press, 255–266.

Azhgikhina, N. (1997) 'Heaven's Better Half', *Current Digest of the Post-Soviet Press* (henceforth *CDPSP*), 49, 3: 20.

Baiduzhii, A. (1994) 'Demographic Catastrophe Has Become a Reality', *CDPSP*, 46, 5: 19.

Borzenko, V. (1994) 'Abortion in Russia: in the Light of Public Opinion', *CDPSP*, 46, 10: 16–17.

Bridger, S. (1992) 'Young Women and Perestroika' in L. Edmondson (ed.) *Women and Society in Russia and the Soviet Union*, Cambridge: Cambridge University Press, 178–201.

—— (1996) 'The Return of the Family Farm: a Future for Women?' in R. Marsh (ed.) *Women in Russia and Ukraine*, Cambridge: Cambridge University Press, 241–254.

Bridger, S. and Kay, R. (1996) 'Gender and Generation in the New Russian Labour Market' in H. Pilkington (ed.) *Gender, Generation and Identity in Contemporary Russia*, London: Routledge, 21–38.

Bridger, S., Kay, R. and Pinnick, K. (1996) *No More Heroines? Russia, Women and the Market*, London and New York: Routledge.

Brui, B. (1993) 'Poka politiki sporiat, Rossiia vyrozhdaetsia', *Nezavisimaia gazeta*, 23 September: 6.

Bruno, M. (1996) 'Employment Strategies and the Formation of New Identities in the Service Sector in Moscow' in H. Pilkington (ed.) *Gender, Generation and Identity in Contemporary Russia*, London: Routledge, 39–56.

Buckley, M. (1989) *Women and Ideology in the Soviet Union*, Hemel Hempstead: Harvester Wheatsheaf.

—— (1990) 'Social Policies and New Social Issues' in S. White, A. Pravda and Z. Gitelman (eds) *Developments in Soviet Politics*, Basingstoke: Macmillan, 185–206.

—— (ed.) (1992) *Perestroika and Soviet Women*, Cambridge: Cambridge University Press.

—— (1993) *Redefining Russian Society and Polity*, Boulder, San Francisco and Oxford: Westview Press.

—— (1997) 'Adaptation of the Soviet Women's Committee: deputies' voices from "Women in Russia"', in M. Buckley (ed.) *Post-Soviet Women: From the Baltic to Central Asia*, Cambridge: Cambridge University Press, 157–185.

Buehrer, J. (1992) 'Women demand a role in reforms', *Moscow Times*, 18 September: 9.

Buijs, G. (ed.) (1993) *Migrant Women: Crossing Boundaries and Changing Identities*, Oxford: Berg.

Clements, B. E., Engel, B. A. and Worobec, C. D. (eds) (1991) *Russia's Women: Accommodation, Resistance, Transformation*, Berkeley and Oxford: University of California Press.

Cockburn, C. (1991) 'Democracy without Women is no Democracy', *Feminist Review*, 39: 141–148.

Corrin, C. (ed.) (1992) *Superwomen and the Double Burden*, London: Scarlet Press.

de Haan-de Vogel, O., Tuender-de Haan, G. and van der Zande, A. (eds) (1993) *From Problems to Strategy: Materials of the Second Women's Forum, Dubna, 27–29 November 1992*, Hilversum: Ariadne Europe Fund.

Einhorn, B. (1993) *Cinderella Goes to Market: Citizenship, Gender and Women's Movements in East Central Europe*, London and New York: Verso.

El'tsina, N. (1992) ' "Ia ne pervaia ledi, ia prosto zhena prezidenta Rossii" ', *Wel My* (Russian edn), 11 (August): 1, 9, 14.

Eremicheva, G. (1996) 'Articulating a catastrophic sense of life' in A. Rotkirch and E.

Haavio-Mannila (eds) *Women's Voices in Russia Today*, Aldershot and Brookfield USA: Dartmouth, 153–163.

'Ethnic Georgians harassed in Moscow, says Embassy', *Summary of World Broadcasts*, SU/2881 B/3: 6.

Evtushenko, A. (1993) 'Vybory mestnogo znacheniia nakanune general'nogo srazheniia', *Komsomol'skaia pravda*, 13 April: 1.

Faludi, S. (1992) *Backlash: The Undeclared War against Women*, London: Vintage.

Frolov, D. (1994) 'Bureaucrats Show Concern for Multiplying the Nation. By Making all Abortion Clinics Charge Fees', *CDPSP*, 46, 10: 16–17.

Funk, N. and Mueller, M. (eds) (1993) *Gender Politics and Post-Communism: Reflections from Eastern Europe and the Former Soviet Union*, New York and London: Routledge.

Gerasimova, T. (1966) 'Elderly Women – a Challenge to Russia' in Anna Rotkirch and Elina Haavio-Mannila (eds) *Women's Voices in Russia Today*, Aldershot: Dartmouth, 175–185.

Gilligan, C. (1982) *In a Different Voice: Psychological Theory and Women's Development*, Cambridge, Mass. and London: Harvard University Press.

Golovachov, V. (1996) 'A miracle: the economy is in crisis, but life is improving?', *CDPSP*, 48, 44: 18–19.

Gorbachev, M. (1987) *Perestroika: New Thinking for our Country and the World*, New York: Harper & Row.

Goryachev, V. (1997) 'Rhapsody Played from Someone Else's Score', *CDPSP*, 49, 5: 18–19.

Goscilo, H. (1993) 'New Members and Organs: the Politics of Porn', *Carl Beck Papers*, 1007, Pittsburgh: University of Pittsburgh.

Grafova, L. (1997) 'How Can We Save the Russians Still in Chechnya?', *CDPSP*, 49, 1: 11–12.

Grebesheva, I. (1992) 'Abortion and the Problems of Family Planning in Russia', *Planned Parenthood in Europe*, 21, 2 (May): 8.

Hearst, D. (1995) 'Patriot or Puppet?', *Guardian*, 2 January: 9.

—— (1997) 'Hostages to Prejudice and Fortune', *Guardian*, 2 May: 16.

Heldt, B. (1992) 'Gynoglasnost: Writing the Feminine' in M. Buckley (ed.) *Perestroika and Soviet Women*, Cambridge: Cambridge University Press, 160–175.

Iuriev, E. (1996) 'The Landscape after the Battle', *CDPSP*, 48, 3: 18–19.

Ivanova, E. (1992) 'There Are More Women in Russia Than Men. The Demographic Situation Today', *CDPSP*, 44 , 28: 22.

Kay, R. (1996) 'On Their Own Terms: Grassroots Women's Organisations in Contemporary Russian Society', unpublished paper presented to ESRC seminar on 'Feminism and Women's Movements: the Way Forward', University of Bath.

Khamrayev, V. (1995) '"Women for Solidarity" Want to Calm "Nervous" Society', *CDPSP*, 47, 13: 14.

Kharlamova, T. (1996) 'Sindrom unizheniia na fone liubvi', *Rossiiskaia gazeta*, 31 May: 27.

Khotkina, Z. (1994) 'Women in the Labour Market: Yesterday, Today and Tomorrow' in A. Posadskaya (ed.) *Women in Russia: a New Era in Russian Feminism*, London and New York: Verso 85–108.

Khudiakova, T. (1991) 'Zhenshchiny ukhodiat s politicheskoi stseny', *Izvestiia*, 23 October: 2.

—— (1992) 'Gosudarstvo mozhet zadushit' sem'iu v ob"iatiiakh liubvi', *Izvestiia*, 25 November: 2.

—— (1994a) 'We Could Turn into a Country of Pensioners', *CDPSP*, 46, 5: 19.

—— (1994b) 'Ella Pamfilova reanimiruet ideiu sotsial'noi reformy i nadeetsia na podderzhku prezidenta', *Izvestiia*, 24 May: 2.

Kigai, N. (1996) 'Family Planning, Russian-style', *CDPSP*, 48, 31: 10–11.

Klimenkova, T. (1994) 'What Does Our New Democracy Offer Society?' in A. Posadskaya (ed.) *Women in Russia: a New Era in Russian Feminism*, London and New York: Verso, 14–36.

Kokurina, Y. (1996) 'Furor over Fetuses is Legitimate', *CDPSP*, 48, 1: 17–18.

Kon, I. (1997) 'Sexual Counter-Revolution in Russia', INFO-RUSS List, 9 March.

Konstantinova, V. (1994) 'No Longer Totalitarianism, But Not Yet Democracy: the Emergence of an Independent Women's Movement in Russia' in A. Posadskaya (ed.) *Women in Russia: a New Era in Russian Feminism*, London and New York: Verso, 57–73.

Koshkareva, T. (1996) 'Sostoitsia li politicheskaia reabilitatsiia Borisa El'tsina?', *Nezavisimaia gazeta*, 10 November: 1–2.

Kravchenko, T. (1995) 'Ne tak strashen chert', *Literaturnaia gazeta*, 17 May 1995: 4.

Kuznetsova, L. (1988) 'Val i Valentina', *Rabotnitsa* 9: 22.

Lapidus, G. W. (1978) *Women in Soviet Society: Equality, Development and Social Change*, Berkeley: University of California Press.

Lavrov, A. (1996) 'Polovina regionov strany ne predstavlena v Dume', *Rossiiskie vesti*, 2 April: 1–2.

Lebedeva, E. (1996) 'Pri nalichii osnovanii . . . ', *Moskovskie novosti*, 39 (29 September–6 October): 27.

Lerner, G. (1986) *The Creation of Patriarchy*, Oxford: Oxford University Press.

Levina, A. (1992) '"Iarmarka" vakansii, ili 5 sposobov bor'by s zhenskoi bezrabotitsei', *Rabotnitsa*, 2: 10–11.

Likhanov, A. (1996) 'Social Factor: The Situation of Children in Russia', *CDPSP*, 48, 48: 8–10.

Lipovskaia, O. (1992) 'New Women's Organisations' in Mary Buckley (ed.) *Perestroika and Soviet Women*, Cambridge: Cambridge University Press, 72–81.

Lipovskaya, O. (1992) 'Gender Bender', *This Magazine*, 25 (May): 24–25.

—— (1994) 'The Mythology of Womanhood in Contemporary "Soviet" Culture' in A. Posadskaya (ed.) *Women in Russia: a New Era in Russian Feminism*, London and New York: Verso, 123–134.

Lissyutkina, L. (1993) 'Soviet Women at the Crossroads of Perestroika' in N. Funk and M. Mueller (eds) *Gender Politics and Post-Communism: Reflections from Eastern Europe and the Former Soviet Union*, New York and London: Routledge, 274–286.

Liuka, G. (1992) 'Russian Authorities Decide to Concern Themselves with Children and Parents', *CDPSP*, 44, 23: 25.

Lovenduski, J. (1986) *Women and European Politics: Contemporary Feminism and Public Policy*, Brighton: Harvester.

Marsh, R. (1992) 'Olga Lipovskaya and Women's Issues in Russia', *Rusistika*, 5 (June): 16–21.

—— (ed. and transl.) (1996) *Women in Russia and Ukraine*, Cambridge: Cambridge University Press, 1996.

—— (forthcoming) 'An Image of their Own? Feminism, Revisionism and Russian Culture', in R. Marsh (ed.) *Women in Russian Culture*, Oxford: Berghahn.

Materialy XXVIII S"ezda KPSS (1990) Moscow: Politizdat.

Meek, J. (1994) 'Weakest are Sacrificed on Altar of Privatized Homes', *Guardian*, 1 June: 10.

Miliband, R. (1989) *Divided Societies: Class Struggle in Contemporary Capitalism*, Oxford: Clarendon Press.

Milič, A. (1993) 'Women and Nationalism in the Former Yugoslavia', in N. Funk and M. Mueller (eds) (1993) *Gender Politics and Post-Communism: Reflections from Eastern Europe and the Former Soviet Union*, New York and London: Routledge, 109–122.

Millinship, W. (1993) *Front Line: Women of the New Russia*, London: Methuen.

Mitchison, A. (1988) 'Ulster's Family Feminists', *New Society*, 83, 1312 (19 February): 17–19.

Morozov, A. (1996) 'Attempt to Combat Illegal Abortions', *CDPSP*, 48, 31: 11, 24.

'Mrs Yeltsin Interviewed on her Husband's Personality and Prospects' (1995), *Summary of World Broadcasts*, SU/2478 B/1 (5 December).

Nadezhdina, N. (1996) 'Strana bezdetnaia', *Trud*, 31 May: 4.

Pankova, M. (1993) 'Alevtina Fedulova: "Zhenshchina tozhe chelovek"', *Nezavisimaia gazeta*, 6 March: 6.

Pavlychko, S. (1992) 'Between Feminism and Nationalism: New Women's Groups in the Ukraine', in M. Buckley (ed.) *Perestroika and Soviet Women*, Cambridge: Cambridge University Press, 82–96.

—— (1996) 'Feminism in Post-communist Ukrainian Society', in R. Marsh (ed.) *Women in Russia and Ukraine*, Cambridge: Cambridge University Press, 305–314.

Pervyshin, V. (1993) 'Unichtozhenie', *Molodaia gvardiia*, 8: 3–8.

Pierson, R. R. (1987) *Women and Peace: Theoretical, Historical and Practical Perspectives*, London and New York: Croom Helm.

Pilkington, H. (1992) 'Russia and the Former Soviet Republics', in C. Corrin (ed.) *Superwomen and the Double Burden*, London: Scarlet Press, 180–235.

—— (ed.) (1996a) *Gender, Generation and Identity in Contemporary Russia*, London: Routledge.

—— (1996b) 'Can "Russia's Women" Save the Nation?: Survival Politics and Gender Discourse in Post-Soviet Russia', in S. Bridger (ed.) *Women in Post-Communist Russia*, Interface: Bradford Studies in Language, Culture and Society, no. 1, University of Bradford, 160–171.

—— (1997) '"For the sake of the children . . . "': gender and migration in the former Soviet Union' in M. Buckley (ed.) *Post-Soviet Women: From the Baltic to Central Asia*, Cambridge: Cambridge University Press, 119–140.

Polenina, S. (1996) 'Brachnyi kontrakt mozhno teper' zakliuchit' i v Rossii', *Izvestiia*, 6 March: 11.

Politkovskaya, A. (1997) 'Betrayed Three Times – 140,000 Russian Citizens Are Now Doomed to a Struggle for Survival', *CDPSP*, 49, 7: 16–17.

Popov, A. (1989) 'Eta drevniaia igra', *Moskovskii komsomolets*, 18 August: 4.

Popov, G. (1990) 'Perspektivy i realiia', *Ogonek*, 50 (December): 5–8.

Posadskaya, A. (ed.) (1994) *Women in Russia: a New Era in Russian Feminism*, London and New York: Verso.

Predvybornaia platforma ob"edineniia 'Zhenshchiny Rossii' (1993) Pre-election pamphlet, Moscow.

Randall, V. (1987) *Women and Politics*, Basingstoke: Macmillan.

Rash, K. (1989) 'Vsekh tsarstv dorozhe', *Pravda*, 22 February: 3.

Rasputin, V. (1990) 'Cherchez la femme', *Nash sovremennik*, 3: 169.

Remennick, L. I. (1993) 'Patterns of Birth Control' in I. Kon and J. Riordan (eds) *Sex and Russian Society*, London: Pluto.

Rimashevskaia, N. M. (ed.) (1991) *Zhenshchina v obshchestve. Realiia, problemy, prognozy*, Moscow: Nauka.

Ronina, G. (1988) 'Chernoe i beloe', *Sel'skaia nov'*, 1: 28.

Rotkirch, A. and Haavio-Mannila, E. (eds) (1996) *Women's Voices in Russia Today*, Aldershot: Dartmouth.

Ruban, V. (1992) *Berehynia*, Kiev: Ukrains'kyj pysmennyk.

Rubchak, M. (1996) 'Christian Virgin or Pagan Goddess: Feminism Versus the Eternally Feminine in Ukraine' in R. Marsh (ed.) *Women in Russia and Ukraine*, Cambridge: Cambridge University Press, 315–330.

Rule, W. and Noonan, N. (eds) (1996) *Russian Women in Politics and Society*, Westport CT: Greenwood.

'Russians are Beginning to Die at a Slightly Lower Rate' (1996) *CDPSP*, 48, 6: 18–19.

Sargeant, E. (1996) 'The "Woman Question" and Problems of Maternity in Post-communist Russia' in R. Marsh (ed.) *Women in Russia and Ukraine*, Cambridge: Cambridge University Press, 269–285.

Sazonov, V. (1993) 'Novyi simbioz: obshchestvennoe mnenie o zhizni, prervannoi vrachom, i svoboda propovedi', *Nezavisimaia gazeta*, 12 August: 5.

Semeinyi kodeks Rossiiskoi Federatsii (1996), Moscow: SPARK.

Semenova, G. (1992) 'Zhenshchiny i rynok: vyzhivat' – ne vyzhidat", *Rynok*, 16, September: 1.

Shafran, E. (1994) 'Izgnanie ploda: pochemu zhenshchiny v Rossii boiatsia rozhat' ', *Izvestiia*, 26 January: 8.

Shishina, Sof'ia (1994) 'Kakie uzh deti zdes' i seichas?', *Moskovskie novosti*, 25, 19–26 June: 8.

Skliar, I. (1994) 'Zhenshchiny pri den'gakh', *Rabotnitsa*, 3: 16–17.

Skoptsova, L., Tuender-de Haan, G., Weijer, P. and van der Zande, A. (eds) (1993) *Directory of Participants: Second Independent Women's Forum, Dubna, Russia, 1992*, Hilversum: Ariadne Europe Fund.

Slater, W. (1994) 'Female Representation in Russian Politics', *Radio Liberty/Radio Free Europe Bulletin*, 3, 22, 3 June: 27.

Stacey, J. (1983) 'The New Conservative Feminism', *Feminist Studies*, 9, 3: 559–583.

Stites, R. (1978) *The Women's Liberation Movement in Russia: Feminism, Nihilism and Bolshevism*, Princeton, NJ: Princeton University Press.

Temkina, A. (1996) 'Entering Politics: Women's Ways, Gender Ideas and Contradictions of Reality' in A. Rotkirch, and E. Haavio-Mannila (eds) *Women's Voices in Russia Today*, Aldershot: Dartmouth, 206–234.

Terekhov, V. (1993) 'Rossiiskie selianki odni nivu ne podnimut', *Nezavisimaia gazeta*, 12 August: 1–2.

Tiurin, G. (1995) 'Kodeks stroitelia matriarkhata', *Nezavisimaia gazeta*, 10 November: 6.

Toktal'eva, G. (1989) 'Olia i Iulia', *Sobesednik*, 46 November: 11.

Tolstaya, T. (1990) 'Notes from Underground', *New York Review of Books*, 37, 9: 3–7.

Toporov, V. (1991) 'Dnevnik "Literatora"', *Literator* (Leningrad), 21: 7.

Tutorskaia, Svetlana (1996) 'Mama, vse li ty produmala, koga reshila menia rodit'?', *Izvestiia*, 30 January: 5.

'V Rossii zhivet 148.4 milliona chelovek. Chislennost' naseleniia prodolzhaet umen'shat'sia' (1994) *Nezavisimaia gazeta*, 5 May: 6.

Valiuzhenich, G. (1994) 'Pochemu ushla Ella Pamfilova', *Argumenty i fakty*, 5: 3.

Vasil'eva, L. (1989) 'Pervye lastochki na tsirkuliare. Razmyshleniia posle S"ezda o roli zhenshchiny v obshchestve', *Pravda*, 24 June 1989: 3.

'Verkhovnyi Sud ne udovletvoril zhalobu Galiny Starovoitovoi' (1996), *Segodnia*, 6 May: 1.

Vitkovskaia, G. (1996) 'Migranty stremiatsia v Rossiiu', *Literaturnaia gazeta*, 11 July: 3.

Vladimirov, I. (1996) 'Obsuzhdaiutsia problemy peremeshchennykh lits', *Nezavisimaia gazeta*, 2 April: 3.

Voronina, O. (1988) 'Zhenshchina v "muzhskom obshchestve"', *Sotsiologicheskie issledovaniia*, 2: 104–110.

—— (ed.) (1992) *Feminizm: perspektivy sotsial'nogo znaniia*, Moscow.

—— (1994) 'Virgin Mary or Mary Magdalene? The Construction and Reconstruction of Sex during the Perestroika Period' in A. Posadskaya (ed.) *Women in Russia: a New Era in Russian Feminism*, London and New York: Verso, 135–145.

Walker, M. (1986) *The Waking Giant: the Soviet Union under Gorbachev*, London: Michael Joseph.

Waters, E. (1992) '"Cuckoo-mothers" and "Apparatchiks": Glasnost and Children's Homes' in M. Buckley (ed.) *Perestroika and Soviet Women*, Cambridge: Cambridge University Press, 123–141.

—— (1993) 'Finding a Voice: The Emergence of a Women's Movement' in N. Funk and M. Mueller (eds) *Gender Politics and Post-Communism: Reflections from Eastern Europe and the Former Soviet Union*, New York and London: Routledge, 287–302.

White, N. (1997) 'Women in Latvia and Lithuania', in M. Buckley (ed.) *Post-Soviet Women: From the Baltic to Central Asia*, Cambridge: Cambridge University Press, 203–218.

White, S. (1993) *After Gorbachev*, Cambridge: Cambridge University Press.

Zabelina, T. (1996) 'Sexual violence towards women' in H. Pilkington (ed.) *Gender Generation and Identity in Contemporary Russia*, London: Routledge, 169–186.

Zakharova, N., Posadskaia, A. and Rimashevskaia, N. (1989) 'Kak my reshaem zhenskii vopros', *Kommunist*, 4: 56–65.

Zdravomyslova, E. (1996) 'Problems of Becoming a Housewife', in A. Rotkirch and E. Haavio-Mannila (eds) *Women's Voices in Russia Today*, Aldershot: Dartmouth, 255–266.

6 Back to the future

Nationalism and gender in post-socialist societies

Tanja Rener and Mirjana Ule

INTRODUCTION

Of the three great dispositions of modernity/modernization – the nation-state, industrialization, and the urban way of life – one element, the nation-state, is dangerous and potentially anti-modern. Despite its constitutive nature, the nation-state is modern only when it is tightly bound into the mechanisms of the other two elements, which prevent it from realizing the principles upon which it is founded. Distinct from industrialization and urbanization, which are founded upon modern principles of individualism and rationalism, nationalism as the substance of every nation-state feeds itself from entirely different sources: the community and sentiment. Here it is difficult to overlook the similarities with one of the presuppositions that may be of a central and constitutive nature within modernization – the social construction of (the female) gender.

The thesis that we are bringing forth is not new. One of the essential contributions of the new social history of the family lies in the realization that the small nuclear family based upon sentiment is not a consequence of the processes of modernization but was, on the contrary, a condition and basis for modernization. But for the family to play its own modern productive role it had to remain anachronistic, that is, pre-modern. The construction and maintenance of the pre-modern elements of the family became the social domain of the female gender. Family privacy together with its spatial dimension became the symbolic, the imaginary, and the real place of women. Women's 'goodbye' to individuality and rationality in favour of a community based on sentiment was in fact a precondition for a politically public and bourgeois civil society.

Modern interpolations of women into mothers and wives occur together with the shaping of modern nation-states. The similarity of these parallel processes is therefore double: the 'national' and 'woman' are foreign to modernity even though they are indispensable and constitutive. Their social function is analogous: with the help of sentiment, they construct the community or at least the image of community.

For this reason generalizations of nationalist discourse should be taken extremely seriously. These articulate themselves in forms such as 'The nation is one big family' or the concept of 'the motherland'. Even though those who utter these generalizations do not seem to take them seriously, we must take them word for word to understand their ideological productivity. We take these hypotheses as the cue for our analysis of the outbreak of nationalist passion and conflict in former socialist states.

NATIONALISM AND WOMEN IN POST-SOCIALIST SOCIETIES

All post-socialist countries have in common certain problems as well as slogans that they wish to use ideologically to contain and articulate these problems. The basic common problems are: the establishment of a market economy of goods, work and capital; unarranged ownership relationships; an underdeveloped rule of law; national and social conflicts; and political instability. The fundamental ideological and political answers to these problems are reprivatization; the ideal of the nation state; entry into European associations; and the rehabilitation of traditional values.[1]

Post-socialist societies have reclaimed the status of the privileged subject that was once held by certain social groups and classes (for instance the working class, youth, the party) and given this status to new groups and classes (entrepreneurs, new political parties, churches). Some social groups witnessed the 'redelegation' of their social status (social subjectivity). Women, who in socialism were supposed to have achieved their social and personal emancipation and equality with men and who were one of the preferred 'social subjects' within the ideology of socialist societies, became in post-socialism once again the target of a special ideological interpolation, even though this interpolation is now of a radically different nature.

In the ideology of socialist societies, women were one of the social subjects of emancipation and revolutionary change. In post-socialist societies they became the targets of redelegation into 'mothers who should ensure the biological survival and moral progress of the nation', 'the guardians of the home', and the 'guardians of privacy'. Thus, instead of the former (mostly economically enforced) 'proletarization' and (politically enforced) 'emancipation of women', we are now dealing with the domestification of women which is also economically and politically enforced.[2] The foremost tendency of the domestication of women does not lie in the desire for women to give up their jobs and 'return to the family', but rather the internalization of the classification into public men and private women.[3]

The redelegation of social status into the field of privacy is accompanied by the mass social pacification of women. This is particularly evident if we compare the current weak political activity of women in post-socialist countries with the mass participation of women in various demonstrations and movements for the implementation of democracy, civil society and the rule of law at the end of the 1980s. It is true that political and economic conditions differ in various post-socialist societies (from relatively hopeful conditions in Hungary and the Czech Republic to extreme misery in Albania, Romania, and the countries of the former Soviet Union, to war in Croatia, Serbia, Bosnia, Chechnia and Azerbaijan) but, as far as women go, their political passivity and absence from public life is very evident (Funk and Mueller 1993).

What is most important here is the long-term connection between the ideological domestication of women and traditional and conservative views related to the social role of gender, the relationship between the private and the public, politics in general and in the nation-state. We see this connection in the idea of a society that has pledged itself to some kind of organic whole (this whole being represented by the 'nation') that overcomes all internal conflict through a process of social homogenization. In this light, differences and conflicts within society are interpreted as opposition to the whole, as different kinds of conspiracies (for instance, the conspiracy of the supporters of former socialist governments) or as acts of hostility by foreign elements (for instance, as acts of hostility carried out by 'foreign minorities' or by neighbouring countries) and not as preconditions for social progress. This exterior projection of social conflicts, the helplessness or refusal to see them as the result of the inner dynamics of society and its problems, can temporarily ease a situation of conflict in the imagination and within the processes of ideological projection – but it also makes them insoluble and traumatic in the long run.

From whence does this pre-modern view of society originate? We think that it is a necessary result of the contradictions within the fundamental ideological options of post-socialist societies: reprivatization, the establishment of nation-states, the way into Europe, and the return of traditional values. The concepts and ideas about nationally homogeneous social entities that the nationalist political programmes offer succeed in bridging the gaps between these options.

The project of reprivatization, accompanied by a trust in 'Europe', helps reaffirm in people a paradoxical mixture of expectations. These expectations anticipate that the process of reprivatization will be swift and that it will represent an improvement in living conditions, as well as maintaining the preconceived unity of the social community and reconciling it with itself.

The idea of strengthening the nation-state and the return of traditional values help form and reinforce these expectations. The idea of an autonomous nation-state serves as the political and historical secessionist superstructure of the organic understanding of recapitalization – that is, the conversion from a (post)socialist to a modern market economy society. Meanwhile the return to traditional values (home, nation, God) ensures that individuals within their microcosms (in private and within the family) can cope with the perils of this process.

The trinity of the home, nation and God, are ideally suited to the organic self-understanding of society. The 'home' signifies the illusion of a guarded and organic non-conflictual community; the 'nation' signifies a large family to which all individual action must be subservient; and God signifies the transcendental self-conception of one's own life as unforeseeable fate. Thus, all the fundamental ideological conceptions (and premises) of social reform in post-socialist societies coincide with each other. They represent a mechanism of defence against the challenges of the present and the future, instead of being merely temporarily rational and productive.

The ideological views of 'real socialism' and new national collectivism are both opposed to individual ways of life that are not subservient to the collective 'vision' and 'self image'. Both views stand against those differences among individuals that cannot be reduced to some social type (class, gender, religion, nationality). Within these ideologies, the individual is understood to be 'free' only if his or her individual action belongs to the superstructure of supra-individuality, as is the case in a nationally defined role.

THE REDELEGATION OF PRIVACY

The ideological options promoted in post-socialist societies are not far removed from their socialist predecessors, even though they have the image of modernity. Socialism represented the constant defence against the Western world, as well as a defence against the market, competition, conflicts within society, economic and political pluralism and antagonism. 'Real existing socialisms' were a mixture of pre-modern and industrial societies founded upon concepts of organic and non-conflictual societies.

In socialist societies the slogans of equality between the sexes and the liberation of women quickly revealed their own contradiction. The employment of women led to a new dependency and burdened women instead of offering economic emancipation. The political activation of women resulted in their formalistic and ritualistic participation in the lower strata of the power structure, whereas toward the top of the political pyramid of power their participation was drastically minimized (Rener 1985). In addition, women did not have any special reason to participate in such empty and ritualized political activities which only ate up their already tight 'spare time'.

As a result of the long-term lack of civil society and of a modern, relatively autonomous, private and public sphere in socialist societies, we cannot expect that in the few years since socialism began to collapse a modern civil society – and within it a corresponding private sphere which would be the social base for the formation of the individuality of women and men – would emerge. This is why in post-socialist societies there is no intermediate social sphere which would make public action possible for women without them being forced to relinquish their family roles. This lack of a developed social sphere also signifies that families are left to themselves and atomized. As a consequence, women are faced with the unrealizable task of replacing the social tissue of civil society with family activity. The lack of the social sphere can be replaced neither by the assistance of friends and relatives nor by the participation/involvement of women in the black economy. The privacy into which women are constrained by economic conditions and by post-socialist nationalist ideologies is therefore not a privacy corresponding to the development of the identity of the individual's ego. Rather, this privacy is an asylum for protecting the individual from society – it is a privatized sphere of particular interests.

That is why advocacy of 'the return of women to family' is closely related to national-ideological rhetoric since, according to such conceptions, only women who have dedicated themselves exclusively to their families are capable of preserving traditional values and the national consciousness of new generations. Such engagement in disciplining new generations also disciplines women themselves and subjects them to the authorities and the institutions of society. Neither former socialist, nor present national-oriented policies, allow women to express their individuality and their potential disagreement with the aggression of such ideologies and policies.

Such a position for women is not a historical novelty since it is present in most traditional societies. What is new is that the post-socialist societies, in following national projects (despite their urge to 'catch up with' developed Europe), have ignored the historical shift in the position and perception of women that has taken place in developed European societies. Namely, in modern post-industrial societies there is an increasing tendency towards the individualization of strategies of life, patterns, needs, views and opinions, followed by a decrease in the significance of social identifiers – class, gender, profession, nationality – considered up to now to be more or less life-long (Beck 1986). For a woman, this means that she connects her life, work and needs less and less to her gender identity and especially to her family role.[4]

The attempts to return women to the family in post-socialist societies are contrary to this principal tendency towards the individualization of the way of life and of the formation of identity. These attempts thus put women into pre-modern social conditions instead of putting them into post-modern ones. Pressures experienced by women under such present or future conditions are necessarily transferred to the rest of the population – if not in any other way, then at least by the division of roles within the family. Should a woman, for example, because of unemployment, actually return to the family? This would definitely mean a loss of social identity and of individuality. Inside the family this loss will then reflect itself in the form of tense interpersonal relations, suppressed fears, hopeless attempts at emotional replacements, and so forth. The withdrawal of women into domestic privacy will not, however, be complete because of the economic crisis and low incomes. Women, as always, will be forced to supplement the family budget by working outside their homes.

The result of social pressures will, therefore, not be the mass return of women to their families planned by the architects of national projects. A strongly frustrating, 'para-family' type of existence for women will occur instead. Women, just like unemployed men, will be looking for employment, thus encouraging competition in the labour market which will reduce the value of their work. This reduction of the (already low) value of work might become one of the main sources of profit for private and state enterprises. Undoubtedly, the pressures on women will have a negative feedback as far as the development of democracy is concerned because an eventual social agreement will be reached under conditions of a repressive disciplining and domestication of a large part of the population.

The tendencies towards the domestication of women and the glorification of the family (as the primary bond in the society) are, therefore, an expression of a regressive social process in post-socialist countries. However, we believe that we are not dealing with an irrational regression, but rather with a 'return' to the irrational fundamentals of modernization intended to get post-socialist countries back in touch with the processes of modernization in developed Europe. At this point such tendencies in post-socialist countries intertwine with the nationalist delirium.

Nationalism in the former Yugoslavia has a long and many-sided history, and a new revival of nationalism in the middle of the 1980s led directly to the armed conflicts of the 1990s. However, although the circumstances appear to be 'historical', the nationalist discourse is as a rule anti-historical. It exchanges history for myth, and myth comes to function as history, as fuel for what then follows. The more nationalism in the ex-Yugoslav republics became aggressive, the more its mythology became heroic and 'masculine'. Nationalism grew alongside increasing misogyny. It could even be argued that the deteriorating position of women in the last years of socialism warned of the nationalist outbreak, the war and the decay of the state. Feminist analyses were not successful in breaking through ideological repression and consequently they stayed contextually limited to narrow elitist circles in urban centres.

After the Second World War women in Yugoslavia were rewarded for their massive participation in the anti-fascist struggle with the right to vote and the general obligation of the society to social equality. A great deal of legislative effort was made to achieve gender equality, and the normative position of women was relatively satisfactory. Women benefited from favourable social legislation by the socialist state without any corresponding effort at active political participation.

However, as the memory of the Second World War began to fade, women were dislodged from public life and political representation. In the 1970s, when a new feminist movement appeared, the representation of women in political public life was merely a matter of form and ritual. This was also the moment of the first post-war revival of nationalism. At that time few, if any, detected any connection between the two processes. Internal feminist analyses pointed out that the self-management system, celebrated as a great Yugoslavian achievement, ignored the specific position of women. Feminist critics never launched discussions and debates but helped bring about the rejection and labelling of feminists as enemies of the people.

With the new wave of nationalisms in the 1980s, women became surplus labour because of the economic crisis and nationalist rhetoric portrayed images of women as both mothers of future warriors and guardians of the nation's virtue. During the second half of the 1980s when the great nationalist campaign in all the Yugoslav republics began, and especially at the time of first 'free and democratic elections' in 1990, the nationalists were the only ones who addressed women as their target group. Neither groups and parties in the opposition nor anti-nationalists realized the need to address women in particular, which was a recurring mistake by the Left (Ivekovic 1996).

NATIONALISM AND THE COMMUNITY

When a social phenomenon strikes in such a powerful way as have the 'Yugoslav nationalisms' in the last few years, our astonishment is often expressed in the form of (naive) questions. First, how have acute, destructive and, therefore, deeply anti-social forms of nationalism manifested themselves on the fringes of a Europe that is in the middle of a transition to a post-industrial and post-modern phase? Second, why is nationalism successfully dropping its anchor in the less aggressive half of the population – that is, why is it becoming a real power among women? These two questions are, of course, naive because they are put in the wrong way. Modern Yugoslav nationalisms are not a residual element of the nineteenth century. They are not a retrograde and regressive expression of societies undergoing modernization. Rather, they are a materialization of the dark side of the same Europe that professes amazement at the aggressive eccentricity of the Balkan ethnic communities.

Nationalism is not anti-social. On the contrary, it is an extremely social response to the so-called crisis of industrial modernity. In a world where the permanent restructuralization and differentiation of society represent a condition for growth and expansion, the non-differentiated and totalizing 'we' plays the role of an asylum or a therapeutic environment of protection and mutual solidarity. Not so long ago it seemed that such a social role would be played by the family. But the social struggle of women (above all, feminism) which laid claim to a consequential modernization (the possibility of autonomous individualization for women), has been a cause of destabilization. That is why the Yugoslav search for surrogate communities through nationalism is such a vulgar and unfortunate, yet vanguard, consequence of the problem of community that is unsolved by modern societies.

The three rules that condition communities are a tendency toward egalitarianism, a sharing of ideas and sentiments, and a severe selectivity when dealing with the Other (the latter being a constitutive, rather than a marginal and disturbing, element). It is only with identification and excommunication of the 'Other' that one can recognize unity and community.

It is only by differentiation from Others, and by rejecting them, that 'we' become 'We'.

Systems of real socialism, seemingly suppressing the national element intensely, have actually followed the same thought pattern: while promising communalism they have demanded, first and foremost, faith. That is why 'socialist' life habits, which remain our daily *forma mentis* despite the breakdown of socialism, remain an extreme basis for nationalist sentiments. The (national) community as a transfunctional, transrational, and transindividual entity is regaining its social value precisely in boundary situations. By not being directly dependent on the modern social structure, the community is a social form that under conditions of rapid change can become predominant. Nationalist experience as a collective experience has the following basic attributes:

- On the level of thinking, there exists a common and unique truth.
- On the level of sentiments, there exists something that is good on its own behalf, something that represents an absolute object for Eros, with pleasure and duty thus becoming one.
- On the level of interpersonal social relationships, there exists a promise of community and a tendency towards breaking up the existing social barriers in the name of common truth and common (authentic) sentiment.

When elements of the community's national experience are institutionalized, a deadlock occurs; barbaric totalitarianism then becomes the only possible outcome. Since national unity does not and cannot exist, but is at the same time a premise for the national experience of the community, it is achieved by means of repression and moral stigmatization of the Other and/or of those in opposition to this national experience.

NATIONALISM, SENTIMENT, AND EROS

In communities faith comes first, it is more important than action. The will to 'be together' is what counts; outcomes, failures/successes, and losses/profits are a secondary issue compared to the genuineness of this sentiment of faith. What we are interested in here is not the political uses and abuses of nationalism but rather the secret of nationalism's attraction. We wonder what it is that makes individuals not only recognize themselves as members of some national community but also willingly give up their everyday life and contingency for the sake of the national community.

It seems that women in the former Yugoslavia have an ambivalent attitude toward nationalism. But in any case they have no trouble finding themselves in its social matrix, regardless of whether they reject nationalism or accept it. This is so either because they accept their own elements of the community and sentiment as a traditionally female milieu and thus see in this affirmation and legitimization of that which every 'normal society' frowns upon and undervalues; or they reject the nationalist matrix as being nearly identical to the one that women have been able to escape through employment, their own social struggle, 'a change of consciousness', or otherwise. That is why we can safely claim that in the former Yugoslavia nationalism is extremely unattractive to feminists. The peace movement and local humanitarian aid were mostly organized by women during the war in the former Yugoslavia. Women supported these activities massively where they made sense. Those who had to defend themselves, those who were attacked and bombed – as was the case in Bosnia and Herzegovina – did not have the time and energy for pacifism, they had to struggle for their lives first.

By asserting that nationalism relates particularly to women (that it is a sexualized experience), we do not mean that it suits them. Quite the contrary, our claim regards men as actors. Nationalistic metaphors of the family are stories that speak of men as sons and fathers (of the nation) and as lovers (of the home/motherland). Nationalism always trades in historical regressions in the form of the return to national myths and legends. The 'homeland/nation as the mother' expresses the infantile regression of the return to the mother's breast, it is the affirmation of the dual relationship between the mother and the (lost) son. In the conditions of post-socialist societies, such regression has an extra meaning: the stress is on return of the lost son, who under the socialist 'brotherhood and unity of the nations' lost his real mother and was adopted instead by the 'socialist community', which turned out to be a wicked stepmother. This is also why the return is so sincere and so violent. How could we otherwise understand the unintelligible and unimaginable heroic acts of personal sacrifice taking place in the struggle for Us (for our nation) if it was not for this ecstatic, erotic investment?

Such a strong experience of national sentiment, which strengthens according to the degree of the suffering/bleeding of the mother, is as enthusiastic as it is dramatic. It is similar to an exceptional and fantastic sexual act. It is the promise of the realization of an extreme desire. It is love as death. Of course, it is also attractive to those who do not live through such experience. If it is true, as Julia Kristeva states, that (apart from wars and the stock exchange) Europe is bored to death, then surely Europe's gaze towards the Balkans offers voyeuristic pleasure?

The imaginary of Yugoslav nationalisms is intertwined with sexual phantasmagorias. Here we also note that stories of women actually speak of men. In the case of Yugoslavia, the sexual phantasmagorias showed themselves as the main agent of national sentiment. This imaginary started with the stories of alleged (nationalistic) rapes in Kosovo in the early 1980s. The actual concrete situation and context of the transgression were unimportant. What was important was the national identity of the raping phallus. Castration stories had a similar mobilization effect in the escalation of the Serbian–Croatian conflict. They were reported more or less on a daily basis by media on both sides of the conflict. The horror of deformed bodies is always the horror of castration, regardless of whether the act is the putting out of eyes, the cutting of ears and tongues or (if castration was explicit) the slashing of the sexual organs. The morbid fury thus showed its real face: this was not a simple extermination of the enemy but much more – an act to prevent the enemy from having any sexual relationship with the 'Motherland' as his 'object of desire'.

THE OPPOSITION TO THE BAN ON ABORTION AS A SYMBOL OF OPPOSITION TO THE DOMESTIFICATION OF WOMEN AND TO NATIONALIST POLICY

Socialist systems that lasted for over fifty years undoubtedly left profound traces in the people who lived in these systems, regardless of whether they have rebelled and regardless of the degree of their rebellion. We who live in the post-socialist societies are probably unaware how deep inside us lies the atavistic inclination to leave the resolution of our own economic and social problems to somebody else. We are also not aware of our willingness gladly to put ourselves in the custody of authorities, 'powerful' people, or influential institutions, and how much we tend to minimize the shock caused by change, by using organic concepts of society, the state, the nation, enterprise and the family as psychological buffers. The shift from socialist society to a genuine market-based society will therefore be more difficult than most people imagine and will cause quite a few frustrations as well as opposition.

Hence, it is plausible that expectations and presumptions about the future will remain within the circle of relations concerned with coping with the 'shock of the new'. It is also no surprise that even intellectually advanced political and economic programmes carry those shocks inside them. At this point traditional values on one side, and mythology about the national state on the other, become more useful. The domestication of women is easily included in the defence mechanisms of society since it is a natural reaction to the former underestimation of (and threats toward) privacy, the family, religion and nationality, and represents a seeming reaffirmation of 'real womanliness'.

When the nationalists became the authority, programmes for increasing birth rates and against abortion appeared. In Serbia a 'Resolution on Population Renewal' was proposed as a bill. In Croatia the 'Concept for the Demographic Renewal of the Population', written by a conservative priest, became a starting point for government policy. In both cases feminist lobbies protested and in Slovenia women and feminists succeeded in preventing the implementation of a proposal on the prohibition of abortion.

In Slovenia we witnessed angry debates and conflicts in Parliament, as well as in public, over the right to abortion. The pressure of public opinion, especially of various movements and women's organizations against attempts to abandon the right to abortion, were so strong that an article has been included in the Slovenian Constitution providing women (and men) with the liberty to decide about the birth of their children (Ule 1991). All of the women who stood up in public against the threat to the right to abortion were aware that their basic human rights were being jeopardized. We knew that the pressure would not stop at the right to abortion but would continue until we became obedient subjects of the new rulers. That is why opposition to the ban on abortion was not just a particular, women's, protest. It was also a general protest that succeeded in delegitimizing the political forces aimed at limiting the basic human rights of women (Ule 1991). We presume that such considerations can be applied to similar protests of women throughout the post-socialist world (for example, in Poland, Hungary, and the former German Democratic Republic).

The political protest of women against the cancellation of their basic rights are an efficient remedy for the pseudo-organic concept of national unity and for the tendencies towards the domestication of women. The more the leaders of national policies count on the assumption that women will allow their own depolitization and domestication without offering significant resistance, the larger are the cracks (which are caused by women's protests) in the imaginary tissue of the national unity.

The same goes for the men who protest against the same pressures that would turn them into an obedient and faithful labour force (the slogan 'Work and pray!' was publicly presented by some Slovenian ministers) or, which is even worse, into cannon-fodder. The protests of men also serve to prevent the attempts to silence and depolarize the public, and these protests open fissures in the construction of national unity. Minor yet important steps have been taken towards disassembling organic ideologies and related socio-economic projects.

The attitude towards women in post-socialist countries can be understood as a symptom of the attitude towards democracy. The struggle for peace in the Balkans, for ending the war, should also include the struggle for democracy. But it seems that no one cares about this basic fact. For women, the new nationalist regimes in the ex-Eastern Bloc and in Yugoslavia, the so-called 'new democracies', are neither new nor democratic. On the contrary, the attitude towards women and minorities shows the limited comprehension of democracy in those countries. Women's rights and their position are most endangered in the sphere of labour rights and rights connected with the body. Although the situation within the former Yugoslavia differs from one country to another, they share a common misogynist atmosphere. On the territories which were pushed into the war through nationalist delirium, women were forced backwards by at least half a century.

NOTES

1 In her article 'Women's Rights in East Central Europe: Back to Cinderella?' (1990) Barbara Einhorn stated that we are dealing with the triumvirate of

rational values: the home, the homeland (nation) and God; these illustrate the search for new spiritual and ethical values in post-socialist societies. In fact, we are dealing with the rebirth of the values that the old regime violently repressed and which were (in themselves) legitimate. However, what is dangerous is that they are being used to manipulate; that is, the revived values serve as the ideological backbone for the reduction of the already achieved and well-settled economic, social, health and political rights of women.

2 The essential characteristic of nationalist ideologies and socio-political strategies of the domestification of women is that they do not accept women as individuals with their own ways of life and needs but rather as the bearers of roles defined in advance. It is true that in nationally defined collectives women are put on a pedestal of motherhood as saintly guardians of the home and family, but at the same time through this position they are tightly controlled and contained.

3 Here we are dealing with the equalization of the three different categories: public–private, political–apolitical, and man–woman. This equalization is quite common in sociology and serves to justify the real or just the 'surface' apoliticalness of women. In their article 'The Politics of Public Man and Private Woman' Siltanen and Stainworth (1984) criticized this theoretical domestication of women. They believe that women's disinclination for political activity is the result of quiet resistance to the kind of confrontational politics that has been appropriated by men as their own domain. Women's scepticism towards politics can therefore also be the sign of a realistic analysis of current political conditions and a rejection of instrumental calculation within politics and trade union activity. A lot of evidence points towards political processes being anchored within privacy as well as towards the differences between the public sphere and political awareness. Also, the activity of men within the public sphere has its own private origins, as well as women's privacy having its political meaning and expression ('the personal is political!') (Ule, Ferligoj and Rener 1990).

4 The stronger the tendency towards individualization the more important is the individual contribution of people to the products of their work, especially in terms of knowledge and capability for communication and control. With the passing of industrialism, the difference is increasing between new individuality, which is developed through an individual's activities, and privatism, which comprehends individuality as possession, manifesting itself predominantly in the private sphere. This difference between the two kinds of individualism is typically manifested in comprehension of gender roles and relations between the genders. Whereas privatistic individualism observes the differences between the genders and their roles only through their typified and uniform image, the new individualism recognizes individuality and also roles of genders.

BIBLIOGRAPHY

Bahovec, E. (ed.) (1991) *Abortus*, Ljubljana: Skupina zenske za politiko.

Beck, U. (1986) *Risikogesellschaft*, Frankfurt: Suhrkamp/M.

Einhorn, B. (1990) 'Women's Rights in East Central Europe: Back to Cinderella?', unpublished paper, Glasgow: University of Glasgow.

Funk, N. and Mueller, M. (1993) *Gender Politics in Post-communism: Reflections from Eastern Europe and the Former Soviet Union*, New York: Routledge.

Habermas, J. (1972) *Prassi politica e teoria critica della società*, Milan: Bompiani.

Ivekovic, R. (1996) 'Kako nacionalizem in vojna prizadeneta zenske', *Delta*, 1–2, 2: 7–13.

Rener, T. (1985) 'Yugoslav Women in Politics', Selected Issues, *International Political Science Review*, 3, 6: 347–354.

Siltanen, J. and Stainworth, M. (1984) 'The Politics of Public Man and Private Woman' in J. Siltanen and W. Stainworth (eds) *Women and the Public Sphere: A Critique of Sociology and Politics*, London: Hutchinson.

Ule, M. (1989) 'Kriza industrijske moderne in novi individualizem', *Druzboslovne razprave*, 6, 7: 66–76.

—— (1991) 'Javno mnenje o splavu' in E. Bahovec (ed.) *Abortus*, Ljubljana: Skupina Zensk za politiko.

Ule, M., Ferligoj, A. and Rener, T. (1990) *Zenska, zasebno, politicno*, Ljubljana: ZPS.

Vajda, M. (1981) *The State and Socialism. Political Essays*, London: Allison & Busby.

7 Women's rights and political conflict in Yemen 1990–1994

Maxine Molyneux

INTRODUCTION: A DIVIDED STATE

On 7 July 1994 army units loyal to the government of President Ali Abdullah Salih, backed by the militia of the Islamist Reform Grouping or Islah (*al-tajammu' al-yamani lil-islah*), entered Aden, the capital of the former southern Yemeni state, thereby in effect unifying North and South Yemen under one rule for the first time in modern history. Thus ended, through a military offensive launched two months earlier by the president, the interim period that had prevailed since the former North and South had agreed on unity in May 1990.

Few countries in the world can be as 'divided' as Yemen, a country the majority of which had never experienced even the centralizing of colonial rule, and where a series of civil conflicts have, since the early 1960s, enhanced the position of tribal forces *vis-à-vis* the state. The now unified country was, until 1990, formally divided into two states, North and South. Within each there are, moreover, profound variations of region, tribe and religious sect. In the south, in addition to tribal division, there are marked contrasts between the capital, Aden, the tribal hinterland of the west, and the eastern districts, the Hadramaut. In the more populous north, where no central government has ever consolidated itself, a weak state faces tribal groups that are autonomous in military and social organization, while the population is split between the Zeidi Shi'ites and Shafei Sunnis. If a formally united state does now exist it presides over a most centrifugal society, one made all the more diverse by an influx of guns and the retribalization that has affected the South since 1994.

The discussion that follows will examine changes in women's rights between 1990–1994. This was the 'transitional period' agreed on with the introduction of unity in May 1990 and which continued through the elections of April 1993 and the ensuing months of tension and conflict (Carapico 1993; Detalle 1993).[1] Up to July 1994, and despite the 1990 agreement and the subsequent elections, Yemen remained, in large measure, two countries. A formal government and Constitution presided over two state machineries, including two armies and two political and security apparatuses, neither of which was prepared to yield ground significantly to the other and engage in a complete merger. The uncertainties and distrust inherent in this situation were to emerge much more clearly after the April 1993 elections. Mounting stress led progressively to a situation of great tension, and then to the civil war that exploded at the end of April 1994, when president Salih launched his offensive against the south (Kostiner 1996; Naim 1993; Watkins and Makin 1993).

This is not the place to go into the history of this 'unification' process, nor to examine the reasons why a process initially embarked on in a political and constitutional manner should have ended in civil war (Braun 1992; Dunbar 1992; Hall 1991; Halliday 1990: Chapter 4). The purpose here is, rather, to examine how one aspect of state policy in Yemen, that pertaining to women's rights and status, was affected by this 'unification' process: such a study may illuminate both the particular issue of gender–state relations and how these were affected by some of the conflicting political currents operating within Yemen in this period.

Along with other areas of policy, changes in the legal and social position of women formed an important, and complex, part of the transition through which the Yemen passed in the early 1990s: as elsewhere in the Islamic world, the codification and implementation of the law reflected the impact of various political and social, as well as strictly legal, factors. As the following analysis will seek to show, the evolution of legislation on the family and on women in Yemen during the four-year 'transition period' was as much a microcosm of the overall shifts and conflicts in Yemeni politics, as it was a reflection of a strictly jurisprudential process. It demonstrated both the relative weakness of women as a distinct social and political force and, at the same time, the importance which some parties attributed to this question.

Prior to unification in 1990, the difference between the two Yemeni states was graphically reflected in, amongst other domains, the legislation pertaining to the family and to women's rights. While that of the Yemen Arab Republic, or 'North' Yemen, represented a more conservative legislative approach embodying both secular Arab nationalist and religious elements, that of the People's Democratic Republic of Yemen (PDRY), or 'South' Yemen, was, despite certain concessions to Islam, a secular code, arguably the most egalitarian in the Arab world. During this period the division between the two political and legal systems was eroded, in effect by the prevailing of the northern code over the southern. This involved, among other changes, the adoption, after parliamentary and some press debate, of a new Decree of Personal Conditions, under presidential decree in March 1992 (Republic of Yemen 1992). The fact that it was introduced during Ramadan was probably deliberate, reflecting the hope that its promulgation would not attract undue hostility, especially in the South. Although subject to ratification by the parliament, this decree was, under the Yemeni Constitution then in force, legally binding: it therefore reflected the balance of influence and power within the new state. But precisely because there was widespread disagreement about where power lay in the new state the drafting, introduction and, even more so, the implementation of the new law were themselves objects of dispute and conflict in the society. The family law was, therefore, both a reflection of the changed situation in Yemen and itself part of this political process, prior to and subsequent to its promulgation. The discussion that follows will examine the different fates of these two bodies of legislation.

FAMILY LAW PRIOR TO 1990

Before 1990 then, each of the Yemeni states had distinct, indeed contrasting, family laws and constitutional positions *vis-à-vis* women. In the North, there had been no national family law until 1979. The result was that legal matters pertaining to the family were settled in accordance with a variety of authorities and interpretations of *shari'a*. In the Zeidi areas, the more politically conservative part of the country, *ijtihad* or interpretation of *shari'a* was generally more favourable to women than in the Shafe'i regions where more orthodox constraints, mediated through the Sunni interpretation of the law, applied. But this variety of legal practices was compounded by the prevalence in tribal areas, the majority of the country, of elements of tribal law, known elsewhere as *'urf*, but in Yemen also as *akham al-aslaf* (rules of the ancestors) (al-Hubaishi 1988; Dorsky 1986; Dresch 1993; Mundy 1979). The codification and interpretation of law in North Yemen followed a pattern found throughout the history of Islamic societies: in the absence of a strong central state, legal practice and interpretation varied. As Gabriele vom Bruck (1992–1993) has shown in regard to Zeidi marriage law and practice, the legal system was characterized above all by heterogeneity and, in the modern era, by considerable pragmatism with regard to interpretation.

With the end of the civil war in 1970 and the subsequent consolidation of the republican regime, measures were taken to promulgate a constitution and legal codes based on the *shari'a*. The Constitution was announced in 1970, followed by laws on inheritance, wages, endowments, evidence and compensation in 1976 and the family law itself in 1979. The drafting process took several years and reflected conflicts both between Zeidi and Shafe'i on the one hand, and between religious-oriented Shafe'is and more secular legal experts on the other. In the words of one constitutional authority in the latter group who was closely involved in the process: 'In the end we got half of what we wanted'.

This new family law, while permitting polygamy and the male right to unilateral divorce (*talaq*) also introduced a measure of protection for women. As for the Constitution, it made vague references to the equality of men and women but within a framework of respect for the authority of Islam and the *shari'a*. Shari'a was 'the source of all laws' (Article 4), and where no clear codified law existed the courts were enjoined to pass their judgements in accordance with the general principles of *shari'a* (Article 153). In contrast to the South, the state made little effort, formal or practical, to alter the social and economic position of women.

In the PDRY a very different situation prevailed (al-Shamiry, 1994). With the adoption of 'scientific socialism' by the regime that came to power with the British withdrawal in 1967, a new secular Constitution was adopted, first in 1970 and then in revised form in 1978. In 1974 a family law was also introduced. In the 1978 Constitution (People's Democratic Republic of Yemen 1979) Islam was recognized as 'the state religion' (Article 47) but the legal and constitutional legitimacy of the state was not based on this, but on 'the people', and in particular on 'the interests of the working class' as expressed through the Yemeni Socialist Party (Articles 1, 2, 3, 6, 8). In this framework the equality of women was spelled out, thus Article 35 stated:

> All citizens are equal in their rights and duties irrespective of their sex, origin, religion, language, standard of education or social status. All persons are equal before the law. The state shall do whatever it can to realize this equality by means of providing equal political, economical, social and cultural opportunities.

Article 36 went further, asserting that:

> The state shall ensure equal rights for men and women in all fields of life, the political, economical and social, and shall provide the necessary conditions for the realization of that equality. The state shall also work for the creation of the circumstances that will enable the women to combine (*sic*) between participation in the productive and social work and her role within the family sphere. It shall render special care to the vocational qualifying of the working women. The state shall, further, ensure special protection for the working women and the children and shall establish kindergartens and nurseries for the children and all other such means of care as to be specified by the law.

Further articles enjoined the right to employment, social security, free education, free medical care, and accommodation (Molyneux 1980, 1982).

In the family law of 1974 this implicit secularization was taken further. The principle of free choice marriage was established. A minimum legal age for marriage was fixed at 16 for women, and 18 for men. Polygamy was prohibited, but allowed in exceptional cases such as barrenness or incurable disease. The bride-price or *mahr* was reduced to 100 Yemeni dinars, equivalent to around twice the average white-collar monthly salary. Article 17 of the code stipulated that both spouses should bear the cost of supporting the family. Some of the most controversial elements related to divorce: unilateral divorce by the male, *talaq*, was now banned, and all divorces had to go through the courts. Men no longer had automatic right of custody but male children were normally to remain with their mothers until the age of 10 and daughters to the age of 15, with the courts retaining the right to make decisions in terms of the best interests of the children (Molyneux 1985).

This law was in many respects similar to the most radical legislation hitherto introduced in the Arab world, namely in Syria and Tunisia: their influence was in part the result of the involvement of legal experts from both countries in the South Yemeni drafting process rather than direct political contacts. However, it was introduced in a political situation far more radical than that which had prevailed in these states, by a regime committed to a programme of socialist modernization, including a change in the position of women. The law, as in other socialist states, not only reflected a different view of gender relations and of women's place in society, but also of the significance of juridical reform: it was one of several instruments designed to alter society and linked to other mechanisms, such as mass campaigns, changes in education and employment and a reduced place for the role of religion (Halliday 1987). This context is important to bear in mind in examining what happened to family law following the 1990 unification: the apparent abandonment of the policies embodied in the law of 1990 can only be understood in the much broader context of political change in Yemen, North and South, during this period.

LEGAL CHANGE IN THE TRANSITION PERIOD

When the two Yemens entered the 'transitional period' in May 1990 the new unified government and regime proceeded to enact a single legal system, one in which most of the specific, socialist or secular, elements of the South were displaced in favour of the laws and customs prevailing in the North. The new Constitution had been drawn up as early as 1981 by a committee drawn from both states (Hall 1991: 22–39). It reproduced the position of the northern constitution on the role of Islam which was thus proclaimed to be 'the religion of the state' (Article 2) and *shari'a* designated as 'the main source of legislation'. Article 18 guaranteed 'to all its citizens, equal political, economic, social and cultural opportunities'; Article 20 stressed that work was 'a right, an honour and a necessary tool for the advancement of society'; and Article 27 restated the commitment to equality before the law. The Constitution therefore allowed for the equality of men and women but established a legal framework tied to the *shari'a* and omitted many of the commitments to state intervention on behalf of women contained in the PDRY Constitution of 1978.

The Constitution was in the main a secular document embodying the modified Arab nationalist consensus of the North Yemen regime, derived from its Nasserist origins in the 1960s. A similar perspective was to be found in the joint 'Programme of National Construction and Reform' of the two ruling parties, the General People's Congress (GPC) and the Yemeni Socialist Party (YSP), issued after unification and which was intended to outline a broad political programme for the transitional period (Republic of Yemen 1991). The discussion of women's rights appeared in a section on

'Social Problems' after sections devoted to illiteracy, tribal vengeance and the narcotic *qat*; it also made a number of generic modernist pronouncements. However, even leaving aside the commitment of the new state to their implementation, the policies enjoined were markedly less radical than those which had been called for and to some extent effected in the south. The Programme of National Construction and Reform declared 'Support for the development of women's participation in political, economic, social and cultural life', by means of:

- Promoting the emancipation and freeing of women from traditional customs and traditions, in order to enhance their effective participation in society.
- Providing opportunities for women to study and work.
- Promoting the work of women's associations, especially in the fields of developing motherhood and care for children, training for household work, acquiring certain skills, and involving educated women in literacy work amongst other women, in consideration of this as a national, human and religious obligation.
- Vigilance with regard to the high level of bride-prices, the organization of lavish marriages, in connection with which the government organized national conferences to pay attention to these social manifestations.

In effect, the indications about women's social and economic role were removed from the joint constitution and appeared, in a significantly altered form, in this political document. Yet, even had it represented a realistic state commitment to promoting women within the limits identified, it would have marked a definite contrast with the policies to which the YSP had hitherto been committed.

THE POLITICS OF MARRIAGE

The codification of a new family law can only be understood in the context of the broader changes taking place in Yemen in this period. On the one hand, it appeared as if, quite simply, the southern law of 1974 had been abandoned and the northern one of 1979 applied to the whole of Yemen. The new law, embodied in the Decree of March 1992 (Republic of Yemen 1992), reproduced the 1979 northern law with a few changes: these were not concessions to the southern law, but incorporated elements from the Arab League's Unified Model Arab Personal Statute Law (*mashru' qanun al-ahwal al-shakhsiyya al-arabiyya al-mouhid*), which had been prepared by the League's Council of the Ministers of Justice. Thus Chapter 1, Section 2 of the new law laid out general principles on marriage. Article 12 permitted marriage by a man of up to four wives 'on condition of equitableness (*'adl*), otherwise only one'. Four conditions were laid down: that there should be 'legitimate benefit'; that the husband should be financially able to support more than one wife; that the woman must be told that the man who wants to marry her is married to another; that the existing wife is told that her husband wishes to marry again. The minimum age for marriage, by men or women, is 15 years (Article 15). Marriage by compulsion (*ikrah*) of either male or female is invalid (Article 10), but when it comes to specifying what constitutes 'consent' for a woman a distinction is made between a woman who has already been married, who has to give explicit consent, and a woman for whom this is the first marriage, for whom silence constitutes consent (Article 23). The third section of Chapter 1 has a detailed discussion of the handling of the bride-price (*mahr*).

Chapter 2 of the new law discusses the ending of marriage, either through dissolution through the court (*faskh*), pronouncement of divorce by the husband (*talaq*), or death (Article 43). The section on dissolution allows the woman to petition for divorce on a number of grounds, including the traditional grounds of the husband failing to practice *kafa'a*, or equal treatment of his spouses. Other grounds include addiction to drugs or alcohol, or refusal to work when the man is capable of so doing (Article 51). Prolonged absence without providing support or indicating his whereabouts is also grounds for divorce – a significant factor in a country with large-scale male out-migration (Article 52). *Talaq* is defined in conventional terms as an utterance repeated three times (Articles 58 and 59), although it is for a period revocable: thus the husband has the right to return to his wife during the period of '*iddat*, the legally prescribed period after divorce when a woman cannot remarry. The divorced woman is not entitled to reverse this verdict in the courts, but she is entitled to compensation if the judge considers the *talaq* to have been conducted unfairly (Article 71). In regard to custody of children, this is normally given to the woman provided that she remains a Muslim and does not work outside the home unless provision is made for child care. On the other hand, a husband may transfer children from one wife to another, the conditions being that the second is 'equal or better in the level of caring and culture', and that the first wife requests more money than the normal amount (Article 144).

This impression of a victory of the northern legislation over the southern is, however, somewhat misleading and needs to be set in the context of at least three other operative factors. The first is that the PDRY law, enacted in 1974 at the height of the Aden regime's commitment to a 'transition to socialism', had encountered some opposition within the country, especially outside Aden. In 1974 itself, as part of the UN's International Year of Women, the regime had created a number of residential colleges for women where they lived apart from their families. Protests from the families had, in some governorates, forced the government to send the women home (Molyneux 1982). Enthusiasm for the law among the leadership was already being eroded long before the regime itself unified with the North.[2] For instance, the control on bride-price was not being enforced, the attendance of girls at school in the Hadramaut and elsewhere was allowed to fall to negligible levels, and there was less willingness to support the legal requirement for husbands to provide divorced wives with housing. In numerous ways, the law was being circumvented: for example, a man who wanted to marry a second wife and who had secured the agreement of his first wife to do so, could achieve this by the subterfuge of divorcing the first, marrying the second with the period of '*iddat* relevant to the first, and then revoking his initial divorce. There was also an external dimension: as part of the overall conflict between the PDRY and Saudi Arabia, the latter's radio broadcasts had attacked the 'atheistic' legal reforms in South Yemen, making particular mention of the appointment of women judges in family courts (BBC *SWB* 1970).

Against this background, by the early 1980s the Family Law, along with other 'socialist' laws, was coming under review and the government set up a committee to investigate proposed changes. There was talk of introducing a period of '*iddat* for men, but this was never implemented. No changes were actually introduced into the 1974 law, but this was in part a result of the political crisis in the country prior to, and after, the explosion of intra-regime factionalism in 1986. It can, therefore, be said that to a considerable extent the leadership of the YSP had itself lost confidence in this law when the unification process began in 1990.

SOCIALISM IN RETREAT

The loss of support for the 1974 southern family law was compounded by a much broader loss of confidence in the 'socialist' orientation of the regime, which led the YSP to yield on a number of issues after May 1990. In its broadest context, the YSP had lost faith in the ability not only to maintain socialism in a part of Yemen, but in the whole socialist transformation project, as exemplified in the USSR and East Germany. Under the influence of *perestroika* and in the aftermath of the 1986 civil war, they had already revised their positions on a range of issues (Yemeni Socialist Party 1987). Thus the state's control on the economy was loosened, by allowing a greater role for private ownership of industry and agriculture, emigration was permitted, and the role of Islam was enhanced. When unification did occur a measure of political pluralism had already been introduced and much of the regime's claim to a socialist revolutionary authority had been aban-doned.[3]

This process, a precondition for the 1990 unification agreement, was accelerated in the transition period itself. Thus property expropriated in the revolutionary changes after 1967 was restituted, political exiles returned safely to Aden, some of the Sultans ousted in 1967 came back to their tribal areas, sometimes to warm welcomes, and foreign businesses, mainly in the oil sector, were active in Aden. As a result of the 1990 unification the YSP yielded ground across the board on the social policies that had been their distinctive mark: the narcotic *qat*, whose consumption was limited to two days a week by a 1977 law, became, as it had always been in the North, freely available; the public sale of alcohol was now banned, although informal distribution networks continued to operate, and the beer factory at Sira Island off Aden continued to function (allegedly for export only). In the rural areas the tribes, largely disarmed after 1967, rearmed with enthusiasm as the country as a whole was flooded with cheap weapons after the end of the wars in Ethiopia. The retreat on the Family Law was, therefore, linked to a much wider process. Reform of the position of women had always been part of a broader social and political project and of the YSP's intervention in society through the state: once that project and the party's interventionist capacity were disabled, policies designed to promote greater equality for women also foundered.

The capitulation of the YSP was, however, only part of the overall political process in the now unified Yemen. While the regime in the North had succeeded in prevailing over its former rival in the South in relation to social legislation, it was conducting another campaign, this time in league with the YSP and other secular forces, against the Islamist challenge in the form of the Islah Party. The Islah, itself a coalition of tribal forces, urban Islamists and conservative merchants, presented itself as a rival to both the GPC and the YSP and gained a place in the ruling coalition at the 1993 elections. But in the period prior to the elections it had opposed the new state's Constitution and legal system on the grounds that it was not Islamic.

Among other 'social' questions, it paid considerable attention to women: Islah had a women's section, and a corresponding analysis of the 'Islamic' solution to the women question. It blamed Western influence for inappropriate ideas of conflict between the sexes, and of identical social roles for men and women, laying greatest stress on the need for women to achieve equality with men by playing their role in the home: while most Islamists did not, in principle, oppose the right of women to go out to work, they regarded this as possible only with the permission of the husband and as subordinate anyway to the domestic duties of women. Another target of the Islah was co-educational schooling, what they termed 'social mixing' (*takhallut al-ta'alim*) *Takhallut* (from *khalata*, to mix, commingle or confuse) has a suggestion of disorder or confusion. Later, at a conference of *ulema* held to celebrate the defeat of the YSP in July 1994 (*al-Hayat* 1994) its communiqué called for

> the end of co-education in schools and beginning of the process of changing the school curriculum (amending the curriculum in a way which can form a basis for religious belief, correct concepts, and eradicate all the effects of cultural invasion). The cultural invasion was a key cause behind the recent destruction and crisis.

Social difficulties of all kinds were blamed on Yemen's deviation from the path of true Islam.

While Islah articulated a neo-traditionalist position on women, it was not on this question that the most overt disagreements occurred, but rather on two other related questions. First, Islah wanted the draft constitution amended so that *shari'a* became the 'sole' (*al-masdar al-wahid*) rather than the 'main' (*al-masdar al-ra'isi*) source of legislation. This campaign, backed up by demonstrations and press articles, paralleled that of Islamists in other Arab countries at the time. Second, Islah supported state funding for a large number of religious schools, the 'scientific institutions' (*al-mu'ahid al-'ilmiyya*) that had been set up in the 1980s and through which (in part *via* the Egyptian Islamist teachers working in them), it exercised considerable influence. This latter issue was the most controversial one before the joint parliament that sat from 1990 to 1993: more than any other question, it polarized opinion within and outside the parliament, not least because the schools, and by implication Islah, were seen as acting in some way as collaborators of Saudi Arabia.

The significance of these two issues – the revision of the Constitution and the funding of the schools – is that on both the Islamists lost. In other words, the process of policy formation in the new republic, while involving the YSP in ceding to the northern regime on a range of sensitive matters, also involved a successful rejection of the Islamist option by the transitional state. This meant that in the field of legislation, including that of the new family decree, the Islamists were not dominant. Much depended, as had previously been the case, on contingency, on the interpretation put on the law by the courts and, more broadly, on the political response in the country to the new laws.[4]

POLITICAL FACTORS: DRAFTING AND IMPLEMENTATION

This general context to a large extent determined the actual formulation and implementation of the new Family Code. Between the initial unification agreement of 1990 and the proclamation of the presidential decree in 1992, the authority of the old southern law had already been undermined: men were able to enter into polygamous unions in the south without fear of prosecution, and could obtain divorces from their southern wives more easily by going to northern courts. In a parallel process, state support for the employment of women declined, and many of the women employed at the textile factory in Aden, the largest factory in the south, were dismissed (Molyneux 1982). Within the legal revision process itself, conducted by the Constitutional Committee and the *Shari'a* Committee of the unified parliament, the northern representatives were divided between a secular group, who wanted a proper compromise between the two family law codes, and a group of supporters of *shari'a*. But what was crucial in the victory of the latter was the fact that the representatives of the South themselves made no significant effort to defend their law, abandoning the 1974 family code much as they had the other distinctive, secular and socialist laws on social practices. The result was a victory for the northern position, based on *shari'a*: despite claims that the outcome was a compromise, it decidedly was not.

Popular reaction was somewhat more mixed. In the North there was virtually no public discussion of the change in the law, either in the press or on the part of political parties.[5] In the South, on the other hand, there was considerable outcry: a demonstration in Aden joined by hundreds of women was held on 27 April under the auspices of the recently formed 'Organization for the Defense of Democratic Rights and Freedoms' (*Aden* 1992). This was an umbrella organization with around 5,000 members, some of them active in the capital Sana'a, and which included many lawyers, opposed both to the new law and to other reversals of hitherto prevailing norms in the south.[6] The demonstrations denounced the new law and there was a stream of correspondence in the press (i.e. in the press of the former PDRY).[7] In contrast to cases of thorough re-Islamization of the law (e.g. in Iran after 1979), women continued to work in the judicial system as both judges and lawyers.

However, despite these signs of opposition the new law was enacted and imposed by the courts. In the first place, there was no formal legal protest: although within the Supreme Court there is a constitutional division to which anyone may file an application against the constitutionality of legislation, no case of such an appeal regarding the Decree was recorded. Within the legal system itself, the cases on divorce were held by the courts at the local level, the courts of first instance: appeals were then possible first to the appeal courts of each of the eighteen provinces, and then to the Supreme Court, within which there was a Personal Status Division. Of the five judges in this Personal Status Division four were from the North, and the president was a traditional northern *shari'a* judge. The latter's view, and that of the others from the North, was that the pre-1990 northern law was consistent with *shari'a*, whereas that of the South was not.

A RETROGRESSIVE UNIFICATION

The results of this shift in law, and in overall political and social context, were predictable. There are no statistics on either divorce or polygamous marriages, but informed opinion confirms that the incidence of unilateral divorce by men rose substantially. In particular, men divorced first wives by the device of marrying a second, moving them into the home, and then divorcing and expelling the first, thus circumventing the problem of custody. There was also a significant rise in the level of the bride-price, fixed by the 1974 law at 100 dinars: by the mid-1980s it had already begun to rise, and the average rose to between 2,500 and 5,000 dinars, reaching 25,000 dinars in some cases, which, even allowing for inflation, was a major increase (at the official rate for 1992–1993, 10 dinars were equal to US$1). The overall economic situation acted as a constraint both on polygamy and on the bride-price, but despite this the ending of state controls had a noticeable impact.

The reasons for this shift have already been examined: the general aban-donment by the YSP of its commitment to 'progressive' or secular social policies, the comparative weakness of the South within the overall unifica-tion process, and the disenchantment at both official and popular levels with the socialist government. The decline in the economic situation in Aden after unification, in part a result of deliberate diversion of aid and invest-ment by the North, also contributed to this depressed atmosphere, since it led to a significant fall in women's employment. But there is one further factor that merits attention, namely the relative ineffectiveness of organized opposition by women in the South itself in the face of this shift. The official women's organization, the General Union of Yemeni Women (GUYW), beyond organizing some demonstrations, did little by way of legal advocacy to protect or secure women's rights. Various explanations are given for this relative inaction, including the belief that the mass of the population were so preoccupied with general economic and political issues that they had little time for this question; and the lack of political leadership from the top of the YSP. This indicates that the GUYW was more a tool of the party leader-ship than an expression of support from below.

Opinions on this change are ultimately derived from different political and ideological affiliations of key actors. Those opposed to the secular legal system in the South welcomed the changes as a return to the 'genuine', 'traditional', situation of Yemeni women. Secular and independent observers, however, argued that since the social reforms in the South had been imposed from above they were bound to fail, and that progress could only be made when the initiative came from below. More hard-line elements within the YSP argued that since the southerners had not fought to acquire or defend the 'revolutionary gains' of the previous regime they deserved what they got.

CONCLUSION: POLITICS IN COMMAND

The fate of family law in the 1990–1994 transitional period serves as much to illuminate the overall pattern of development in Yemen as to define the particular position of women. The latter were affected not only by changes in law but by the clear shifts in state policy, and by the economic difficulties which both parts of Yemen endured as a result of Sana'a's stance on the invasion of Kuwait, which led to severe economic pressure from the Gulf states and the West. The changes were, however, neither absolute nor mono-lithic: social and political conditions varied as between North and South, and a degree of diversity, a product both of the past pluralism of Yemen and of the enduring North–South split, prevailed. The continued presence of women in the judiciary in the South, and the different attitudes of the press between North and South, were indices of this.

This diversity was, however, most evident within the core organs of the state, the parties and the security forces, where, despite the creation of a unified government after May 1990, no unification of state apparatuses occurred. Paradoxically, the election of 1993, far from pushing this process forward, acted as the catalyst for a new, more overt reassertion of the different political interests and priorities of North and South, and led to the crisis of late 1993 and the war of April to July 1994. It was significant that many of those, in North and South, who favoured a greater degree of secularism and modernity in the legal system also favoured federalism, since they sought to limit the power of the more conservative elements within the state and the legal system. What this suggested for the position of women, and for legislation pertaining to the family, was not immediately evident since questions of this kind were simply not priorities in the political disputes that divided the country. If, however, such a decentralization had been achieved, or, even more so, if Yemen had again split into two halves, with a return to some more 'progressive' legal system in the South, and to associated social policies on education and employment, then it would have been possible to envisage some corresponding improvement in the position of women in the South at least.

In the event, the victory of the northern forces in the 1994 war led to the destruction of the southern state and the residual space for social and political diversity that had prevailed during the transitional period (Halliday 1995; Hudson 1994; Human Rights Watch 1994; Kostiner 1996). The political and military subjugation of the South, coupled with the economic cost of war, siege and looting meant that the South as a whole had lost much of the distinctive modern character it possessed (*Le Monde* 1994a; 1994b). Women were doubly affected – by the cost of the war in general and by the influence which the Islamists now held in the government in Sana'a and, through the militia, on the streets of Aden itself.[8] One of the first acts of the Islah after the fall of Aden was to convene a 'victory conference' of *ulema* which condemned the heretics (*mulhidin*) in the South. It called for the revision of the Constitution to make *shari'a* its sole basis, for the introduction of Islamic punishments 'corresponding to "the book and tradition"', and for an Islamization of the state's educational and informational policy (*al-Hayat* 1994). What this would mean in practice, and how far the northern regime of President Salih would now concede to the Islah, remained open questions.

Two almost immediate indications of the changed atmosphere, as far as the South was concerned, were evident in the fields of women's dress and deportment and of education. From the start of the school year classes were segregated, and from 1995 onwards schools were to be single sex. Textbooks in history and other subjects were brought from the North to replace those used in the South. Instruction in English, which had previously started at the age of 9, now began at 13. Within a few months, the Constitution was duly revised: Article 3 now read 'Islamic Shari'a is the source of all legislation'. The chapter on 'Social and Cultural Foundations' (formerly Chapter 4, now Chapter 3) included a new article on women: 'Women are the sisters of men. They have rights and duties, which are guaranteed and assigned by *shari'a* and stipulated by law' (Republic of Yemen 1994). In 1997 Islah also began, in the context of the parliamentary elections, to agitate for a revision of legislation pertaining to women: they proposed to reinstate the right of minors to marry, and to alter the law pertaining to testimony in court so that women would no longer have the same rights as men in this context.

In the aftermath of the war, the situation in Yemen remained as uncertain as ever with intensified economic problems and a pervasive breakdown of law and order, especially in the South. As before, the question of women's rights was dependent upon the overall destination of that country's politics and the balance of forces prevailing within it. Amidst a general pattern of human rights violations those against women continued. Women prisoners were often held long after their sentences had elapsed, on the grounds that no male relative had come to collect them. Women were on occasion detained for *khilwa*, defined in an earlier northern code as the unauthorized meeting of an adult male and adult female who are not close relatives (Amnesty International 1997). The intersection of gender with the new post-1994 system was graphically demonstrated in June 1996 when riots broke out in the Hadramaut coastal city of Mukalla. Two southern women had initiated a lawsuit against the police for wrongful arrest and rape whilst in detention. In the course of this case, the (northern) state prosecutor remarked that all southern women were 'whores'. Riots broke out and the police fired on unarmed demonstrators, wounding seventeen people. The court in the end found in favour of the women, but on grounds of depriva-tion of liberty, not of rape. Moreover, the official response illustrated all too clearly the view that the now dominant northern authorities held of the southern population (Human Rights Watch 1997: 310).

The impact of these political conflicts on women has been compounded by the appalling social conditions in which many of them live and which the state has done so little to alleviate. Surveys of poverty in Yemen indicate that, in a country with an already low per capita income, the position of women is especially bleak: in 1992, for every 100 boys enrolled in primary school, there were only 41 girls, as against a developing country average of 86 (World Bank 1996). Yemen has the highest infant mortality rates and female morbidity rates in the whole of the Middle East and North Africa and the highest rate of fertility. The state has come under pressure from international institutions for its failure to address the issue of poverty, including that of women, and Amnesty International has criticized, among other violations, the treatment of women prisoners, who are regularly shackled and subjected to other mistreatment (Amnesty International 1997). There is little sign, however, of this pressure being heeded. The regime has contrived to squander its limited income, derived to a large extent from oil, on military expenditure and dubious acquisitions of political influence. Outside the main cities, no effective administrative or legal system operates. Critical voices have also been harassed: opposition media that flourished in the 1990–1994 period have found it more difficult to publish. Parliamentary elections in April 1997 gave an appearance of constitutional order, but served only to consolidate the hold of the presidential party.[9] The Islah went into formal opposition and its more extreme proposals for the Islamization of the legal system were rejected by parliament, but, as part of the ceaseless manoeuvring of Yemeni politics, the president continued to court Islah and to accommodate its influence in the educational system. If the future for Yemen as a whole offers few grounds for optimism, for those without power, among whom women predominate, it looks even grimmer.

ACKNOWLEDGEMENTS

Maxine Molyneux would like to acknowledge many people, not all of whom it is possible to name, who have assisted with the preparation of this study. She particularly thanks the many Yemenis who have, over the past two decades, provided information on the legal process and political background. Thanks also go to Anna Wurth, Susanne Dahlgren, Eric Watkins and Gabriele vom Bruck for help with information and sources, and Lu'ayy al-Rimawi and Fred Halliday for assistance with translation.

An earlier version of this article was published by the *Middle East Journal* 49, 3: Summer 1995.

NOTES

1 Technically, the 'transitional period' ended with the elections and the constitution of a new coalition government; in effect, the transition lasted till the outbreak of war in late April 1994.
2 Information from Yemeni legal experts and from Anna Wurth.
3 'Pluralism' (*ta'addudiyya hizbiyya*) involved allowing a variety of parties to organize, publish newspapers and hold meetings but not to have access to power.
4 Information from a member of parliament in the transitional period.
5 One notable exception to the northern indifference on these questions was that of Dr Raufa Hassan of the Social Research and Women's Studies Unit, of Sana'a University College of Arts, who openly called for reform of the position of Yemeni women. She also ran as a candidate in the 1993 elections. She was denounced in the press for her deviation from Islam and was not in the end elected. In an interview with *Frontline News Television* (London) in April 1993 she had stated: 'What I have to work for is to establish credibility for me as a woman politician capable of doing the things, and building an image. We have to work peaceably with the other world, by expressing ourselves by words and not by guns' (transcript 'Yemen: Test Case for Democracy', April 1993: 2). In the 1997 elections she adopted a similar, apparently solitary, stance (Pearl 1997).
6 Information supplied by Susanne Dahlgren.
7 For example, the article by A'ida Ali Said, a member of parliament for the YSP and president of the executive committee of the Union of Yemeni Women in *Saut al-'Ummal* 30 April 1992.
8 The reaction of many Adenis to the northern victory was to make plans to emigrate. This was especially noticeable among educated women who saw little future in a society dominated by the Islah militia. At a meeting with Adenis soon

148   *Maxine Molyneux*

after the northern victory the US ambassador is reported to have asked what the US could do for the South: the unanimous reply was '10,000 green cards'.
9 There were fewer women candidates in 1997 than in the 1993 elections. Of the 301 members elected to the new parliament, 2 were women. Women's percentage of the country's registered voters rose from 19 per cent to nearly 30 per cent and in some provincial capitals the turnout for women was higher than for men. In the rural areas, on the other hand, there were places where there were no ballot boxes for women and where women's access to polling stations was restricted (*Yemen Times* 1997).

BIBLIOGRAPHY

Aden (1992) weekly journal: 28 April.
Amnesty International (1997) *Ratification Without Implementation: the State of Human Rights in Yemen*, London: March 1997.
BBC *SWB* (1970) BBC *Summary of World Broadcasts* Part 4, 'The Middle East and North Africa, ME/35681/A5', London: 21 December.
Braun, U. (1992) 'Ein anderer Fall von Vereinigung: Jemen', *Aussenpolitik, Zeitschrift fur internationale Fragen* 43, 2: 174–184.
Carapico, S. (1993) 'Elections and Mass Politics in Yemen', *Middle East Report* 23, 6: 185 November–December.
Chipaux, F. (1994a) '*Nouvelles menaces sur le Yemen*', *Le Monde*, 22 September.
—— (1994b) '*Loi de la jungle dans le sud du Yemen*', *Le Monde*, 28 September.
Detalle, R. (1993) 'The Yemeni Elections Up Close', *Middle East Report* 23, 6: 185 November–December.
Dorsky, S. (1986) *Women of 'Amran: A Middle Eastern Ethnographic Study*, Salt Lake City: University of Utah Press.
Dresch, P. (1993) *Tribes, Government and History in Yemen*, Oxford: Clarendon Press.
Dunbar, C. (1992) 'The Unification of Yemen: Process, Politics and Prospects' *Middle East Journal* 46, 3: 456–476.
Hall, S. (1991) *Yemen: The Politics of Unity*, London: Gulf Centre for Strategic Studies.
Halliday, F. (1987) '"Islam" and Soviet Foreign Policy', *Arab Studies Quarterly* 9, 3: 219–233.
Halliday, F. (1990) *Revolution and Foreign Policy: the Case of South Yemen 1967–1987*, Cambridge: Cambridge University Press.
Halliday, F. (1995) 'The Third Inter-Yemeni War', *Asian Affairs*, June: 131–140.
al-Hayat (1994) daily paper: 14 July.
al-Hubaishi, H. A. (1988) *Legal System and Basic Law in Yemen*, Worcester: Billing & Sons Ltd.
Hudson, M. (1994) 'Unhappy Yemen, Watching the Slide Toward Civil War', *Middle East Insight*, May–August: 13–19.
Human Rights Watch (1994) *Human Rights in Yemen During and After the 1994 War*, New York: October.
—— *Human Rights Watch World Report 1997*, New York.
Kostiner, J. (1996) *Yemen. The Tortuous Quest for Unity, 1990–94*, London: Royal Institute of International Affairs/Pinter.
Molyneux, M. (1980) *Peuples Méditerranéens*, 12: July/September, 147–172.
—— (1982) *State Policies and the Position of Women Workers in the PDRY 1967–1977*, Geneva: International Labour Organization.
—— (1985) 'Legal Reform and Social Revolution in Democratic Yemen: Women and the Family', *International Journal of the Sociology of Law*, 13.
—— (1991) 'The Law, the State and Socialist Policies with Regard to Women; the

Case of the People's Democratic Republic of Yemen 1967–1990' in D. Kandiyoti (ed.) *Women, Islam and the State*, London: Macmillan.

Mundy, M. (1979) 'Women's Inheritance of Land in Highland Yemen', *Arabian Studies*, 5.

Naim, M. (1993) 'Yemen: Nordistes et Sudistes tentent de surmonter leurs divisions', *Le Monde*, 9 December.

Pearl, D. (1997) 'As Democracy Looms in Yemen, Women Begin to Enter Politics', *Wall Street Journal*, 28 March.

People's Democratic Republic of Yemen (1979) *Constitution of the People's Democratic Republic of Yemen*, approved by the Supreme People's Council, 31 October 1978, Aden: 14 October Corporation.

Republic of Yemen (1991) Chamber of Deputies, *Barnamaj al-Bana' al-Watani wa al-Islah al-Siyyasi wa al-Iqtisadi wa al-Mali wa al-Idari* (Programme of National Construction and Political, Economic, Financial and Administrative Reform), issued 15 December.

—— (1992) al-Jumhuriyya al-Yamaniyya, Wizarat al-Shu'un al-Qanuniyya, *al-Qirar al-Jumhuri b'il Qanun Raqm 30 l-Sana 1992 b'Sh'an al-Ahwal al-Shakhsiyya* (Republican Decree Law No. 30 for 1992 on Personal Status), Mu'assassa, 14 October. Text also in *al-Jarida al-Rasmiyya* (*The Official Gazette*) 6, 3: 1–64, 31 March 1992.

—— (1994) *The Constitution of the Republic of Yemen*, amended on 1 October 1994, translation from the Information Services and Translation Center, Sana'a.

Roth, K. (1994) 'What Saudi and Yemeni Religious Authorities Had to Say About the Yemen War', *Institute of Current World Affairs*, Hanover, NH: ICWA.

al-Shamiry, N. (1994) 'The Judicial Background in Democratic Yemen', in B. Pridham (ed.) *Contemporary Yemen: Politics and Historical Background*, London: Croom Helm.

vom Bruck, G. (1992–1993) 'Enacting Tradition: the Legitimation of Marriage Practices Amongst Yemeni *Sadah*', *Cambridge Anthropology* 16, 2: 54–68.

Watkins, E. and Makin, P. (1993) 'Yemen's Crisis Threatens the Country's Unity', *Middle East International*, 19 November.

World Bank (1996) *Republic of Yemen Poverty Assessment*, 26 June.

Yemen Socialist Party (1987) *al-Wathika al-Nakdiyya al-Tahliliyya* (The Critical-Analytical Document), Aden.

Yemen Times (1997) 5 May.

8   Communal violence, civil war and foreign occupation
Women in Lebanon

Kirsten Schulze

In prolific language
men lay waste the land

Tear it up with gunfire
crash it with terror
bury it under the dead

In the spiral of ages
in the black winds of hatred
love is too light.

André Chedid Ceremonial of Violence (1976)

INTRODUCTION

Lebanon as a deeply divided society combines conflicting cultural, religious and political elements which are often presented in the over-simplified binary structure of Christianity versus Islam, and Western versus Arab cultural identity. The common perception of the position of women portrays Christians as more 'liberated' than their Muslim counterparts and, while this is true to a certain extent, it is a matter of degree rather than kind. Women of all communities are still defined primarily as daughters, sisters, wives and mothers. Before the civil war in 1975 only 19 per cent (*Al-Raida* 1995) of women worked outside the home and those that did reflected orthodox patterns of occupational segregation by being employed mainly as teachers, nurses, factory workers and secretaries (Sabban 1988). Under a modern occidental guise, Lebanese society was a traditional one wherein the division into a female-private and a male-public domain was evident (Karamé 1995: 87).

Lebanon's second civil war, which lasted from 1975 until 1990, has had a fundamental effect on the role of women. Women of all religious traditions became involved in the war and thereby 'claimed' a place in the public sphere either through combat, support functions, or employment outside the house. Thus the civil war raises four key issues which will be explored in this chapter: it questions war as an activity limited to combat; it raises the issues of womanhood and femininity within the context of women becoming active in conflict; it explores to what extent women's movements have been able to bridge the gaps of this divided society; and finally it poses the question of whether Lebanese women, through their involvement, have been able to shift into the public domain after the war and take up positions in business and politics.

By discussing gender relations before the war; women's roles in the civil war; their positions in family and religion, women's education and employment; and finally their place in current day society undergoing national reconciliation, this chapter shows that fifteen years of civil war did not significantly change the situation. Although some women were actively involved in combat and in peace movements, and many more became the breadwinners, the war did not provide a springboard for female participation in politics. To the contrary, it will be argued here that the war in many ways served to reinforce the existing male-dominated social structure. Women remain confined by cultural traditions, Lebanese conceptions of womanhood and the divisions in Lebanese society which were present not only throughout the war but have continued during the current politics of transition. Thus, not unlike women in the Algerian war of liberation (Cooke 1993; Helie-Lucas 1988), or in the Iranian revolution (Azari 1983; de Groot 1996), Lebanese women subordinated the struggle for equality to the nationalist struggle, stating that the achievement of women's rights had to be postponed (Karamé 1995: 391). In practical terms this meant, for instance, that after laying down their arms Lebanese women until 1993 still required the signature of a male parent to obtain a passport or open a bank account. Moreover, Lebanese nationality still is only passed down through the father.

THE NATURE OF DIVISIONS IN LEBANON

Lebanon is composed of twenty-three ethnic and religious minorities which include the Maronites, Greek Orthodox, Greek Catholics, Armenians, Sunni, Shi'a, Druze, and Jews among others. They all at some point in history fled to the safety of the Lebanese mountains to avoid persecution in other areas of the Middle East. The present state was created by the French mandatory powers on 30 August 1920 from the predominantly Christian area of Beirut-Mount Lebanon, to which the Muslim provinces of Tripoli and South Lebanon were added, in order to make it economically viable. The net effect, however, was the disruption of the demographic balance, resulting in discord between the traditional Maronite Christian ethos, which underlay its creation, and the heterogeneous composition of its population (Rabinovich 1986: 21).

The most apparent cleavage within the society was, and remains, the Muslim–Christian one. The Christians as an ethno-religious group had traditionally looked towards the West for protection, culture and identity. The Muslims, by contrast, had looked to the surrounding Arab nations. Yet,

Christians and Muslims should not be regarded as homogeneous groups. Intra-faith rivalries have in the past erupted between Maronites, Greek Orthodox and Armenians, as well as between Sunni, Shi'a and Druze. To these were added feuds between clans and rivalries within families. Thus, the idea of a common national identity was, and still is, elusive in comparison with past loyalties to specific communities and memories of old enmities.

Historically divided along sectarian, regional and family lines, several attempts were made at creating national unity, such as the constitution of 1926 and the National Pact of 1943. The latter was specifically designed as an agreement among the different minorities which asserted Lebanese independence and sovereignty. Christians were not to seek Western protection and Muslims were not to attempt to make Lebanon part of a larger Arab Islamic state (Hudson 1985: 44). Political and administrative representation was accorded by sect. Seats in the parliament were allotted via a system of proportional representation, based on the 1932 census. The census calculated the Maronites to be 29 per cent, the Greek Orthodox 10 per cent, the Greek Catholics 6 per cent, the Armenians 4 per cent, other Christians 1 per cent, the Sunnis 23 per cent, the Shi'a 20 per cent, the Druze 6 per cent, and others, such as the Jews, 1 per cent of the Lebanese population. The overall Christian population totalled 50 per cent, the Muslims 49 per cent, and others 1 percent (Hanf 1994: 88). The census identified a Christian majority of 6:5 and divided the parliamentary seats accordingly. Moreover, the presidency was allotted to the largest Christian sect, the Maronites, while the premiership was bestowed upon the largest Muslim sect, the Sunnis. It was a carefully balanced system which worked provided the respective populations did not increase too rapidly. Lebanon's weak geographic position, however, made this system vulnerable to external intervention from neighbouring Syria, Israel and the PLO, each of which exploited Lebanon's divisions.

Neither the 1943 National Pact nor any other unifying measures succeeded in erasing the felt primordial loyalties in Lebanese society. Thus, in times of political and economic instability many Lebanese returned to their sectarian loyalties and communal identity. Two civil wars, the first in 1958 and the second lasting from 1975 until 1990, were fought over conflicting communal visions of the state (Salibi 1976). Society disintegrated along religious lines and sectarian militias were established to defend communal interests. In the second civil war the army disintegrated and several minorities 'invited' foreign powers such as Syria, Israel and the Palestinians to 'join' the conflict in order to further their own interests.

One of the reasons for this lack of national unity lay in the nature of the inter-communal arrangements which essentially served the interests of the commercial and financial elites (Sunni and Maronite) rather than the population as a whole (Schiff 1989: 10). However, the real impetus for civil war came from the demographic changes accompanied by the widening socio-economic gap. The census of 1932 had not been updated and, accordingly, a demographic restructuring of parliamentary seats and government roles had not occurred. Yet, the population growth of almost 4 per cent for the Shi'a, 3 per cent for the Sunnis, 2 per cent for both the Maronites and the Druze, and 1 per cent for the Greek Catholics, had changed the demographic reality significantly (ALPF 1971). As a result the Maronites, who still held the presidency, no longer were the largest minority. Nor were the Christians as a whole a majority in Lebanon. The Shi'a, who incidentally had no significant political representation and were also among the poorest segments of the population, had become the largest minority. Lack of political, economic and social power made them into the main challengers of the pre-1975 confessional structure. The civil war provided the Shi'a community with the organization, arms and self-conscious identity to demand equal participation and full franchise (Schiff 1989: 19).

Fifteen years of fighting over the identity of the state and political hegemony came to an end in 1990. The long-term question of whether Lebanon is essentially Western, Christian, Maronite, Phoenician or Arab, Muslim and Middle Eastern – whether the state should remain consociational or be secularized – has been overridden by the Syrian occupation of the country, which still prevails. Some scholars, such as Theodor Hanf (1994), believe that the absence of violence, the refocusing on rebuilding the state and the growing resentment towards the Syrians will serve to create a type of national unity; others are less optimistic.

PARADIGMS OF GENDER RELATIONS BEFORE THE 1975 WAR

Women in Lebanon have to be viewed within the context of its social divisions. Both Muslim and Christian women are defined by patriarchal cultural norms. Their roles within their respective ethno-religious traditions have been both complex and contradictory. On the one hand, nationalist movements invited women to participate more fully in collective life. On the other, they reaffirmed the boundaries of culturally acceptable feminine conduct and exerted pressure on women to articulate their gender interests within the terms set by nationalist discourse (Kandiyoti 1996: 9).

Christian women identified either with one of the various Christian nationalisms, ranging from 'Maronitism' to 'Lebanonism' or saw themselves simply as more Western (Phares 1995). This meant they were Western-oriented, and political activism, while acceptable, was not necessary – neither was working outside the home nor becoming highly educated and relatively independent. It should be said at this point that not all Christian women were Maronite nationalists and that the level and quality of education available to girls also varied greatly across the socio-economic classes. In the 1960s and 1970s, young Maronite women were as active in the youth movement of the Kataib party as their menfolk, even joining paramilitary organizations, thereby providing them with a stepping stone into combat during the civil war (Karamé 1989).

Muslim women, on the other hand, were faced with the complex problem of choosing Islam as a sole identity or as complementary to an Arabist or socialist-nationalist orientation. The strong identity of cultural authenticity with Islam has meant that feminist discourse could only legitimately proceed in two directions: either denying that Islamic practices are necessarily oppressive; or asserting that oppressive practices are not necessarily Islamic (Kandiyoti 1996). Muslim women's difficulties of finding a place for themselves in a patriarchal yet changing society have been exacerbated with the emergence of Islamic resurgence throughout the Middle East. Politicized religious ideologies have had a tendency to transform women into one-dimensional symbols of cultural purity and religious rectitude (King-Irani 1995).

Among Muslim women, Sunnis living in Beirut as well as in the north were the most socially and politically conservative. Bound by Muslim tradition on the one hand and urban middle-class conservatism on the other, they were neither politically active nor visible. Shi'a women, who before the war were living in the rural south were often less well educated than either their Maronite or Sunni counterparts. They were not politically active in the public realm but did play an integral role in Shi'a society and the agricultural economy: Shi'a Islam in some respects has a more liberal attitude towards women, as instanced by granting them equal inheritance rights.[1]

In the late 1960s and early 1970s large numbers of Shi'a began migrating to the southern suburbs of Beirut to escape the deteriorating economic situation in the South (Johnson 1983). Lebanon's *laissez-faire* economy had promoted economic and social divisions, resulting in the neglect of the rural areas (Calic and Perthes 1994). However, life in the city for the migrant peasants was only marginally better. Urban poverty forced many Shi'a women into paid employment. Concurrently, the increasing calls for political mobilization by leaders, such as Musa al-Sadr, advocating a distinctly Shi'a, rather than Arab national, identity propelled the Shi'a as a whole into the Lebanese political arena with demands for social, political and economic equality.

From an economic perspective, developmentalism serves as a paradigm for Lebanese women, recognizing the class structure evident in Lebanese society. Indeed, overlapping class and community structures reinforced confessionalism (*ibid.*: 15). Shi'a women were perceived as 'rural, uneducated, overly fertile and male-dominated' (Kandiyoti 1996: 10), in effect as representing traditional views of them as docile, if not oppressed. Christian women in general, and Maronite women in particular, but also Beiruti Sunni women, were 'urban, educated, and companionate' (*ibid.*) representing the modern image of womanhood. Druze women fall somewhere between these two stereotypes; never having been subject to the same Islamic traditions, Druze society has a more egalitarian, even communitarian nature (Firo 1992). However, it needs to be stressed that these were the predominant perceptions, leaving room for exceptions such as well educated Shi'a women who were middle- and upper middle-class. The class structure within the confessional groups gives the binary developmental paradigm an additional dimension. Most Shi'a, and many Maronite, women were lower- to lower middle-class, while most Sunni women were upper middle-class. The class aspect is important as it sheds light on the conservatism of Sunni women. The urban–rural perspective illuminates the political inactivity of Shi'a women compared to Maronite women.

Employment for Lebanese women as a whole was restricted to low paying work in the textile industry and equally low paid work in the service sector which, however, was socially more acceptable because it was perceived as a nurturing activity. For a short period before the war international organizations attempted to improve the marginalized situation of women by including them in developmental organizations. With the outbreak of the civil war, this short-lived programme was replaced with relief work directed at displaced women and children.

Viewed from the public/private dichotomy which is often applied to the Middle East, Christian women were more likely to enjoy a role in the public sphere, whereas Muslim women were more confined to the private sphere. However, there have been a number of Muslim women who stand out as exceptions to this general rule. Perhaps the most compelling exception in the 1930s was the Druze matriarch, Sitt Nazira Junblatt who, widowed while still young, governed the Junblatt clan, raised her two children and conferred with foreign diplomats in her salon in Beirut (Abu Izzedin 1984; NARA 1951). A more recent example is Sitt Rabab as-Sadr Charafeddine who, since the early 1970s, has been organizing women's programmes and activities for the Shi'a.

In the years leading up to the civil war of 1975 gender issues had a relatively low priority, although some key achievements were gained: in 1952 Lebanese women attained the right to vote; in 1959 Christian women obtained the right to equal inheritance; and in 1974 Lebanese women acquired the right to travel. The most significant achievement during the war was the annulment in 1983 of all punishments relating to contraceptive measures. And, in 1988, the first women were recruited into the Lebanese Army under General Michel Aoun. Indeed, since 1990 Christian women have become a prime target for recruitment in order to obtain a representative confessional balance.

In short, it was not unusual for Maronite women to be politically active before the civil war as it was acceptable in their cultural, ethno-religious context and compatible with their community's conception of womanhood; women who were less politically involved, such as the Shi'a, or who were absent from the public realm, such as the Sunnis, were also playing out preconceived roles. As society and state started to collapse in the early 1970s, gender issues became even less important in the face of the nationalist discourses which started to engulf Lebanon.

THE CIVIL WAR

The brutal civil war which erupted in 1975, costing 150,000 lives (out of a population of 3 million), and which led to the displacement of two-thirds of the population, had its roots in the divisions within Lebanese society. The confessional system which had been created to maintain the balance of interests between the communities collapsed because it no longer reflected demographic realities. The distribution of governmental offices, not revised since the census of 1932, meant that the Maronite community which held the presidency had lost its majority, while the Shi'a community, which had an insignificant stake in Lebanese politics, had expanded to become the largest community. The reason for the collapse of the confessional system, however, lay not only in its structure but in the fact that primordial allegiances and particularistic identities at a communal level had already eroded civil culture at a national level. It was the durable affiliations of family, clan and sect in the social system which led to crisis (Khalaf 1987; Schiff 1989: 9).

The civil war split the country along sectarian and confessional lines. More accurately, Lebanon was divided into those who aimed to uphold the political *status quo* – which in essence meant Maronite political dominance – and those who challenged it. Inextricably intertwined with the issue of political representation was the vision each community held of Lebanon as a state. The Maronites were fighting to maintain their hegemony and to promote Lebanon as a Western and Christian, or at least independent, Levantine state. Armenians, Greek Orthodox, Protestants, Melkites and Jews generally supported the *status quo*. Divisions, however, were visible over the question of whether the Christians' future lay in assimilation and a pro-Syrian orientation or secession and alliance with Israel.

The Shi'a aspired to equality in all realms: social, political and economic. During the war their agenda also took on an Islamic and anti-Zionist character. Split into Amal, Islamic Amal and Hizballah supporters, their political aims ranged from increased representation within the Lebanese system to its replacement with an Islamic one.

The Sunnis had an Arab nationalist agenda. Seeking to maintain their relative dominance over the Shi'a, they supported the Palestinian cause and, having no militia of their own, they relied upon the Palestinian *fedayeen* to represent them militarily, thus joining the anti-*status quo* forces of the Lebanese Nationalist Movement. The Druze were also part of this coalition. Their aims were a more socialist and secular Lebanon with an Arab orientation.

Thus, from an internal perspective the civil war was about power, political representation, religious and communal identity and economic and social inequalities. Added to this was the vital strategic position of Lebanon in the wider Arab–Israeli conflict. With Syria on its eastern and northern borders, Israel on its southern border, and the PLO headquarters and a large

Palestinian refugee population in Lebanon, it became a battlefield of the Arab–Israeli conflict once the state collapsed. Lebanese territory was used by the Palestinians to attack Israel; Syria intervened in 1976, attracted by the power vacuum and the opportunity to reclaim Lebanon as part of Greater Syria. Israel invaded in 1982 to expel the PLO and Syria from Lebanon, seeing the situation as a way to extend its own hegemony over the Levant. And while these external factors did not cause the civil war, it has often been argued that they served to prolong it.

WOMEN ON THE FRONT LINES

Women of all communities were caught up in the conflict and were faced with the choice of either actively becoming involved or trying to avoid the fighting. Active involvement took two forms: fighting for the respective nationalist cause; or protesting against the communal violence. Each involved risking their lives in defence of their country.

There were three Christian all-female militia units in addition to some mixed units. Between 250 and 300 young Christian women took part in combat, although 3,000 had received military training in the preceding years (Karamé 1995: 379). In 1982, during the Mountain War, women fighters constituted 7 per cent of the Lebanese Forces' combatants (Shehadeh, unpublished paper). Not unlike their male counterparts, these young female soldiers had decided to take up arms to defend their community, their way of life, their image of Lebanon as a state. However, they did not anticipate that their engagement would subsequently yield occupancy of political office (Karamé 1989: 184). Obstacles to female involvement in the fighting came from two sources: parents and society. Parents feared for both the safety and the reputation of their daughters: a sullied reputation would jeopardize the prospect of marriage. Nevertheless, parents accepted their daughters' involvement on patriotic grounds. Society tolerated female 'warriors' since they were perceived as temporary, often not being taken seriously by their male counterparts or those in politically important positions.[2] The degree of female participation in combat was highest during 1975–1976, before the militias were organized into more regular forces. With the regularization of the conflict came the introduction of heavy weapons training from which women were excluded.

Muslim women also became involved in the conflict, but rarely on the front lines (Maksoud 1980). They acted in a more predictably supportive capacity performing roles concerning logistics and communications. They comprised 5–10 per cent of the Progressive Socialist Party militia where their function was predominantly medical or administrative (Shehadeh 1995: 5). Women made up 30 per cent of Amal and had their own Women's Affairs Department which was subordinate to the Executive Council. They were not involved in military activities but served in auxiliary functions. The most visible Muslim female soldiers were those of Hizballah, which was formed in 1982. Following the Israeli invasion of Lebanon, some Shi'a females volunteered and were trained to fight but, in fact, never entered into combat.[3] The only exception was the 16-year-old female suicide bomber who carried out an attack against Israeli soldiers in April 1985.

Consistent with Muslim tradition, there is complete segregation between males and females in Hizballah. Moreover, women were relegated to the second line of defence (Reeves 1989: 7), meaning demonstrations and parades rather than combat. The function of armed women demonstrating for a revolutionary cause has been seen as a means of mobilizing young men rather than according women equality in arms (Stiehm 1988). Revolutionary movements promoting a traditional and religious ideology, such as Hizballah, use the image of women with guns to shame and blackmail men into service. If the Iranian Revolution supplies a guide, female Hizballah soldiers will find themselves politically marginalized as soon as the revolutionary objective has been achieved. The Ayatollah Khomeini, immediately upon taking power, began a campaign to 'drive women back into the sphere of domesticity' (Ahmed 1992: 232). The political climate in Iran shifted from innovation and insurrection to consolidation, conformity and repression; 'Islamic' politics asserted male power and authority as central aspects of politics (de Groot 1996: 44).

Female Hizballah fighters already seem to have disappeared in post-war Lebanon,[4] despite the fact that the armed resistance against Israel in South Lebanon continues. The main role of female Hizballah supporters today is to send their husbands and sons into battle. Attitudes such as 'we mothers will never tire of producing martyrs' (Shehadeh *op. cit.*: 7), 'armed struggle is a normal right'; and 'we are all involved in the armed struggle through contact with a martyr's family and support of those women who have lost a son or husband',[5] are characteristic of the self-ascribed roles of Shi'a women.

During the course of the civil the war Lebanese women of all communities also became very active in non-violent activities. They staged peace marches, hunger strikes, sit-ins, and submitted petitions to national and international peace organizations. On many occasions they stood in the line of fire trying to prevent the kidnappings which had given the civil war a new macabre twist (Accad 1994). Women also tried to appease fighters by visiting refugee camps and military headquarters and placing flowers in the muzzles of guns (Stephan 1984). There were also occasions when women attempted to dismantle the militia checkpoints where individuals were being kidnapped. Moving from East Beirut to West Beirut, from Lebanese Forces' checkpoint to Progressive Socialist Party checkpoint, they 'were speaking in the name of spouses, mothers, and sisters. They wanted the butchery to stop' (Accad 1994: 44). Women blocked the passage ways dividing the two sides of the capital, and stormed into local television stations to interrupt the news in order to ensure that their demands were broadcast.

Yet, despite female involvement in combat and female non-violent political activism, the Lebanese civil war served to maintain gender identity, war being profoundly gendered, synonymous as it is with male space. Some insist that the importance of war in social existence, the allocation of economic resources and cultural models, lies at the root of masculine domination. Indeed, Arab society in general and Lebanese society in particular, has prided itself on male leadership through the *za'im*, the epitome of the 'macho man' (Accad 1994: 41). He embodies the perceived masculine values of conquest, domination, competition and war. He is 'the gifted person who commands the deference of the many for the well-being of all' (Beyoghlow 1989: 29). Before the civil war, the *za'im* was the political and secular leader of his community. During the war he became its military leader along with a new, younger generation of militia leaders. Afterwards he resumed his traditional role, based on notions of political and social differentiation, class privilege, or class status. Thus, it can be seen that he never relinquished the control of his community, making it difficult even for women involved in combat to assume decision-making positions.

Nationalist movements, whether Maronite, Shi'a, Arab nationalist or greater Syrian, are inherently traditional, patriarchal, and sexist in organization and language. Women are called upon to join nationalist movements; when they are needed they may carry arms and fight, but ultimately they are still seen as 'other', as inferior to men (Davis 1983). In ethnic conflict and war, women's positions in general worsen as it becomes more difficult for them to express themselves politically outside the nationalist framework. Thus war, in the end, becomes a male event with predominantly male fighters and a masculine nationalist discourse and agenda. Females can be fighters and fight as well as, or better than, their male counterparts, but ultimately they are functioning within a patriarchal system. The masculinity of civil war is never more evident than through the use of rape as a tactic of warfare; rape not to violate women as such, but as a way of shaming the males of their community who are supposed to protect them.

EDUCATION AND EMPLOYMENT

The changes in women's education and employment very often are reflective of the social, economic and political position of women in society. Lebanese girls have always been privileged within the Arab world; since the nineteenth century in the *mutassarifiyah* (province) of Mount Lebanon and the coastal cities there was an equal amount of schooling for girls and boys. Most Lebanese children were sent to religious schools if the parents could afford them. By 1970, 44.9 per cent of students enrolled in private (religious) schools and 44.5 per cent of those in public schools were female.

During the civil war the number of females in public, as opposed to private, education increased. This has been attributed to the destabilizing economic situation and inflation which led to a prohibitive rise in the costs of education. Parents who could afford to send only one child to a private school preferred to send their sons rather than their daughters (Khalaf 1995). As a result girls suffered more than boys from the fall in educational standards in public schools which accompanied the conflict (Perthes 1994).

In the labour market women did not fare any better. The war economy created a new extremely wealthy upper class and also enriched the traditional elites through import–export trade, currency speculation and corruption. Minimum wages, however, fell to a quarter of their pre-war value (Hamdan 1992). This particularly affected women of the lower and lower middle classes employed in factories and the service sector, and inadequately educated housewives who had been forced into the labour market by the war. A survey conducted in 1984 established that two-thirds of Lebanese women were working from economic necessity. The type of work for 40 per cent of women was determined by their lack of qualifications. For another 18 per cent the choice was made by the family (Chicani-Nacouz 1988). Only 8 per cent were pursuing a career of their choice.

Since the end of the war middle-class families have found it increasingly difficult to pay the tuition fees for the better schools and universities (Abou Mrad 1991). Despite this fact, female university enrolment has almost doubled from 25 per cent in 1973 to 48 per cent in 1993.[6] This increase has been attributed to the opening of university branches in all regions of the country, making it easier for females to study whilst living at home. Most women, however, study literature, the humanities, education and social sciences, preparing them for gender-segregated, and hence socially acceptable, employment in the service sector.

Women in Lebanon have had easy access to education, especially compared to other Middle Eastern countries. This, however, has not enabled them to reach decision-making positions within the public and private sector commensurate with their educational attainment, capabilities and experience (King-Irani 1995: 3). The main obstacle for Lebanese women of all communities has been traditional gender socialization based on notions that women cannot and should not exercise decisive power. Assumptions that 'a woman cannot be a successful worker while also being a loving wife and mother' go hand in hand with the message many girls receive from their families: that above all, they need to find someone to look after them. Thus, many young women take up employment without planning a career, anticipating that they will not continue to work after marriage (Mourabat 1995: 14).

While the civil war and rural–urban migration forced many women to enter the labour market, they have only recently been moving into the professional sector in significant numbers. Yet, women are still under-represented in professional syndicates; in 1993 they constituted only 7 per cent in the engineers' syndicate, 14 per cent in the doctors' syndicate and 20 per cent in the lawyers' syndicate (Lebanese National Commission 1995). More women have been appointed in the public sector as a whole. With a solid education and hard work they are able to progress to the supervisory level – at which point they encounter the glass ceiling. In 1995, a total of 114 out of 1,414 supervisors (all employment sectors combined) were women. However, only 16 out of 242 reached managerial or executive positions, a mere 3 per cent (Mourabat 1995: 13). For this number to increase, two major changes need to take place. First, a change in the patriarchal assumption that women cannot and should not hold decision-making posts. Second, a change in the attitudes of the women themselves, who need to believe themselves capable of transcending traditional gender socialization.

RELIGION AND FAMILY

As the family and religious structures in Lebanon are essentially patriarchal, the privileging of males in the public sector reflects gender relations in the private sphere. At the core of gender relations are traditional concepts of women as the property of men and of women embodying family honour. Such beliefs have led to intra-communal as well as inter-communal violence against women.

Domestic violence, in particular, has been regarded as a 'normal, ordinary feature of life' (Osseiran 1995: 7). Women of all communities and all social classes have been victims of domestic violence and Lebanese laws tend to reinforce the helplessness of battered women. For instance, a mother is not awarded custody of her children over the age of 7, no matter how violent the father (Yared 1994). If a woman does opt for divorce and loses her children to her husband, many Muslim families will then forbid the woman to remarry, hoping that if her ex-husband remarries the custody of the children will revert to her. Thus, the combination of laws and traditions places many women of all confessions in the position of 'choosing' to endure domestic violence, given that the other option is divorce, loss of custody and in many cases 'imprisonment' by their own families.

While women of all confessions are, and have been, victims of abuse, the proportions for the different communities vary. As in most Middle Eastern states, jurisdiction on personal status matters lies with the religious courts of the various confessions. The percentage of court cases involving domestic problems in both the Catholic (Maronite, Greek Catholic and Armenian Catholic) community and the Druze community is low. In the Greek Orthodox community, domestic violence is the subject of 50 per cent of court cases and in the Sunni community it is at the centre of most court actions (Hamadeh 1994). In all cases women registering the complaint have to prove through witnesses or an official medical report that the husband has been physically abusing them. Even then this does not mean the women will get a permanent separation; only within the Druze community is battery considered sufficient ground for divorce. Catholic and Greek Orthodox courts will only grant temporary separation unless the risk to the woman is perceived to be life threatening.

According to Islam the husband is actually permitted to beat his wife if she does not respond to him sexually or she is considered rebellious. The Koran's *sura* (verse) on women advises husbands to 'admonish those you fear may be rebellious; banish them to their couches and beat them'.[7] One of the spiritual leaders of the Lebanese Shi'a community, Sayyed Mohammed Hussein Fadlallah, who is often associated with Hizballah, maintains that by virtue of his role as financial provider the husband has the right to use force in order to preserve the marriage.[8]

Domestic violence is further exacerbated by the concept of shame. A woman who is raped or battered is considered to bring shame upon herself and her family (Osseiran 1995: 7). Male family members according to this doctrine have traditionally possessed the right to kill the woman who brought shame upon the family and thereby restore the family's honour. In most courts of law, murder for family honour is still accepted as a defence and sentences are usually light. A vicious twist to the values of honour and shame was added during the civil war when militia members of one community raped women of the other community in order to humiliate them 'militarily'.

Religious attitudes, Middle Eastern cultural values, the respective communities' conceptions of womanhood, and Lebanon's legal and political system, have made it difficult for women across the communal divide to attain even a semblance of equality. Traditional attitudes still remain intact after the end of the war and will continue to influence female self-perception. For instance, Sitt Rabab, in looking at the changing role of women in the Shi'a community, has voiced concern that women may become 'too harsh'. Her view on male–female relations reveals some of the barriers women still face: 'It may be very easy to dispute and argue with her husband, but it is much braver and stronger to bear him silently'.[9]

Despite such views, the issue of domestic violence has led recently to the establishment of women's groups which have attempted to bridge the communal and confessional gaps in Lebanese society. In June 1995, a Women's Tribunal was held in Beirut where women shared their experiences of domestic, social and political abuse. While it has not resulted in the elimination of violence against women it has led to increased inter-confessional communication and a desegregation of communities which were polarized at the end of the civil war.

NATIONAL RECONCILIATION AND SYRIAN OCCUPATION

Unlike many young Lebanese men who had sought and gained political power through their patriotic engagement in militias, Lebanese women did not harbour the same aim or opportunity (Karamé 1995: 390). The primary reason for this failure to translate engagement during the war into a clear public voice is that political power in Lebanon has not only been sectarian and male, but it has also been the domain of certain families: such as the

Gemayels, the Franjiehs, the Khourys, the Chamouns, the Junblatts, the Sulhs, the Karamés and others (Hanf 1994: 75). Accordingly, any female seeking greater political involvement, particularly on the national level, has to overcome the obstacles of religion, family patronage and gender.

In addition, women have to change their own perceptions which, of course, have been shaped by society. Politics is still to a large extent regarded as 'dirty' and 'immoral': women do not see it as desirable to become politically involved at the national level. Indeed, there are no women ministers and only three seats in the 128-seat parliament are currently held by females.[10] This low number not only indicates the reluctance of the patriarchal society to accept females as politically equal, but also suggests the reluctance of women to demand such equality. Even more telling is the way these three women captured their seats.

Only 29 per cent of the Lebanese population participated in the parliamentary elections of 1992 (Murani 1993: 14). Bahia al-Hariri, a former teacher, is the only Muslim female who gained a parliamentary seat in Sidon. During her election campaign religious traditions prevented her photograph appearing on posters. Instead, her brother's picture was portrayed with her name written below. The fact that her brother, Rafiq al-Hariri, is a wealthy businessman who was appointed Lebanese Prime Minister by the Syrians, raises questions regarding her political independence. But even her brother's name did not protect her from criticism. Hizballah objected to her candidacy and called upon Muslim voters to cross out her name on the ballot and replace it with that of a male Sunni Islamist (Perthes 1994: 65).

The credentials of Nayla Mouawad, a Maronite and the widow of the former president, are also based on patrimonic grounds. She had pursued a career as a journalist when she decided to stand for her late husband's seat in Zghorta. Maha Khoury Assad, also a Maronite and the sister of a Kataib Member of Parliament who was assassinated in 1983, stood unopposed for the Byblos seat.[11] It is questionable whether she would have won without the Christian boycott of the elections in 1992. More importantly, though, it can be argued that all three women can be seen as an extension of the politics of a male family member – brother or husband. They are certainly not the women who were involved in the militias. Yet, in the case of Hariri and Mouawad it is interesting that they had a non-confessional, integrative political profile and both received many votes from outside their own confessional groups. These cross-confessional votes, however, should not be overemphasized, especially since the prevailing view of these women is that 'nowadays, if a woman reaches power, she cannot do anything but officiate, appear at cocktail parties and cut ribbons'.[12]

While Lebanese women have had a relatively low profile in national politics, they have played a role behind the scenes supporting individual candidates or issues. In the Druze community the most prominent woman is Hawla (Junblatt) Arslan. A member of the Sidon branch of the Junblatt clan she has been politically active on behalf of her son, Faisal. Through her family connections she has been able to set the agenda for one of the two major factions within the Druze community. In the Maronite community one of the key female players is Solange Gemayel, the widow of president-elect Bashir Gemayel, who was assassinated in 1982. Another female activist is Laure Moghaizel, widow of MP Joseph Moghaizel. She was the founder of the women's committee within the Maronite Kataib party in 1948, but later transferred her allegiance to the Democratic Party. Throughout the civil war she was involved in anti-war campaigns, human rights and feminist issues. In the Shi'a community the most prominent woman is Sitt Rabab al-Sadr, sister of the cleric and community leader Musa al-Sadr, who disappeared in 1978. These women have remained politically active since the outbreak of the war.

Lebanese women have also played a role in conflict resolution. In 1985 one of the female units of the Christian Lebanese Forces started to pursue more peaceful means to conflict resolution, and in May 1988, it officially became a pacifist movement, believing that non-violence was the way to achieve the restoration of the Lebanese state and, ultimately, national reconciliation. On the one hand, the adoption of a non-violent approach is a more formal continuation of the *ad hoc* campaigns started during the war. On the other, it represents a shift from active combat – which was tolerated by society during the war even though it was still seen as a male prerogative – to the socially acceptable and traditional role of the woman as the peace-seeker.

This peace-making role, however, was of limited success since it requires power to make peace. In the absence of power, many of the gaps between the different confessional groups or the social classes have remained. Indeed, the war reinforced the confessional structure. For instance, whereas before the war intermarriages were not uncommon, during its course they declined significantly (Perthes 1994: 59). Many Lebanese youngsters today are not familiar with the neighbourhoods of the other communities since one of the results of the war was the strengthening of confessional solidarity and religiosity (Khashan 1992). This trend is a stumbling block to inter-community relations and has not been addressed by the two post-war Karameh and Sulh governments which showed no interest in organizations trying to promote inter-confessional dialogue. The present government, though, has taken a more integrative path by promoting the view that there were no losers in the war and that everyone should participate in the political, economic and social reconstruction of the country.

With the end of the war international organizations began to stress the issue of gender and development in the context of reconstruction. While these aims were welcomed by many Lebanese women, their implementation attracted a considerable amount of criticism. This was specifically aimed at the type of vocational training a number of aid agencies were providing for rural Shi'a women in South Lebanon. Women who were essentially peasants, and who would have benefited from technical agricultural training, were instead being taught how to knit and weave.

A national response to the increasing prominence of women's issues was the establishment of the 'Lebanese Women's Council' as an umbrella organization for 120 women's organizations dealing mainly with charity, handicraft, children and family. None of these organizations in Lebanon could be described as feminist. However, the Beijing women's conference of September 1995 has prompted some interest, specifically with regards to women's rights. The Lebanese Human Rights Group has taken up the fight to repeal laws discriminating against women.

On the business front, women have been marginally more successful than on the political front. Na'maat Ken'aan, Director General of the Ministry of Social Affairs and the first Lebanese woman to hold such a high position, has stated that the primary gain for the Lebanese woman from the war is that she has found her place alongside men in the workplace (Ken'aan 1995: 41–45). Wafa Yunis, Manager of Bank Audi's Verdun Branch, supports this view by pointing out that 60 per cent of the banking sector's personnel are women.

The overall picture, however, is rather bleak. Women in the workforce have increased from 19 per cent in 1970 to 28 per cent in 1995. Yet, as the National Report on Lebanon to the Beijing Conference noted, 'women are virtually absent from the crucial political and economic decision-making process. Women also do not scale the administrative ladder as quickly as their male counterparts' (Lebanese National Commission 1995). This observation is shared by Laure Moghaizel (1995): 'I don't see any improvement in the way society looks at women. Women were powerless, and still are, in all domains: in the trade unions, in the municipalities, in politics, even in the family'.

The final obstacle in the path of female political emancipation is the Syrian occupation of Lebanon. The Taif Accord of 1989 is generally regarded as signalling the end of the civil war. Yet, after fifteen years of fighting it was little more than an updated version of the National Pact of 1943. Just as the latter had provided a convenient agreement between neo-feudalists and the commercial and financial bourgeoisie, the Accord affirmed the confessional system and presented an equally convenient arrangement for the same warlords, businessmen and notables. The only real change came in the relationship between Lebanon and Syria. The Treaty of Friendship and Brotherhood in 1991 formalized the Syrian military presence and Syrian political hegemony over Lebanon. Most political decisions on foreign and defence policy and many on domestic policy require a stamp of approval from Damascus. The authoritarian and patriarchal Syrian regime under Hafez al-Asad[13] has negatively influenced the possibility of a major shift towards Lebanese female political involvement and equality. Indeed, Syrian military occupation has superseded the civil war as a means of reinforcing the existing male-dominated social structure.

CONCLUSION

Victory and defeat have in a way become meaningless categories in a context where violence has become endemic. The realization that nothing more could be gained militarily led to the return to the very formula for conflict resolution which had existed up to 1975. While demographic adjustments were made to balance power between the various communities, efforts to include women in the power-sharing structure remained conspicuously absent. Patriarchal, feudal and religious elements underlying Lebanese society still make it extremely difficult for a woman to enter the public realms of politics, but the years of the civil war have hinted at what might be possible.

What the war has shown is that Lebanese women by choice, as well as by necessity, were involved in roles ranging from active combat, to support, and keeping the family fed. Thus it can be said that female participation in the conflict superseded the limited 'male' definition of war as combat action. Further, the involvement of Lebanese females in the respective nationalist struggles redefined society's conception of womanhood as a whole, but only temporarily. This reveals that there exists a certain amount of flexibility of gender boundaries, yet Lebanese women remain unwilling to stretch them too far as they are often restricted by their own self-perception. This also explains to some extent why those women involved in combat were unable, and in many cases did not attempt, to move into a more public political position after the war. They have, however, had limited success in bridging the communal gap in Lebanon with regard to women's issues, such as discrimination, domestic violence, education and rights within the family.

As a result of the war, Lebanese women have entered the labour market in increasing numbers and continue to enjoy one of the highest levels of education in the Middle East. Yet, they still face almost insurmountable obstacles in reaching decision-making positions. The reason for this lack of significant political advance lies in the nature of nationalisms in Lebanon. Their conservative hierarchies have prevented women from challenging the social order; such a challenge would have been perceived as a betrayal of the respective nationalist causes. Thus, the Lebanese civil war from 1975 to 1990, rather than liberating women from religious, family, and social constraints has served to bolster the male-dominated traditional social structure, itself reinforced by the continuing Syrian occupation.

ACKNOWLEDGEMENTS

I am grateful for Rick Wilford's and Kari Karamé's helpful comments and suggestions. Moreover, I would like to thank the LSE Staff Research Fund for contributing to the financing of my visit to Lebanon.

NOTES

1 According to Islam, a man generally inherits twice as much as a woman. In Sunni Islam, the inheritance of a family which has only daughters is traditionally bequeathed to the brother or nephew(s) of the father. In Shi'a Islam, the daughters are able to inherit.
2 Author's interview with Antoine Bassil, Middle East editor of the Kataib Party's newspaper, *Al-Amal*, 4 July 1995.
3 Author's interview with a female Hizballah activist, 30 March 1996.
4 *ibid.*.
5 *ibid.*.
6 In 1990, 66.2 per cent of Egyptian women were illiterate.
7 *The Koran*, Surat al-Nisa, Verse 34.
8 Interview with Sayyed Mohammed Hussein Fadallah, 1994.
9 Interview with Rabab as-Sadr Charafeddine, 1995.
10 The 128 seats were allocated on a confessional basis as follows: 34 Maronite; 27 Sunni; 27 Shi'a; 14 Greek-Orthodox; 8 Druze; 8 Greek-Catholic; 5 Armenian Orthodox; 2 Alawi; 1 Protestant; 1 Armenian Catholic; 1 other.
11 In Muslim areas there was an average of 95 candidates for ten seats.
12 Interview with Mona Khauli, 1995.
13 Syria does have a women's quota for its parliament. This, however, rather than an expression of state feminism, is consistent with Ba'athi socialism. Moreover, women's representation is essentially cosmetic.

BIBLIOGRAPHY

Abou Mrad, H. (1991) 'Y-a-t-il une solution à la fuite des cerveaux?', *Les Cahiers de l'Orient* 24: 45–54.
Abu Izzedin, N. M. (1984) *The Druzes: A New Study of Their History, Faith and Society*, Leiden: E. J. Brill.
Accad, E. (1994) 'Gender and Violence in Lebanon and Yugoslavia', *Al-Raida* 11: 65–66.
Ahmed, L. (1992) *Women and Gender in Islam: Historical Roots of a Modern Debate*, New Haven: Yale University Press.
Al-Raida (1995) 'Women in Post-War Lebanon', 2, 1 and 2: 58–59.
ALPF (Association libanaise du Planning familial) (1971) *La famille au Liban*, Beirut: ALPF.
Azari, F. (1983) 'Women of Iran: The Conflict with Fundamentalist Islam' in A. Tabari and N. Yeganeh (eds) *In The Shadow of Islam*, Colorado: Boulder Press.
Beyoghlow, K. A. (1989) 'Lebanon's New Leaders: Militias in Politics', *Journal of South Asian and Middle Eastern Studies*, 12, 3: 28–36.
Calic, M.-J. and Perthes, V. (1994) *Konflikte im Libanon und in Bosnien-Hercegovina: Ein Strukturvergleich*, Ebenhausen: Stiftung Wissenschaft und Politik.
Chedid, A. ([1976] 1995) 'Ceremonial of Violence', quoted in *Al-Raida*, 70 and 71: 50.
Chikhani-Nacouz, L. (1988) 'Maternité et travail au Liban', in *Women and Economic Development in the Arab World*, Beirut University College: Institute for Women's Studies in the Arab World.
Cooke, M. (1993) 'Wo-man: Retelling War Myth' in M. Cooke and A. Woolacott (eds) *Gendering War Talk*, Princeton NJ: Princeton University Press.
de Groot, J. (1996) 'Gender, Discourse and Ideology in Iranian Studies: Towards A New Scholarship', in D. Kandiyoti (ed.) *Gendering the Middle East*, London: I. B. Tauris.

Firo, K. (1992) *A History of the Druze*, Leiden: Brill.
Hamadeh, N. K. (1994) 'Battered Women in Lebanon: Religious Courts', *Al-Raida*, 11: 65–66.
Hamdan, K. (1992) 'The Future Role of the Lebanese Economy', *The Building of the Second Republic and the Problems of Peace in the Lebanon*, Beirut: Al-nadi al-thaqafi al-arabi.
Hanf, T. (1994) *Coexistence in Wartime Lebanon: Decline of a State and Rise of a Nation*, London: I. B. Tauris.
Helie-Lucas, M.-A. (1988) 'The Role of Women during the Algerian Liberation Struggle and After' in E. Isakson (ed.) *Women and the Military System*, New York: Harvester Wheatsheaf.
Hudson, M. (1985) *The Precarious Republic: Political Modernization of Lebanon*, Boulder: Westview Press.
Johnson, M. (1983) 'Popular Movements and Primordial Loyalties in Beirut' in T. Assad and R. Owen (eds) *The Middle East*, New York: Monthly Review Press.
Kandiyoti, D. (1996) 'Contemporary Feminist Scholarship and Middle-East Studies' in D. Kandiyoti (ed.) *Gendering the Middle East*, London: I. B. Tauris.
Karamé, K. H. (1989) 'L'expérience des jeunes militantes: Etude de cas et conséquences éducationelles' in L.-M. Chidiac, A. Kahi and A. N. Messara (eds) *La Génération de la Relevé: Une pédagogie nouvelle pour la jeunesse libanaise de notre temps*, Beirut: Publications du Bureau Pédagogique des Saints-Coeurs.
—— (1995) 'Girls' Participation in Combat: A Case Study from Lebanon' in E. W. Fernea (ed.) *Women and the Military System*, New York: Harvester Wheatsheaf.
Ken'aan, N. (1995) 'Interview', *Al-Raida* 7: 70–71.
Khalaf, M. (1995) 'Women and Education in Lebanon', *Al-Raida*, 11: 68.
Khashan, H. (1992) *Inside the Lebanese Confessional Mind*, New York: University of America Press.
King-Irani, L. (1995) 'A Decade of Power and Progress for Women?', *Al-Raida* 11: 69.
Lebanese National Commission (1995) *National Report Submitted to the Fourth World Conference on Women*, Beirut: LNC.
Maksoud, M. (1980) 'Les adolescents libanais et la guerre: Attitudes et réactions des jeunes de classe térimale à Beyrouth et en banlieue', unpublished Ph.D. thesis, University of Paris.
Moghaizel, L. (1995) 'Interview', *Al-Raida*, 7: 70–71.
Mourabat, Z. (1995) 'Has Gender Anything to do with Management Style?', *Al-Raida*, 11: 69.
Murani, N. M. (1993) *Nuwab '92*, Beirut: Dar a-Mu'allif.
NARA (National Archives and Records Administration) (1951) *Foreign Service Despatch*, RG59, Box 4076.
Osseiran, H. (1995) 'The Women's Tribunal', *Al-Raida*, 11: 69.
Perthes, V. (1994) *Der Libanon nach dem Burgerkrieg: Von Taif zum gesellschaftlichen Konsens?*, Baden-Baden: Nomos Verlagsgesellschaft.
Phares, W. (1995) *Lebanese Christian Nationalism: The Rise and Fall of an Ethnic Resistance*, Boulder: Lynne Reiner.
Rabinovich, I. (1986) *The War for Lebanon: 1970–1985*, Ithaca: Cornell University Press.
Reeves, M. (1989) *Female Warriors of Allah: Women and the Islamic Revolution*, New York: P. Dutton.
Sabban, R. (1988) 'Lebanese Women and Capitalist Cataclysm' in N. Toubia (ed.) *Women of the Arab World: The Coming Challenge*, London: Zed Books.
Salibi, K. (1976) *Crossroads to Civil War 1958–1976*, London: Ithaca Press.

Schiff, F. (1989) 'The Lebanese Prince: The Aftermath of the Continuing Civil War', *Journal of South Asian and Middle Eastern Studies* 12, 3: 7–27.

Shehadeh, L. R. (n.d.) 'Women and War: Lebanon As A Case-Study', unpublished paper.

Stephan, W. (1984) 'Women and War in Lebanon', *Al-Raida*, 30: 3.

Stiehm, J. H. (1988) 'The Effects of Myths about Military Women on the Waging of War' in E. Isakson (ed.) *Women and the Military System*, New York: Harvester Wheatsheaf.

Yared, N. S. (1994) 'Battered Women in Lebanon: Their Stories', *Al-Raida*, 11: 65–66.

9 Islamization and modernization in Malaysia

Competing cultural reassertions and women's identity in a changing society

Norani Othman

INTRODUCTION

When Malaysia was granted independence by the British colonial government in 1957, Islam and Malay politics were the main formal reference points in the conceptualization of the independent new state structure. Even though a federal form of constitution based on parliamentary democracy was the basis of the 1956 drafting of the Constitution, Islam became the official religion and pre-eminence was given to the political status of the Malays in the constitutional arrangements of the new state (see Suffian, Lee and Trindale 1978).

The federal constitution established in 1957 specified that

> Islam shall be the religion of the state of Malaya, but nothing in this article shall prevent any citizen professing any religion other than Islam, to profess, practice and propagate that religion, nor shall any citizen be under any disability by reason of not being Muslim.

This set the trend whereby ethnicity and religion became central components of identity politics and political negotiation in contemporary Malaysia. Islam gained ascendancy as the Muslim Malays dominated the alliance of several political parties which had been ruling the country since independence. As we shall see from this chapter, within this constitutional arrangement the question of state policies of Islamization in Malaysia is exclusively within the administrative and political power of the Malay components of both federal and state governments. Under its Constitution the powers of the central or federal government, as in many newly developing states, are overwhelming. Discussions of Malaysian politics, and especially of the local circumstances and conditions of various Islamist initiatives, tend to focus upon the fact that Malaysian society is not exclusively Muslim but is religious and culturally pluralist. While this cultural and religious plurality and its restraining effects upon any impatient or absolutist agenda of social and legal Islamization are undeniable, another equally important but far less widely discussed issue is the state's formal constitutional structure. It is this structure with its division of powers between central government, on the one hand, and the state administrations and their royal figureheads, on the other, which gives rise to tensions and conflicts over competing jurisdictions – that of political rivalry over Islamic religious matters – particularly in relation to Islamic legal administration.

However, since independence the central government has increasingly expanded its political influence over matters of Islamic policy and administration, proceeding with the consent of the sultans or Malay rulers but working deftly around their constitutional entitlements and the religious bureaucracies and courts of the various state administrations. As a result, notwithstanding the constitutional formalities, in political reality the central government plays a significant, and increasing, role in the area of Islamic law, administration and Islamization policies. Areas of overlapping interest and competing jurisdiction pose complex questions. It is within this context of such political negotiation and tension that many Islamization policies in Malaysia (which bear on women's lives in the family, society and the state) are articulated and promoted.

Malaysian women, just as in the general process of their political mobilization, played mainly supporting or auxiliary roles in the political and cultural projects of Islamization. The political mobilization of Malaysian women – Malay, Chinese and Indian – took place solely within the party system. There were no cases of individual women or of women's groups that sought and won elected office outside of the political parties. Political activities for women were thus largely confined to women's wings within the relevant parties. Each political party in Malaysia had separate women's wings which, due to their recent advent, rarely interacted with one another (see Dancz 1987). The role of women in those parties remained slight, as evidenced by their participation in both internal and public party affairs. The separation of women into an auxiliary political wing is an expression of the traditional public role assigned to them. The justification, as expressed by the first *Ketua* (head) of the Kaum Ibu UMNO ('Group of Mothers' or 'Women's Group of the United Malay National Organisation' (now known simply as WANITA UMNO or UMNO Women)) in 1946 when that women's section was founded, still remains unchallenged. Women were said to be:

> reluctant to assert themselves before men and therefore needed the shelter that the wing provided because they were shy and uncomfortable before men. They simply would not speak out at meetings attended by men and women. A separate wing provided women with a way of involving themselves in the affairs of the parties while holding to Islamic customs that separated the public activities of men and women.

(Dancz 1987: 226)

The other non-Malay political parties such as Malaysian Chinese Association (MCA) and the Malaysian Indian Congress (MIC) formed their own women's wings in the 1970s, following the same traditional cultural norm of assigning women's public or political role as supportive of and auxiliary to the men's. Against such a background, recent political reassertions, such as Islamization movements, are initiatives made by men in their capacity either as leaders of political parties or as religious ideologues, with women members or followers of such movements playing their helpmate roles.

ECONOMIC DEVELOPMENT AND MODERNIZATION

Malaysia is one of the smallest Muslim countries in Asia (in terms of its land and population size) yet it is regarded as one of the most economically developed among Muslim nations.[1] It has experienced very rapid economic growth, particularly since emerging from the recession of the mid-1980s. For example, Malaysia's real Gross Domestic Product (GDP) during the period 1991–1995 grew at an average rate of 8.7 per cent per annum. As a result of such unprecedented growth, real per capita income also grew steadily at an average of 6.1 per cent for the same period (Government of Malaysia 1995, 1996a, 1996b). The fast-growing economy is complemented by rapid changes in many aspects of Malaysian society. Among the socio-economic indicators of growth are the improved level of educational attainment, especially among the post-*Merdeka* (political independence from British colonial rule) generation of Malaysians, the creation of an expanding urban middle class (due to the accelerated pace of urbanization and industrialization in Peninsular Malaysia within the last three decades) and an increasing rate of labour and economic participation among Malaysian women. Greater educational attainment is especially discernible among the Malay population as a direct consequence of the New Economic Policy (NEP) implemented between 1970–1990, an economic development policy introduced by the Malaysian Government after the inter-communal riots of May 1969 in order to correct economic imbalances between the three main ethnic groups.

Profound economic and social changes characterized several post-colonial countries throughout Southeast Asia, notably Singapore, Malaysia and Thailand, such that in the 1990s these countries are acclaimed candidates for global economic status, given the title of newly industrializing economies (NIEs). The structure of these economies has changed, with a significant shift from agriculture into the industrial and service sectors. Accompanying such structural economic change, urbanization levels began to increase due to an influx of rural–urban migration. Even though Peninsular Malaysia was statistically the most urbanized of the Southeast Asian countries in the two decades following the end of the Second World War, approximately two-thirds of its population was still rural, with a significantly larger proportion of its Malay population remaining rural at the time the country was granted independence. For example, in 1970 only 15 per cent of the Malay population was urban compared with 47 per cent of the Chinese.

Malay urbanization, however, proceeded rapidly during the 1970s and 1980s. The Dasar Ekonomi Baru (DEB) or the New Economic Policy (NEP) instituted in 1970 was also influential in changing and raising the economic status of the Malay community through its aggressive pursuit of affirmative action or positive discrimination for Malays and other *bumiputera*[2] groups in the areas of education, employment and access to loans and capital for business and investment. Access to higher education was achieved by Malay and other *bumiputera* groups through incentives provided under the national education policies which grant awards of scholarships and places in higher educational institutions. At the same time, that policy sought to provide girls and boys with equal access to education, irrespective of whether they lived in rural or urban areas. Access to education and an improved level of educational attainment are important indicators of the social status of women, mainly because in a modern economy these open greater opportunities for self-advancement and economic independence. (Boserup 1970; Hijab 1988).[3] Gavin W. Jones describes how rising levels of educational attainment and female labour participation have produced a significant trend of change for many Muslim women in Southeast Asia:

> In a nutshell, the main trend is the change from a pattern of fairly tight control over adolescent females and universal, early, or parent-arranged marriage to one of freer female adolescence, much later, self-arranged marriage, and greater options for non-marriage or very late marriage. A parallel trend is observed in the movement away from high rates of divorce, typically soon after marriage, and from relatively common polygamy.
>
> (Jones 1994: 16)

In 1980, there was an excess of males over females in Malaysian urban areas while equal proportions of both sexes were found in rural areas. However, in 1991, while the urban sex ratio remained unchanged, there was a significant increase in the rural sex ratio to 103 males:100 females, due in part to the increase in the number of male external or foreign migrants employed in the plantation sector in rural areas. The sex ratios among all the three main ethnic groups – Malay, Chinese and Indian – are generally more balanced and similar to the national figure (Government of Malaysia 1991). In the different age groups there are similar slight variations.[4]

Malay women form more than a quarter of the total population of Peninsular Malaysia. Among this population group, 45.8 per cent of those aged between 15 and 64 years are economically active. Another indicator of the high labour participation rates among the Malay female population, is that within the age cohort of 20–39 years, 51.5 per cent of them constitute the total female Malay and *bumiputera* labour force for Peninsular Malaysia (Government of Malaysia 1990, 1991). A similar gender and employment pattern is also found among the Chinese population in which female Chinese form about 14 per cent of the total population of Peninsular

Malaysia. Of the total Chinese labour force, 47 per cent are females in the age group of 15–64 years. Those within the age group of 20–39 years form 55.6 per cent of the total female Chinese labour force. There can be no denial that due to post-*Merdeka* economic changes there was a tendency for women's labour force participation rates (LFPRs) to rise, particularly since the 1970s and in urban areas throughout Malaysia. The rise was especially dramatic among Malay women in Peninsular Malaysia, such that by 1980 in urban areas there was little difference in female LFPRs between Chinese and Malays.

Such changes have been associated with rapidly increasing urbanization of the Malay population and also reflect a very rapid absolute increase in the number of Malay women who are working in urban areas. Structural changes in urban areas appear to have favoured increased female employment (the trend was highest in the 1970s and 1980s) with females heavily represented in export-oriented manufacturing, in community and personal services and in trade and tourism. Part of the reason why Malays did particularly well in employment was due to the government's NEP policy. Additionally, Malay women seem to have benefited more than Chinese women from the growth of the manufacturing sector during the period 1970–1980. In Peninsular Malaysia, female employment in manufacturing industries is estimated to have increased more than tenfold from 22,500 in 1957 to 273,000 in 1970 and 290,000 in 1979. Overall, the female share of manufacturing employment rose from 17 per cent in 1967 to 29 per cent in 1970, 41 per cent in 1976 and 52 per cent in 1979 (Jones 1994: Chapter 2). The largest industry, electronics, was dominated by female workers and in 1980, two-thirds of these women workers were Malays. In the manufacturing sector as a whole, Malay women workers' share of total employment rose from 6.6 per cent in 1957 to 19.4 per cent (of a now much larger sector) in 1980. In services, a sector in which government employment looms large, Malay women did almost as well as in manufacturing, increasing their share of employment from 4.4 per cent in 1957 to 15.5 per cent in 1980. The impetus in the growth of female LFPRs only gradually slowed down in the 1980s, particularly in the years of economic recession in that decade. Between 1980 and 1990, for example, female LFPRs in Malaysia increased only slightly from 45 per cent to 47 per cent.

MODERNIZATION AND ISLAMIZATION

The brief economic background above shows that the position of women generally, and that of Malay women specifically, has undergone significant changes as the Malaysian economy has experienced rapid modernization. Such a transition inevitably alters the socio-economic circumstances of women, including the majority of Malay Muslim women. Partly because of this accelerated change, Malaysia is now seen as an example of a predominantly Muslim country whose social development provides an unprecedented model of the possible and potential role and contribution women can play and provide in a modernizing Muslim society. At the same time, Malaysia is not exempt from the Islamizing agenda of various forces which invariably are perceived and represented as part of the political phenomenon of the resurgence of 'retraditionalizing' Islam worldwide (otherwise popularly known as Islamic fundamentalism).

The focus of this chapter is an examination of the consequences of modernization and Islamization for Peninsular Malaysia, particularly those which affect Malay women. An Islamic resurgence dominated by a 'retraditionalizing' Islam located within a milieu of rapid urbanization and modernization provides a unique opportunity to explore how the two forces of change intersect and bear upon the lives of women. This chapter also examines those issues in the context of economic transformation and the social mobility of both Muslim men and women, providing an analysis of gender identity, the status and power of urban, especially middle-class, women at home and in society, and the extent of their social and religious consciousness. It explores how the state's development or modernizing ideology and other various competing Islamists' ideologies about women and women's role in the family and society are political and cultural projects which tend to be gendered if not gender-biased.

In many ways, the status and position of Malaysian Muslim women is quite distinctive and different from their counterparts in the Muslim heartlands of the Middle East or those Muslim countries of South Asia such as Pakistan, Bangladesh and India. Within the Malay cultural tradition known as *adat*, with its less obvious patriarchal tendencies, Malaysian Muslim women have been perceived to have enjoyed rights, status and roles that are far more egalitarian than in other Muslim societies (Karim 1992).[5] However, the question of the intricate relationship between a 'cultural given' such as *adat*, and 'gender' should not be underestimated here. Issues about gender and culture are not only intertwined but their interrelationship is ever changing according to the economic processes, resources and class situations affecting men and women. When religious reassertions are intensified concomitantly through civil and public legal means, as well as ideological ascendancy, it allows little space for cultural negotiation or adaptation. It becomes a question of politics and the power of those promoting the religious reassertions.

Elsewhere (Othman 1998) I have argued that the 'woman question' in the highly politicized context of Islamization and the social contradictions of modernization of any Muslim society have to be seen in terms of a hegemonic contestation between ideologies, usually that of the state and of influential or radicalized political movements. Both have as their ultimate aim that of shaping and defining human rights, gender identity, rights and duties, as well as the political and citizenship status of women. In the final analysis the struggle for human, especially women's, rights in Muslim countries is a complex one. It involves questions of religion, the validity and hegemony of certain religious interpretations over others, gender bias, patriarchy, the politics of gender and identity. The frequent criticism offered by many Islamists in their discourse on these issues is that Western-influenced conceptions of women's rights and gender equality contradict Islamic principles of gender relations. In current times this criticism can no longer be accepted at face value as both Muslim feminists and human rights activists mount their challenges against it (Othman 1998). These challenges do, to some extent, indicate that in situations where religious orthodoxy is an influential source of the political impetus to impose laws which transgress contemporary notions of rights and freedom, an internal cultural and religiously informed contestation is much needed. That internal contestation has to be initiated by women themselves.

Patriarchal notions of gender relations in contemporary Malaysia, as in most other Muslim countries, are intertwined with the politics of Islamization, nationalism, state-building and the rejuvenation of 'Asian values' and culture. Within these political projects women are linked to the 'demand' of modernization and progress, yet are also charged with ensuring cultural continuity as the basis of society's moral integrity. Women are regarded as central to their country's projects of both cultural rejuvenation and religious orthodoxy. Questions of morality, sexuality and the search for cultural authenticity and religious legitimacy are all implicated in various, and often contradicting, conceptions of the ideal society and in competing agendas for state-building and the pursuit of modernity. Defining Muslim women's rights and freedom is a task that occurs not in isolation but on this complex cultural and political battleground, in the midst of acute polemical contests over Islamization, modernization and cultural relativism.

CHANGING WOMEN'S ROLE AND THE POLITICS OF IDENTITY

Close scrutiny of a number of various case studies reveals that much of the discourse and practice of cultural revivalism in contemporary societies reflects an urgency to assume or regain control of women's bodies in the name of upholding religious and national values. They are the notable if not popular and dominant expressions of a cultural reassertion project aimed at homogenizing notions of gender role and sexuality, thus ensuring a conformity of values and norms regarding gender identity, rights and obligations. These discourses increasingly assign to women the onerous responsibility for the reproduction of the group through family attachment, domesticity and maternal roles. In so many contemporary political and cultural revivalist movements, women are assigned the role of bearers of cultural values, carriers of tradition, and symbols of the community. (See, for example, Kandiyoti 1991; Mernissi 1985; Moghadam 1993, 1994a, 1994b; Mumtaz and Shaheed 1978.)

As scholars and analysts now recognize, such a project almost always consists of competing and often somewhat contradictory views of gender rights and equality in any society, culture or religion. These views are better comprehended by an analysis which specifically looks at some of the underlying cultural tension and gendered dynamics within male–female relationships of that society. Gender relations are defined by the perceptions, beliefs, attitudes and ideology (both traditional and contemporary) of a society and culture. In most Muslim societies the legitimating sources of those views and understanding are often simply and unproblematically taken by men and women to be the *actual* religious principles or some cultural practices validated by the moral values of their religion. Yet religious and cultural values are not necessarily distinct, nor are they easily differentiated. In reality, these demarcations can never be so clear-cut, enabling us to identify easily which values emanate from religion and which originate from a society's culture and tradition.[6]

The relations between religion and culture are complex and problematic, not least in their implications for the issue of sexual and gender inequality. Culture is implicated in behaviour, providing ideological principles for the application of rules, laws and values, foremost among them religious values. An analysis of the political and ideological processes which utilize cultural and religious ideas to mediate and 'determine' male–female perceptions of, and their interaction with, each other is useful. It will provide us with an insight into the dynamics of change as elaborated within the context and politics of cultural identity and religious ideals. Such an analysis hinges upon examining constructions of identity, notions of citizenship rights, sexuality and reproductive rights and obligations within each society.

With this perspective in mind, there are two levels of analysis applied here in discussing the 'woman question' in the modernizing and Islamizing Malay society of Malaysia. First, our analysis is focused at understanding how the Islamization of laws, state and society is implemented. This is crucial for understanding its effects on women as a group, on the institution of the family and on gender relations both within and outside marriage. Such effects can also be discerned by evaluating how Islamization policies affect the quality of access to legal provisions women actually enjoy in order to reclaim rights through existing laws, legal procedures and practice. These laws are family laws or enactments; civil laws generally to do with family, marriage and divorce, domestic violence, custodial rights over children in a marriage or divorce, maintenance rights and claims, and the right of inheritance.

Second, and this is very much related to the first analysis above, we need also to explore the difficulties and problems that Muslim women in Malaysia face almost routinely in their daily lives. The Malaysian state and society increasingly tries to implement numerous policies and social changes that are deemed vital if the society is to be identified as legitimately 'Islamic' as well as fulfilling the demands and 'logic' of industrialization and development. Since these policies are articulated by two main types of authorities, both state and religious, part of this endeavour requires us to review these

issues through the lenses of the state and the various Islamization movements. One is the state and all state-supported or sponsored religious
agencies and functionaries; the other is those ideologues and political
activists, including religious scholars and leaders, who act principally in
political opposition to, or in a manner critical of, the state or government-
sponsored policies of Islamization.

ISLAMIZATION OF LAWS, GENDER AND POWER

A significant aspect of recent Islamization in Malaysia has been the drive to
introduce new rules and a variety of amendments to existing Muslim enactments in all the eleven states of Peninsular Malaysia.[7] The political incentive
and influence of the supporters of the Islamization agenda are felt most in
the arena of Muslim family laws. As an illustration of this tendency, rulings
on various aspects of the Islamic family law have gone through several
amendments since *Merdeka* according to the ebb and flow of neo-
traditionalist views of Islamist groups and the response of the state itself,
particularly that which is embodied in the federal government, in the
promotion of their own Islamic or Islamization policies.

From the end of British rule until the 1970s, Malaysia embarked upon a
programme of rationalizing and reforming its Islamic family laws which was
guided primarily by a modernizing ethos, adapting the law to the effective
and rational working of the modern state machinery and the requirements
of modern life itself. The weaknesses and lack of precision in the legal provisions and procedure relating to Muslim marriage, divorce and the family, as
well as the injustices towards women, were recognized by the state. Others,
including legal experts, noted many gaps and inconsistencies in the letter of
the law itself. Apparently the need to make Muslim family laws consistent
with the equal rights of men and women as declared in the United Nations
Charter and the Universal Declaration of Human Rights was also one of
the reasons justifying the move to legal reform and rationalization (Ibrahim
1965; Raja Mamat 1991). However, the codification of the new Muslim
family statutes under this reform project did not include the participation of
women or women's groups as a matter of principle or procedure.[8] Among
the inconsistencies in the different Muslim family laws in the states at that
juncture (before the reform project was undertaken) was, for example, that in
some states the bride's consent to her marriage was not required, although
other states provided some degree of protection by requiring that the
marriage register be signed by both the husband and the wife.

The Muslim Family Law Act of 1984 was the outcome of the delibera-
tion and reform efforts begun in the late 1970s. It introduced a number of
important changes and a tightening up of various administrative procedures. However, there was great resistance by the more fundamentalist forces
in the Muslim community generally and in the Islamic department of the
various states specifically. They were concerned that secular or modern

considerations in reforming or consolidating the law would replace religious imperatives as they understood them. Many of the states were very slow in adopting or enacting the 1984 Act and when they finally did so in the years between 1989–1991, it was done with further amendments and changes of their own. Some of these amendments were contrary to the original Act in its intent and spirit of providing rights or protection to women. The states of Selangor and the Federal Territories (of Kuala Lumpur and Labuan) were the two jurisdictions which had initially remained faithful to the original draft of the Islamic family law reforms constituted in the 1984 Act. However, even in these two most developed and urbanized states of Malaysia, the pressure from Islamists to 'improve the Islamic character' of the laws became very great. It resulted in several retrogressive amendments being made: in 1988 for Selangor and in 1994 for the Federal Territories.

The rights and protection amended by the individual states were related mainly to matters of divorce, rights and claims for maintenance, and polygamy. Apart from the problem of a lack of uniformity among the states' Islamic family laws, there were other long-standing complaints from women about the problems and injustices they suffer in the *shari'ah* court system and procedure. In early January 1997, in the wake of several states (including Selangor) seeking to initiate more reforms to their Muslim family laws, various women's groups in the country led by the NCWO, AWL and *Sisters in Islam* organized a national workshop centred on a project to submit to the Federal Government of Malaysia two memoranda calling for greater reform and uniformity in the laws, procedure and the court system itself which would ensure justice for both men and women. The titles of the memoranda drafted by *Sisters in Islam* and AWL are: *A Memorandum on Reform of the Islamic Family Laws and the Administration of Justice in the Syariah[9] System in Malaysia*; and *A Memorandum on Reform of the Islamic Family Laws on Polygamy* (*New Straits Times*, 23 January 1997; *Sunday Star*, 3 November 1996).

Many of the presentations and discussions in that workshop highlighted in some detail the problems encountered by women in pursuing court cases of divorce, domestic violence, polygamy and claims for maintenance. Besides the common problems of delays and cumbersome bureaucratic procedures many women also reported prejudice and male bias in the attitudes and the treatment that they received from the various court officers with whom they had to contend. A number of the women participants also recognized that a significant underlying cause of most of these problems is the biased or prejudicial attitudes of an increasingly patriarchal ideology fostered by Islamic resurgence movements since the mid-1980s. Some of these revived patriarchal notions of gender rights are more 'Arabizing' than merely Islamizing and they are often inspired by the Islamists' desire to imitate what they regard as 'authentic' Islamic rule or precedent.

Much has been written recently by scholars and Muslim women activists about the problems occasioned by narrow traditional and literal interpretations of text and the anachronistic codification of religious laws by Islamic authorities in their respective countries (Ahmed 1992; Engineer 1992; Moghadam 1993; Osman 1994; Rahman 1982; Tibi 1988). These are recent elaborations of the debate and argument raised earlier by other Muslim modernist scholars and the Muslim modernist movement of the late nineteenth century, particularly in Egypt. The essentialist and narrowly literalist interpretations offered by traditionalist scholars and ideologues have produced adverse views of women's status as extremely inferior. They also persistently reinforced conservative social and cultural traditions of historical Islam as the normative model to be actualized in all contemporary Muslim societies. Unfortunately, the tensions and social contradictions faced by many Muslim societies undergoing transition and modernization have fostered emphatic efforts by contemporary Islamizing movements to seek the modern day enforcement of restrictive and conventionally codified Islamic social rules and laws. A large part of these religious rules and regulations are manifested in those contemporary Islamists' ideas which define and socially construct woman's identity, her rights and freedom.

CLASS, GENDER AND POWER IN IDENTITY POLITICS

The Islamists' cultural discourse features an uncompromisingly authoritarian construction of identity of the 'ideal woman', the 'ideal family' and society. What is often demonstrated in these constructions is that power is a precondition for effective control, especially when wielded from a claim of religious legitimacy and authenticity. Such control is manifested in efforts to limit the autonomy of women by imposing conformity through the power of identity and the politics of that identity.

Notions of the ideal woman and the ideal society are central to the question of identity politics. The issue of identity politics is pivotal and highly relevant, provided one defines identity in its broadest sense to include such socially defined and often visible characteristics as gender and ethnicity, as well as other aspects of groups and individuals, such as world views, ideologies and religion. The question of choice is also extremely important in this context. For example, when we confront the claim by Muslim women themselves that they willingly resort to 'veiling' or, as in the case of Malaysia, donning of the 'mini telekung' in order to be treated with greater respect or to avoid any kind of possible sexual harassment, either in the streets, on public transport or at the workplace, the essential issue at stake is: why are Muslim women who choose *not* to be veiled not accorded respect and dignity as a matter of general principle? We need also to establish to what extent women are given the autonomous right to choose and/or participate freely in their group's decision-making.

Because identities also represent entitlements to shares of a group's or society's resources, the question of identity and the politics of identity has become a powerful criterion and bargaining chip in the politics of everyday life in the late twentieth century. Conformity (or being compelled by some religious argument to conform) with the common identity, as proclaimed by social or political groups, becomes increasingly important to the group's bargaining power in politics. The number of individuals that abide with or conform to the group's common identity endows the political group with credibility. Pressures within the group to conform are likely to rise as the aspirations of the political group increase. The powerless within the group (often women) are the most likely either to suffer from pressures for conformity or at the very least to bear the brunt and responsibility of dutifully fulfilling the criteria of conformity regardless of how contradictory or inegalitarian their consequences may be. Women often are not autonomous and are denied equal participation in deciding the criteria or bases for group conformity.

To understand the importance of these issues – the politics of identity and the construction of the ideal identity for Muslim women in Malaysia – we must look at the construction of ideology and the justification of public policies concerning women made by the various Islamization movements in the country. In its zeal to resist what are deemed to be 'Western' and alien cultural influences, and despite its claim to be the model of a progressive and modern Muslim state, current Malaysian political discourse manifests dynamics of patriarchy and control similar to those imposed by many of this century's most authoritarian regimes. The political and legal status of women as citizens in the state and their position in the institution of marriage and the family are implicated in the realization of these political constructions.

The citizenship rights and position of Muslim women are often expressed and indicated in the nature of Muslim civil, public and criminal laws and legislation that are regularly introduced or intermittently enforced in Muslim societies as part of their drive to improve the Islamic character of the state. In essence, the citizenship rights of women are compromised or even denied by the Islamic resurgents' narrow perception of the political and civil rights of women. It is a common view among them, for example, that women should not be given the right to hold public office. With the exception of Indonesia, none among the forty Muslim countries of the world allow a woman to be a judge in the relevant *Shari'ah* court. The limited, and limiting, view of woman's capacity and potential as a citizen is also attested to by the position of Islamists and many of the Islamic authorities within and outside the Malaysian Government who oppose the promulgation and implementation of the Domestic Violence Act 1995.

For a period of almost ten years there was widespread consultation and discussion among all Islamic religious authorities and organizations – as well as women's groups – in the country, in the drafting of the domestic violence law. The kinds of opposition that were encountered throughout that process reflected how strongly entrenched is the prevailing ideology. Beyond her position and status as a wife, this ideology does not recognize that a Muslim woman also has the right as a citizen to be given legal capacity and empowerment equivalent to non-Muslim women in order to protect herself against domestic violence. The idea that a Muslim woman can invoke a legal protection (by seeking a court injunction to restrain her violent spouse) is a proposition that many Muslims interpret as 'unIslamic' since it will supersede the authority of the *shari'ah* court in matters of marriage.[10] The actual experiences of many Muslim women who are victims of domestic violence have shown clearly that the *shari'ah* judicial system is not oriented towards taking firm action to restrain or prevent husbands who are the perpetrators of domestic violence. In many cases women were advised to be patient in dealing with their violent spouses and to return to their conjugal homes and seek reconciliation.

Women, as shown by the advice, treatment and counselling given in these cases, have to shoulder the greater burden of responsibility to ensure that the harmony of a Muslim marriage is maintained. The woman is the main-stay of the household and therefore must conduct herself with equanimity in all the daily affairs of her marriage and family life. This extraordinary failure to confront the realities of modern marriage and family life can be explained by the obsession with maintaining an uncritical and idealized notion of the perfection and immutability of the religious principles (as they understand them) that inform all aspects of life for a Muslim.

The recent Islamic resurgence has also popularized some very neo-traditionalist, again unrealistic, ideas of women's domestic roles. These neglect the realities of Muslim women's lives, especially in a modernizing society such as Malaysia. In their conceptualization of the domestication of women, traditional Islamists insist that women are secondary and subordi-nate to men. The Muslim traditionalists' position on women's status is based on their theological view that the female is derivative and secondary, and that men have responsibility (*qawwamuna*) over women (a claim based on their interpretation of a key Qur'anic verse, 4: 34).

Because of their reproductive capability, women are also seen as the transmitters of group values and as agents of socialization of the young. The notion of 'woman as wife and mother' rather than citizen, worker or student, is often dominant. Such constructions now increasingly come from religious traditionalizing social movements as well as the government's programme of social development. Questions of cultural, religious, national, linguistic and sexual identity commanded centre stage in the process of decolonization of many Asian societies. Muslim countries in Asia are no exception. Since the rise of the Islamic resurgence in the late 1970s we find an ascendancy of ideological assertions in both Asian and Middle Eastern Muslim countries which tend to inhibit the public and political participation of women.

Yet the increasing economic role and participation of women during the early period of decolonization in Muslim countries has been an impetus towards their potential liberation. Apart from employment providing some personal economic freedom, the financial contribution of women workers to their families is important and sometimes crucial. With the growing work opportunities for young women either in factories or offices, the earning power of daughters is becoming crucial to the economic well-being of many rural households. Daughters are often more responsible and reliable contributors to the family purse or budget than their brothers (Li 1989; Ong 1987; Young and Salleh 1986). The regular income and remittances of Malay women workers in the Malaysian electronics industry supplement their parents' limited earnings. Their contributions are often used for much-needed expenditure such as the education of siblings and house repairs.

The income earned by married working women is also indispensable to the family budget, not only among working-class households but also in many urban middle-class households where the husband's monthly disposable income is barely sufficient to meet basic expenditure. The current economic burden of an urban lifestyle is not the only reason for the necessity of women's labour force participation. As described above, it is impossible to imagine how economic development can be achieved without the extensive and active participation of the Malaysian female population. This economic imperative will probably be the mainstay of a social development in Malaysia that will help to protect or prevent Muslim women from any further direct assault on her autonomy, social role and public participation.

It is also obvious, however, that a certain degree of devaluation of women has been assimilated into prevalent social attitudes of Malaysian Muslims. To what extent this social contradiction may lead to a backlash or reversal of women's social progress in the future development of Malaysian society remains an open question. Social attitudes that maintain and justify an ideology that devalues women are among the more abstract means of controlling women. In more concrete terms this control is achieved by denying women access to economic, social and political power.

The constraints already imposed on women's access to legal and political rights in Malaysia are, as we have seen, increasing, and have undermined whatever freedom and capacity that existed and was taken for granted in the early formative years of post-*Merdeka* and before the rise of the Islamization movement in Malaysia. Under these circumstances Muslim men and women frequently are exposed now to numerous mixed messages articulated within the mass media, either through the reporting of speeches of various political and community leaders or the public discourse of contemporary social issues and problems of Malaysian society.

ESSENTIALIZING CULTURE AND RELIGION IN THE MALAY POPULAR DISCOURSE

Since the mid-1980s, issues of rape, wife battery and sexuality, together with those concerning religious rules of marriage, divorce and polygamy were reported increasingly in the Malaysian press. This public attention prompted some male politicians, religious officials and authorities (and several women as well) to express a variety of oppressive and rather misogynistic views which had one thing in common. They all emphasized that these problems were the responsibility of women. Frequently it was argued that women either brought these problems upon themselves by their own provocative or careless behaviour, or even if they did not, it was women's responsibility to uphold 'high moral' standards that would restrain men from committing excesses. By holding women responsible, these views blamed women, either as victims or as instigators themselves. Such views were the precursor of the production of an unambiguously gendered discourse regarding questions of morality and social problems within Malaysian society throughout the 1990s.

The periodic monitoring of printed and electronic media in the Malay language, carried out by the author over the years from 1987–1994, provided substantial evidence of the evolution and development of this gendered discourse. Both the printed and the electronic media have been the popular sources for the production and articulation of some disingenuous patriarchal ideas about the working of modern society and the reasons for the breakdown of its values. The target of such text and messages are the Malay masses, both urban and rural, for they make up the bulk of readers and listeners of the Malaysian mass media in the Malay language. For example, since 1989 many religious leaders both from the Government party and the Islamic opposition party, PAS (Partai Islam Se Malaysia, or the Malaysian Islamic Party) regularly display some form of 'moral panic' in their public speeches and *ceramah agama* (religious talk or seminar).

Among their expressed anxieties was the allegedly increasing number of divorces among Muslims, particularly urban Muslims. It is noteworthy that often such expressions of anxiety are followed by two further selective discussions. First, reference is made to the youth of these divorced women and second, to the fact that a majority of them are also working women. No elaboration or discussion is made about the socio-economic characteristics of the men or husbands, nor is there any mention made about the socio-economic situation of these divorced couples. The remainder of the discourse focuses on an exhortation to Muslim couples to intensify their religious knowledge and a recommendation that some official measure be taken to address this problem. Another anxiety often expressed by these same commentators concerns the increasing number of single or unmarried Muslim professional women found in Kuala Lumpur and its suburbs (collectively known as the Klang Valley area). The response to this moral anxiety is a chorus of expert opinion calling for the introduction of a compulsory requirement for all Muslim couples who are about to be married to attend an Islamic marriage preparation course (*kursus bimbingan perkahwinan dan keluarga Islam*).

By early 1990 the first of these pre-marriage courses was provided and by 1994 preparation was under way to make it a compulsory requirement for all Muslims about to be married for the first time. The curriculum for these courses, which was developed by religious officials under the auspices of *Pusat Islam* (Islamic Centre, a federal government department attending to all matters relating to Islam in Malaysia), demonstrated yet again the pre-eminence of a patriarchal Islam in formulating rules and social policy for the Malay community. For example, all discussion of husband–wife relationships in the curriculum of the pre-marriage courses stressed the authority of the husband and stipulated that it is a religious requirement for a Muslim wife to be obedient and submit to her husband's authority. Among the recurrent themes cited in the reading materials used on these courses is that in a Muslim marriage the husband is the final arbiter and figure of authority, while the wife's primary obligation lies in her domestic role. They also state that it is essential that a wife acquire her husband's permission if she wants to go out to work or even to leave the house for any reason or errand.

A similar kind of public discourse was adopted and elaborated in the print media. In the 1990s there was a notable proliferation of popular magazines in the Malay language. The obvious target of their readership is Malay or Muslim women and men. At about the same time, a major national newspaper in the Malay language was also offering several weekly columns as a platform for the discussion of Islam and a range of issues relating to family, marriage, sexuality, gender relations, female identity and behaviour. The 'Islamizing tone' of their discourse is similarly engendering a patriarchal perspective. State-run radio and television programmes also reflect another significant discourse on Islam and the assertion that it must at all times govern and define one's personal and social life. One such popular, hour-long programme (produced in 1993–1994) broadcast live every Tuesday morning enabled listeners in the Klang Valley to phone in and receive immediate information or advice on matters relating to *shari'ah* rules, family laws, personal problems, life and death. The special guest each week was an *ulama* (religious official or scholar) from one of the government departments of Islamic Affairs in Selangor or the Federal Territory of Kuala Lumpur. Again, a similar Islamic discourse is reproduced. Sometimes the consequence of such discussions is merely to accentuate trivia and elevate it to a level of great religious or legal significance. Generally, Islamization discourses whether articulated by the state or counter-state Islamist forces, promote an extremely narrow interpretation of religious principles and cultural values. Their essentialization is inherent in the readiness to adopt wholesale any practice of Muslim Arab society either in the lifetime of the Prophet Muhammad or that of his Companions (the four immediate successors after the death of the Prophet).

A comparative analysis carried out in the 1980s and 1990s of the media and public discourse on Islam and Islamization produced by the religious authorities in the relevant government departments, United Malay National Organization (UMNO), the main Malay component of the ruling political party Barisan Nasional (National Front), those in the opposition political party PAS, and other organizations or political movements such as the banned and now defunct Al Arqam, the Persatuan Ulamak Malaysia (The Malaysian Ulama Association) or Angkatan Belia Islam Malaysia (ABIM) (Islamic Youth Movement of Malaysia) all portrayed an extremely similar image of family and gender relations, women and the Muslim female identity. In their content and form, most of the views, exhortations, sermons and advice offered in the respective discourses manifest an obsessive impulse to inculcate many patriarchal Muslim Arab or Middle Eastern practices of gender and family relations as the unquestionable Islamic norm for all Muslims today. It is an Islamization approach which aims to reassert and strengthen the primacy of historical *shari'ah* as the basis of, and the main legal or jurisprudential reference for, Malay community life and its gender relations. This form of social construction, with its central focus on female identity and control, emerging from both the resurgent Islamic and state ideologies, gave Muslim Malay women very little choice other than to submit themselves to a subordination defined and upheld to be a universal Islamic value.

This imposition of such a patriarchal interpretation of Islam in Malaysia is a compelling example of a contemporary Muslim response to modernity and social change. As noted above, there is a strong convergence between the Islamization project of the state and that sought by resurgent Islamists, whether they support or oppose the state. The difference in their agendas lies only in the extent to which they seek to Islamize the state structure, the economy and the path of economic development. As for the creation of the *ummah* (community of Islam), both the state and its opponents have made similar powerful claims on women, their bodies and minds, as the key element in their competing visions of modern Malaysian society. Several studies of the impact of Islamic revivalism and of economic development on Malay society, women and the body politic have described the dynamics of the rivalry between the state and Islamic revivalists, and their contestation over cultural identity and the imagined community of modern Malaysian Muslims (Nagata 1994; Ong 1995; Shamsul 1994). Ong (1995) has noted that since the 1980s the political rivalry and competition among Islamization projects in Malaysia has resulted 'in the intensification of Malay gender difference, segregation, and inequality' (1995: 183) and their struggle continues 'on other sites, rooted in other class, political, and regional dynamics, but still focused on regulating women, who symbolize the varied ways Islam may be deployed to loosen or control the body politic in an unevenly modernized country' (1995: 186). Ong's analysis rests upon her argument that ultimately 'the state project and the Islamic resurgence must be seen as competing forms of postcolonial nationalism' (one that Ong described as 'soft nationalism') 'that fix upon the Malay family and woman as icons of particular forms of modernity' (1995: 184–186).

My contention is that beyond their representation as competing forms of post-colonial nationalism, both projects must also be seen and understood in the context of a global phenomenon within the Muslim world. Both Islamization projects, whether defined by religious movements or the state, are engaged in a common pursuit *viz.* the elaboration and actualization of Islamic modernity. Despite their political rivalry their conceptions of Islamization demonstrate a common ahistorical Islamic paradigm. Both draw upon the same historically limited understanding of their own Islamic heritage and utilize similar, narrowly interpreted, intellectual sources for the elaboration of their respective visions of the modern *ummah* and the actualization of what others perceive to be an ambiguous and somewhat distorted version of an Islamic culture of modernity.[11]

The formulators and architects of both state and non-state Islamization approaches also share a similar social formation. Whatever their political identification, interest or affiliation, all of them are informed by the same Islamic world view – a 'retraditionalizing' Islam. Theirs is an approach to Islamization which seeks to impose an anachronistically understood Islam onto modern times, one devoid of a modern and Islamically appropriate conception of social relations, established on a basis of equality, between men and women. One simple explanation for the similarity in their conception of Islamization and their discourse on women is that their proponents come from similar educational backgrounds. Common to both is an understanding of a resurgent Islam that yields nothing to the imperatives of current social transformations. Instead they seek to actualize a nostalgic version of Islamic culture drawn from an idealized past.

The ideologues of Islamization projects in Malaysia are currently divided over the support they accord to the two main Malay political parties – PAS and UMNO – as the voice of Malay and Muslim interest. Beyond party affiliation, the prime movers, originators and planners of each of the Islamization programmes share a strong desire for power and legitimacy in order to determine the path of Islam for the Malay community in particular and Malaysian society in general. The current PAS leadership in the state government in Kelantan is perhaps the only group of Islamists who have, especially in its campaigns and propaganda leading up to the 1990 and 1995 general elections, explicitly expressed its political aspiration and commitment to establish an Islamic state in Malaysia should it gain sufficient electoral support. While the leadership of UMNO (particularly the Prime Minister, Dr Mahathir and his Deputy, Dato' Seri Anwar Ibrahim) has declared its commitment to an Islamic agenda which will implement greater 'Islamicity' in all aspects of Malay society, the government also declared that it will remain faithful to the principles of governance of religious tolerance and co-existence, which in themselves are Islamic values and befitting a multi-ethnic society. Yet, when the Kelantan state government began the process of instituting the controversial Islamic criminal laws, popularly known as the *Hudud* laws, the state-sponsored and state-supporting

Islamists remained conspicuously muted and did not openly challenge that policy. When the federal parliament ultimately rejected the implementation of those laws for the state of Kelantan, it did so both on implicit constitutional grounds and explicitly, by stating that the country was not ready for such laws. No political will nor imagination was apparent to seize the initiative and encourage other segments within the community of Muslim intellectuals and activists to open up new debates and provide alternative or critical views of Islamization.

CONCLUSION

Islamization initiatives combined with the country's push towards industrialization, the two politically significant developments in Malaysia these past two and a half decades, provide the contexts within which debates about Muslim women's cultural identity and political status are formulated and defined. Both forces of change have also made Malay and Muslim women the central focus of their discourse and policy-making. Consequently, the issues concerning non-Muslim women are often neglected or marginalized. However, on some issues concerning the legal provisions for women's access to their rights as citizens, non-Muslims have an advantage over their Muslim counterparts. For example, following the joint efforts of many women's organizations to persuade the government to promulgate special legislation to address the various legal and protection problems faced by women who are victims of domestic violence, there was a positive and non-contentious outcome for non-Muslim women in the shape of the Domestic Violence Act (1995). Non-Muslim women also benefited from the enactment of the earlier Law Reform (Marriage and Divorce) Act 1976 which came into force in March 1982. The rights of non-Muslim men to form polygamous marriages, for example, have been abolished by this legislation. As demonstrated by the outcome of the Muslim Family Law Act 1984, the similar objective of reforming family laws so that Muslim women too can benefit from their fast changing roles in society was encumbered and finally hampered by the contestation among male Muslim authorities over the definition and 'Islamicity' of those reform proposals.

This does not mean that non-Muslim women in Malaysia escape the usual range of social and economic problems that are often produced by the neglect of policy-makers and government officials to take into consideration gender specificities and biases in many areas of the nation's numerous development plans since 1957. Non-Muslim women, like their Muslim counterparts, have also to contend with a range of religious teachings, ideas and interpretations (to be found in Confucianism, Buddhism or Christianity as practised in Malaysia) which promote gender hierarchy, bias, and discrimination. The advantage, if any, enjoyed by non-Muslim women over Muslim women in Malaysia, is that to some extent they have escaped any cultural assault at the state level which undermines their existing political rights and civil liberties as currently provided by Malaysian laws. For many non-Muslim women, potential gender discrimination and any backlash against their rights and freedoms can arise within the context of modern patriarchal constraints as well as through the traditional dynamics which govern people's attitudes and behaviour in the institutions of family, marriage and the wider arena of gender relations.

On the other hand, Muslim women are faced with the interaction of the two forces of change which bear directly upon their lives and which have been created by the way the state has advanced its economic modernization policies and its own programme of Islamization. Muslim women themselves helped to formulate the question of their cultural identity on their own terms both as followers and complementary actors in Islamist movements. Some work as activists and feminists in women's organizations to seek equal rights and challenge some of the political and religious efforts to circumscribe their public and domestic roles. The centrality of attention and ideological discourse on Muslim women is likely to filter through to non-Muslim communities and may influence a regeneration of their own patriarchal attitudes towards gender relations within their respective communities. In that context Malaysian women from all ethnic communities need to combine their resources and work together to prevent further erosion of their status. In doing so they may be able to find the political will to ensure greater or equal and effective participation in most of the policy- and decision-making arenas which will ultimately affect them and future generations of Malaysian women.

NOTES

1 Although not an Islamic state, Islam is Malaysia's official religion, professed by almost 53 per cent of the population, most of whom are Malays. The population of Malaysia is about 19.48 million, approximately 52 per cent of whom are Malays who, by definition of the Malaysian Constitution, are all Muslims. Malays, regarded as the main *bumiputera* (the indigenous population already settled in pre-colonial Malaya with their own political system of sultanates), and other *bumiputera* groups (or indigenous ethnic groups) in Sabah and Sarawak, formed about 61.3 per cent of the total population of Malaysia in 1991. Muslims constituted about 58.6 per cent of the total population of Malaysia according to the Malaysian Census Report of 1991; most of them are domiciled in Peninsular Malaysia. The ethnic composition of Peninsular Malaysia's population is as follows: 57.4 per cent Malays, 29.4 per cent Chinese, 9.5 per cent Indians and 2.8 per cent designated as 'others'.

2 *Bumiputera* which means literally 'sons of the soil' was a political status conferred on the Malay people in the Federation of Malaya at the time of independence from British colonial rule. This special status was intended to protect the political interests and pre-eminence of Malays who were the rulers and settlers occupying the Malay peninsula before the coming of the Western colonial powers such as the Dutch, Portuguese and British. During British colonial rule large numbers of Chinese and Indian immigrants were encouraged to settle in British Malaya for they provided the necessary human resources for rapid

economic development at that time. When Malaysia was formed, *bumiputera* status was extended to Malays and all indigenous ethnic groups of Sabah and Sarawak so that the 'affirmative action' of the NEP applies to them as well.

3 Each recognize this general trend while they remain critical of the problems and disadvantages women generally face in seeking employment. Similar observations by other authors also point out these disadvantages: foremost among them is the tendency for women to be segregated towards the bottom of the occupational hierarchies in the industries in which they work. While those views remain true, we cannot deny the liberating effect employment has had on young women. The rapid expansion of urban work opportunities for women has undoubtedly opened up the chance of earning an independent living and escaping the confines of rural society.

4 The death rates of males generally exceeds that of females, so that the natural surplus of males in any birth cohort is steadily eroded until older ages, when the number of women slightly exceeds that of men. This pattern is expected to continue unless modified by excessive age-selective migration (Government of Malaysia 1991).

5 In her study of contemporary *adat* and Islam in a Malay village Karim (1992) argued that *adat* assumes a mediatory role in providing an intimate and intuitive mechanism for re-ordering relationships according to the requirements of culture. *Adat* acts as a neutralizer and produces its own strategies of 'checks and controls'. However, while it may be true that there is a process of adaptation and re-adaptation of indigenous social systems (such as *adat* rules) to forms of social intervention (such as the adoption of Islam as a state religion) in a feudal and traditional society, Islamization in the contemporary era of Islamic resurgence poses a different type of intrusion into the lives of urban and rural Muslims. Islamization as a political movement and as a means of reasserting cultural authenticity by utilizing religious legitimacy has far greater effect in redefining gender relations and its politics.

6 For example, in the Malay context some trends can be observed in the symbolic and ritual reassertions of behaviour derived from *adat*, usually conveniently categorized within the framework of Islam, to strengthen the legitimacy of such institutions, as in the interfusion of *adat* rituals with *sunna* traditions of Islam (customary procedure sanctioned by traditions, in particular sayings and practices of the Prophet Mohammed). The converse situation seems to be apparent at most times, particularly when political movements use religion as their legitimating force (see Othman and Ng 1995).

7 Malaysia is a federation of thirteen states, eleven of which are in Peninsular Malaysia; the other two states, Sabah and Sarawak, are located in East Malaysia on the island of Borneo: all were formerly under British colonial rule. Under the constitutional division of powers between the federal and the state government, Muslim law is a state matter under the constitutional headship of the Malay ruler in nine of the Peninsular states. In the other four states – Penang, Melaka, Sabah and Sarawak – the *Yang Di Pertuan Agong* is the Head of State. The *Yang Di Pertuan Agong* (or Monarch) is the Malaysian Head of State chosen every five years through election by the Council of Rulers among their own number. The existing nine Malay rulers sit in the Council of Rulers with their respective head of state government – the *Menteri Besar* or the Chief Ministers. (The dominant political party in the federal government is the Barisan National (the National Front), with the Malay political component party – the United Malay National Organization (UMNO) – as the dominant member. UMNO is also the dominant party in the state government of Peninsular Malaysia.) The discussion of Islamization of these state laws is restricted to those operating in the eleven states of Peninsular Malaysia,

although in terms of implementing changes or amendments the other two states of Sabah and Sarawak tend to follow the trend of Peninsular Malaysia.

8 Muslim women came together only after the enactment of the state family laws in the Federal Territory (of Kuala Lumpur) when they realized that many of the states of Malaysia had not adopted the 1984 Act and that several of them were only going to enact the new Act after some further amendments of their own. Women's groups such as The National Council of Women's Organization (NCWO), the Association of Women Lawyers (AWL) and the Women's Affairs Division of the Prime Minister's Department (HAWA) jointly held a workshop on the topic 'The Administration of Islamic Laws and the Protection of Women's Rights' in July 1988, to discuss the matter.

9 *Syariah* (other cognates: *syari'e*) is the Malay transliteration of the Arabic word *shari'ah* (Islamic law). In this chapter the Malay transliteration (*syariah*, *syari'e*) is used only when referring to any of the Malaysian *shari'ah* enactments or documents.

10 In fact, when the federal parliament had passed the Act but before its implementation, several influential figures in the government's Islamic Affairs Department opposed the intended legislation, not just some of its details but its jurisprudential foundations. They insisted that the new Domestic Violence Act would undermine the supremacy of the *shari'ah* court in its designated domain over Muslims since it enabled Muslim women to invoke the application of a law other than *shari'ah* against their husbands.

11 Most Muslim modernist scholars, activists and intellectuals in this century have provided ample intellectual, theological and doctrinal challenges to the literalist interpretation and social vision of political Islamists. Unfortunately, Muslim states, regardless of how secular or modern they are, have opted for their own immediate political expediency by adopting less controversial and contentious routes. By sponsoring only Muslim scholars trained within the same traditional mould to provide an Islamization agenda, the state avoids being labelled 'unIslamic'. However, that policy excludes progressive Muslim thinkers and intellectuals from participating in the creation of a discourse and public debate.

BIBLIOGRAPHY

Ahmed, L. (1992) *Women and Gender in Islam: Historical Roots of a Modern Debate*, New Haven: Yale University Press.

An-Nai'im, A. A. (1990) *Toward an Islamic Reformation: Civil Liberties, Human Rights and International Law*, New York: Syracuse University Press.

Boserup, E. (1970) *Women's Role in Economic Development*, London: Allen & Unwin.

Dancz, V. H. (1987) *Women and Party Politics in Peninsular Malaysia*, Singapore: Oxford University Press.

Engineer, A. A. (1992) *The Rights of Women in Islam*, London: Hurst & Co.

Government of Malaysia. (1990) *The Labour Force Survey Report, 1989–1990*, (Department of Statistics Malaysia), Kuala Lumpur: Government Printing Press.

—— (1991) *The General Report of the Population Census*, (Department of Statistics Malaysia), Kuala Lumpur: Government Printing Press.

—— (1995) *The Sixth Malaysia Plan*, Kuala Lumpur: Government Printing Press.

—— (1996a) *The Seventh Malaysia Plan*, Kuala Lumpur: Government Printing Press.

—— (1996b) *The Economic Report 1995/1996*, (Ministry of Finance), Kuala Lumpur: Government Printing Press.

Hijab, N. (1988) *Womanpower: The Arab Debate on Women at Work*, Cambridge: Cambridge University Press.

Hussein, A. (1987) *Status of Women in Islam*, Lahore: Law Publishing Co.

Ibrahim, A. (1965) *The Status of Muslim Women in Family Law in Malaysia, Singapore and Brunei*, Singapore: Malayan Law Journal.

Jones, G. W. (1994) *Marriage and Divorce in Islamic South-East Asia*, Kuala Lumpur: Oxford University Press.

Kandiyoti, D. (ed.) (1991) *Women, Islam and the State*, London: Macmillan.

Karim, W. J. (1992) *Women and Culture: Between Malay Adat and Islam*, Boulder: Westview Press.

Li, T. (1989) *Malays in Singapore: Culture, Economy and Ideology*, Singapore: Oxford University Press.

Mernissi, F. (1985) *Beyond the Veil: Male–Female Dynamics in Modern Muslim Society*, London: Al Saqi Books, (revised edn).

—— (1990) *Women and Islam: An Historical and Theological Inquiry*, Oxford: Basil Blackwell.

—— (1993) *The Forgotten Queens of Islam*, Cambridge: Polity Press.

Moghadam, V. M. (1993) *Modernizing Women: Gender, Social Change in the Middle East*, Boulder: Lynne Rienner.

—— (ed.) (1994a) *Gender and National Identity*, London: Zed Books.

—— (ed.) (1994b) *Identity Politics and Women: Cultural Reassertions and Feminisms in International Perspective*, Boulder: Westview Press.

Mumtaz, K. and Shaheed, F. (1978) *Women of Pakistan: Two Steps Forward, One Step Back?*, London: Zed Books.

Nagata, J. (1994) 'How to be Islamic without Being an Islamic State: Contested Models of Development in Malaysia' in Akbar S. Ahmed and H. Donnan (eds) *Islam, Globalization and Postmodernity*, London: Routledge.

Ong, A. (1987) *Spirits of Resistance and Capitalist Disciplines: Factory Women in Malaysia*, Albany: State University of New York Press.

—— (1995) 'State Versus Islam: Malay Families, Women's Bodies, and the Body Politic in Malaysia' in A. Ong and M. G. Peletz (eds) *Bewitching Women, Pious Men: Gender and Body Politics in Southeast Asia*, Berkeley: University of California Press.

Osman, F. (1994) *Shari'a in Contemporary Society: the Dynamics of Change in Islamic Law*, Los Angeles: Multimedia Vera International.

—— (1996) *Muslim Women in the Family and Society*, Kuala Lumpur: SIS Forum (M) Berhad (reprint).

Othman, N. (1998) 'Grounding Human Rights Arguments in non-Western Terms: Shari'a and the Citizenship Rights of Women', in J. R. Bauer and D. A. Bell (eds) *East Asian Challenge for Human Rights*, New York: Cambridge University Press.

Othman, N. and Ng C. (eds) (1995) *Gender, Culture and Religion*, Kuala Lumpur: Persatuan Sains Sosial Malaysia.

Rahman, F. (1982) *Islam and Modernity*, Chicago: Chicago University Press.

Raja Mamat and Raja Rohana (1991) *The Role and Status of Malay Women in Malaysia: Social and Legal Perspectives*, Kuala Lumpur: DBP.

Shamsul, A. B. (1994) 'Religion and Ethnic Politics in Malaysia: The Significance of the Islamic Resurgence Phenomenon' in C. F. Keyes, L. Kendall and H. Hardacre (eds) *Asian Visions of Authority*, Honolulu: University of Hawaii Press.

Suffian, T. M., Lee, H. P. and Trindale, F. A. (eds) (1978) *The Constitution of Malaysia*, Kuala Lumpur: Oxford University Press.

Tibi, B. (1988) *The Crisis of Modern Islam: A Preindustrial Culture in the Scientific Age*, trans. Judith von Sivers, Salt Lake City: University of Utah Press.

10 Conclusion

Robert L. Miller

A time of transition is a time not of politics as usual but of unusual politics.
(Saint Germain 1994: 27)

INTRODUCTION

The preceding chapters are unified in that they each deal with a society or region undergoing transition. With the exception of Northern Ireland, the future of which is still in doubt, each of these societies has undergone a regime change in the recent past. Consequently, the changes they have experienced have been profound and include significant alterations in the position of women. While the contexts vary widely, the various contributors have been united in their consideration of the links between women's status and the alterations in the social structures of their respective societies. The linkages are in no respect uni-dimensional: as well as being affected by social change, women have been *effectors* of change. Meintjes' account of the roles women have played over the decades of the struggle in South Africa is perhaps the clearest example.

Transition, often equated with democratization (Fukayama 1992), is employed here in broader terms. It refers to profound changes in socio-economic and political structures – rather than the more limited orbit of democratization or transition to a society in which competitive elections are a reality. Democratization, including a broadening of access to political power for groups to whom access was previously denied (in this case, women), is an important, but not the only, aspect of transition. As the contributors demonstrate, in common with the bulk of the literature about the effect of democratization upon women, the extension of franchise rights does not in itself automatically lead to an improvement in women's position: indeed, it may have the contrary effect. Waylen (1994: 329) makes the broad point:

> Institutional democratization does not necessarily entail a democratization of power relations in society at large, particularly between men and women and . . . there is no necessary connection between playing an

important part in any stage of the process of democratization and having any particular role during the period of consolidation.

In this volume, Marsh and Rener and Ule each describe the resurgence of nationalism that has accompanied the collapse of former socialist regimes and the consequent pressure on women to exit the public sphere. Similarly, Othman describes a paradox of Malaysian modernization: *viz.* while Islamization attempts to curtail women's full participation in public life, at the same time women constitute an essential segment of the labour force.

An almost universal phenomenon of successful national liberation movements is that they renege on promises made to their female members during the struggle (Abdo 1993). As political structures are reformulated during transition the sphere of public activity undergoes a process of 'masculinization' leading to women being decanted from institutional politics (Waylen 1994: 353). The re-emergence of gender divisions is not unique; old divisions of class, race, geographical or ethnic origin also are reasserted towards the end of a phase of transition.[1] Women do not necessarily acquiesce passively to this relegation but adopt various strategies to maintain involvement in the public arena. For instance, 'lacking other alternatives, professional African women have [instead of relegating themselves to politically impotent "women's wings" of parties] retreated with their grievances into the non-governmental organization (NGO) sector'.[2] Several of the contributors to this volume provide accounts of these alternative strategies.

Advocates of women's rights tend to be compartmentalized by male activists into 'good' feminists and 'bad' feminists. The criteria employed in order to divide women into the categories 'good' and 'bad' depends upon the male body doing the stereotyping. For 'macho-Leninist' 'comrades-in-struggle', the criterion would be the extent to which a woman is willing to subordinate her feminist ideals to the supremacy of a class analysis and hence assume her 'rightful' place within the ranks of the revolutionary opposition'; for 'progressive' branches of the Catholic Church, the criterion would be the extent to which the woman opposes rights to fertility control and sexual self-determination (Sternbach *et al.* 1992: 402).

Women active in politics are subject to special forms of scrutiny that men escape. For instance, in traditional societies, activist women must contend with the sexual innuendoes that their independent public role will attract (Geisler 1995). Activism will be more acceptable if it coincides with traditional female roles. As Molyneux demonstrates for a traditional Islamic society and Othman for a non-traditional one, women seeking feminist change in Islamic societies can only hope to improve the position of women if they do not challenge the fundamentals of their religion. In Latin America,

> even when women enter politics, they perform in familial-type roles that have been extended to the public arena. The *super-madre*, or conventional female political office holder . . . operates in areas equivalent to a macro

extension of her household expertise, such as social welfare – health care, child care, and literacy programmes.

(Lobao 1990: 188)

As the chapters show, in societies undergoing transition there are many alternatives to the full political participation of women. Instead, women may 'choose' (or be forced into):

- compliance with a male-dominated nationalist project of maternity and relegation to a private domestic sphere within which they are seen, simultaneously, as the prime cultural and sole biological reproducers of the nationalist culture, besides acting as the symbol of the nation's sanctity. The chapters concerned with former socialist societies explicate this most clearly;
- exegesis, where women can attempt to 'square the circle' by reinterpreting the dominant patriarchal ideology to their own benefit. Othman's discussion of *shari'a* provides a clear example of this;
- silence, where the domestic role becomes so all-pervading that women become completely invisible in the public sphere. In the case of *purdah*, for instance, the invisibility can be literal
- exile, where women must leave their community (and perhaps nation) of origin in order to seek self-realization.

Furthermore, a focus upon democratization as the central or sole context of political transition betrays another manifestation of a male-oriented perspective: *viz.* the attention devoted to public activity that privileges formal, elitist political activities over informal, populist ones and continues to bedevil the mainstream study of politics (Miller *et al.* 1996). Party politics remains party politics in transforming societies and the variety of party political activity observed in newly democratized societies is arguably more male-dominated than that in nations where democratic norms are firmly established. Marsh's discussion of the countries that made up the former Soviet Union are the clearest example in this volume.

In a similar vein, while many of the case studies concern societies that are experiencing, have experienced, or show a high potential for, political violence, violence in itself is not a defining characteristic of transition and is not the criterion that has brought this collection together. Transition often carries with it the risk of violence, but its realization is not predetermined. Some constituent parts of the former Soviet Union and the other former socialist societies of central and eastern Europe have now experienced bitter conflicts while others have (so far) teetered on the brink but held back. A universal truism of social science courses of the 1960s and 1970s was that South Africa was doomed to a bloody civil war on racial lines. While the transition of that society has been painful and is by no means completed, the prophecies of apocalypse have as yet proved unfounded.

PATTERNS OF TRANSITION

The main division drawn by most commentators when they discuss societies that have undergone transition in recent times is one between the former socialist societies of central and eastern Europe and societies in the developing world that until recently were subject to authoritarian regimes. In both cases, repressive regimes have been displaced and their apparatus of state terror has been substantially dismantled.

Central and eastern Europe

Commentary and analysis of central and eastern European societies (Rai *et al.* 1992) have been unambiguous in pointing out how the position of women has deteriorated with the transition from 'real socialism'. The features of this deterioration in the former Soviet Union and the former Yugoslavia have been well-documented: the burdens of unemployment and underemployment fall more upon women; the loss of many mechanisms of state social support disproportionately affect women; women's reproductive rights are curtailed; and a general resurgence of patriarchal values associated with a revived hyper-nationalism relegates women to a second-class status. Here, the task for feminist activists in central and eastern Europe is to retain rights formerly given[3] to women during politically repressive periods without being seen to support a return to the old order. This task is complicated because, as Rosalind Marsh observes, anything labelled as having to do with 'women's rights', much less as 'feminist', is even more stigmatized than in Western societies (see also Molyneux 1990, 1994; Racioppi 1995; Rai *et al.* 1992).

The 'solving' of the 'woman question' during Stalinist times was, of course, a myth. Whereas working women in the West may be subject to a double burden of formal employment and domestic labour, women in the socialist nations were not only afflicted with the same double burden (exacerbated by the absence of labour-saving domestic devices, chronic shortages of consumer goods and necessities) they also shouldered a third burden of *required* political activity. State-sponsored women's organizations, no more than mouthpieces for the regime, were totally ineffectual at safeguarding women's interests. It is little wonder that a chance to withdraw to the household, relinquishing two-thirds of an exhausting burden, would be welcomed by so many:

> Ironically . . . socialist state policy on women, which had not achieved their emancipation, succeeded instead in alienating the population from any serious commitment to a feminist programme. . . . the emphasis on 'the woman question', and on the emancipation and promotion of women, could too readily be associated with the dead hand of the same distant and bureaucratic centralizing state, to be resisted and rejected along with its other policies.

(Molyneux 1990: 28)

The unfortunate association between the advocacy of women's rights and the policies of the hypocritical socialist regimes lingers on. Feminists in central and eastern Europe will have to overcome the stigmatization that they have inherited from the pseudo-women's organizations of the recent past before an effective women's movement will be able to gain adherents (Waylen 1994: 350–351).

This affects the interplay of agitation for women's rights in central and eastern Europe now. 'Emancipation from above' meant that there was not a tradition of feminist activism in central Europe. Women were active in the popular movements that led to the collapse of the socialist regimes in central Europe, but their activity was not predicated upon feminism:

> Despite the presence of large numbers of women in the demonstrations, the lack of feminist and women's groups organizing in the late 1980s meant that women were not in a good position to influence the state and the newly active political parties during the very rapid collapse of the old order that has taken place in much of Eastern Europe. Women's movements therefore never played a significant role in bringing about the transition, nor were they poised to play an active role in the postcommunist period.
>
> (Waylen 1994: 347)

One should note that the older state-sponsored women's organizations do not necessarily fade away completely. There is not a clean break between the old organs of 'enforced solidarity' and the new, independent women's organizations. Despite a loss of state support, the previously existing state organizations still enjoy resources in the form of physical premises and equipment, personnel, a level of public awareness and contacts (both within the nation and abroad). Such groups have survived and as women have been faced with dilemmas caused by the economic transformations, have begun to use their remaining limited resources to support women (Racioppi 1995).

New grass-roots feminist organizations have developed with little previous history and, in being distinct from the old mouthpiece groups, they have gained an advantage. This also means, however, that feminist groups in central and eastern Europe have tended to lack traditions of liberal political and psychoanalytical thought and theorizing about women. Hence, their approach has tended to be 'pragmatic' rather than 'strategic/analytical'.[4] Furthermore, as Marsh cogently argues, women's groups in the former socialist nations have to contend with a developing anti-feminist ideology as well as the stigmatization that is a hangover from the old state socialist women's organizations.

Latin America

Latin America provides exemplary cases of societies where democratic transition from right-wing authoritarianism has occurred. In contrast to the 'top down' legacy of central and eastern Europe, Latin American feminism[5] has evolved from grass-roots women's organizations, and not, as popularly assumed, as a North American import (Sternbach 1992). Rather than rejecting feminism as a 'counterrevolutionary diversion', women's and feminist issues have been increasingly integrated into leftist ideology in Latin America during the time of the more prolonged 'people's wars' (Nicaragua and El Salvador) after the early *foquista* movements in Cuba and Columbia (Lobao 1990).[6]

Fisher (1993) divides feminist and women's political activity in the region into four broad types. The most 'popular'[7] are the *movimientos de mujeres* (women's grass-roots organizations), centred upon the need to ameliorate practical problems and which do not employ a feminist analysis (in fact, they may well be suspicious of, or hostile to, feminist standpoints). Struggles for economic survival by women which are characteristic of this type of activity pre-date those for political or national liberation. Many of these grass-roots organizations have received support from progressive elements within the Catholic Church. In parallel with the evolution of individual feminist consciousness by North American and Western European women who learnt their activism in non-feminist organizations, women's grass-roots organizations in Latin America have played a central role in the development of activist skills among women on that continent:

> In the process of organizing around 'survival issues,' many women participants in the *movimientos de mujeres* were empowered both as citizens and as women and consequently often had begun to articulate demands for sexual equality in their homes and communities.
>
> (Sternbach *et al.* 1992: 420)

In reaction to the high level of political oppression that was widespread throughout the region, groups organized around the protection, or recovery, of the victims of such oppression constitute a second category. The Argentinean *Madres de la Plaza de Mayo* is the best known example. Such groups do not ostensibly have a high level of political sophistication but rather are united by the loss of their loved ones. With men effectively removed by repression from the possibility of open, or even clandestine, political opposition, the vacuum was in effect filled by women:

> these . . . regimes limited the amount of public space that was available for political expression. Campaigns of silencing or state terror were directed mainly (at first) against men, because man (sic.) were the visible political actors, whether in Poland or in Peru. . . . As men left the household, either killed, disappeared, jailed, exiled, forcibly recruited into the army, or to join resistance movements, heavier burdens fell on women,

both economic and social. Ironically, it was in many cases the invasion of the private sphere by government authorities that provoked women to enter, however unwillingly, the public sphere. Since men were absent or prohibited from institutional politics as usual, women took up increased political action, often in novel forms.

(Saint Germain 1994: 274)

Ironically, the survival of the women was due in no small part to the patriarchal suppositions of the murderous regimes they opposed. To the authoritarian patriarchal regime, they appeared as unfortunate examples of virtuous motherhood and, because of the passive maternal nature of their protest, these regimes found it difficult to see them at first[8] as a serious threat requiring suppression (Fisher 1992: 109).

Militantes and *políticas*, trade unionists and other political activists, blending left-wing political analysis with feminism, make up a third type. In this group, the distinguishing characteristic is the blend of a feminist perspective with activism associated with some other cause; with the latter taking precedence. Finally, Fisher identifies sole feminists, for whom feminism is the core issue.

While each of these types of activism can be understood to fall under the umbrella of a broadly-conceived 'women's movement', tensions do exist between the types of activism. Furthermore, these tensions are exacerbated with the return to democratic politics that brings with it the re-emergence of divisions of ethnicity and class within the wider movement (MacAulay 1994). One finds sole feminists at an (advantaged) end of a continuum of 'race', class and education with the grass-roots organizations, *movimientos de mujeres*, at the other. This four-fold typology is, though, by no means exhaustive. Distinct from *militantes/políticas* one could, for instance, suggest a fifth category of women involved in active armed struggle within movements of national liberation.

CONCLUSION

The related topics of nationalism and ethnic identity, the interplay between the two, and the manner in which women are affected by, and affect, these phenomena emerged as central concerns of the contributors. In a recent article, Molyneux has succinctly summed up many of the issues that have concerned the authors of the preceding chapters:

These new conservative nationalisms, whether religious or secular in character, are more often than not expressly concerned to relocate women within the family; they advocate versions of the 'separate spheres' argument, and allot considerable importance to redefining women's identities and to their active mobilization. A common feature of such discourses, and one to which many women respond, is the claim that (their definition of) nationalism is the vehicle through which women can find themselves and their 'special qualities' properly valued. This usually means investing the domestic sphere with symbolic value and idealizing women's place within it as mothers. ... Within this discourse, authenticity is often defined as a return to some imaginary past, a natural order when 'real men' and 'real women' occupied their proper place in the social order, women in the home, men in the public realm.

(Molyneux 1994: 307–308)

Yuval-Davis and Anthias (1989) have delineated five ways 'in which women have tended to participate in ethnic and national processes' *viz.*:

• as biological reproducers of members of ethnic collectivities;
• as reproducers of the boundaries of ethnic/national groups;
• as participating centrally in the ideological reproduction of the collectivity and as transmitters of its culture;
• as signifiers of ethnic/national differences – as a focus and symbol in ideological discourses used in the construction, reproduction and transformation of ethnic/national categories;
• as participants in national, economic, political and military struggles.

While different authors have emphasized different aspects of nationalism or ethnic identity, some aspects have played a central part in each chapter. Porter adopts the Yuval-Davis/Anthias typology intact, arguing that 'in Northern Ireland women of *all nationalist persuasions* [Porter's emphasis] participate in each of the five ways, though sometimes differently'. Marsh's application of Milič's four-fold typology of nationalism and its impact upon women – as biological regenerators, as ideological symbols, as participants in national-political discourse, and as participants in conflict – is also derived from the Yuval-Davis/Anthias framework. Like Porter, she is able to provide extensive documentation supporting the existence of each form of participation in ethnic and national processes. Pro-natalism and the sheer competition of numbers in ethnic constituencies provided a context for the contributions from the former socialist nations in which nationalist antagonisms are now reasserting themselves (Molyneux 1994: 308–309).

Boundaries, particularly the barriers to inter-ethnic marriage vigorously maintained by all ethnic communities in Malaysia, contribute to the stubborn persistence of a backdrop of ethnic tension in that society, as is also the case for Northern Ireland. In terms of ideological reproduction, women as the primary socializers of the next generation was a central tenet of several chapters, particularly that for Northern Ireland. Imagery of the daughter and mother remains a potent icon in each of the societies where ethnic conflict is present or lurking near the surface (Molyneux 1994: 309–310). The symbolic role of women in the maintenance of nationalist sentiment was discussed in depth by Rener and Ule. Women are used in rhetorical terms as signifiers to prolong and intensify the pathos of refugee status. They are seen to suffer more from the loss of home and are depicted as having more to gain if the 'lost' homeland is restored (Anthias 1989). Finally, the role of woman as an active participant in struggle is vividly portrayed in Meintjes' chapter on South Africa.

While the discussion in this conclusion has been in the main about repressive regimes and those that have replaced them, the issues apply equally well to any society undergoing profound transition. The problem of women being eased out of the public sphere towards the end of the transition phase appears well-nigh universal. The important questions are conceptual and have more substance than the now extremely well-rehearsed litanies of the ways and means by which women lose out as the transition phase stabilizes. The contributions to this volume leave open to question whether the significant changes undergone by these transitional societies have benefited women in any permanent sense. Assuming the empirical observation – that women are more involved in public activity during times of transition – is correct, *why* is this so? Work from Latin America and the chapter on South Africa here indicate that desperation forms part of the explanation. Women, their families and children are more directly affected by the privations of a transition phase and men may be less effective, or less motivated, in trying to ameliorate these privations. Women may have no choice except to become more active because men are removed from the scene by violence or intimidation. On the basis of past experiences in those societies that have previously undergone profound transitions, women activists around the world are much less likely today to believe that participating and sacrificing for a 'cause' will automatically lead to full inclusion in the public sphere when conditions achieve a new normalcy.

It is, however, possible to argue that the loosened constraints of a transition period allow women a 'window of opportunity' for activity that 'normal' patriarchal conditions do not provide. The chances of realizing these opportunities, however, may be slim but they must be taken. The clearest example of a conscious attempt to grasp this fleeting opportunity can be found in Meintjes' discussion of the Women's National Coalition and the Charter Campaign in post-transitional South Africa. Furthermore, as, or if, women's movements do succeed in enhancing women's involvement in political processes, *will* they actually transform politics? If so, it still remains to be seen whether these transformations will be toward more humane societies with more open access to the public sphere and less hierarchical political processes. As many of our chapters show, in particular that by Molyneux on the Yemen, the recent fate of women in many societies that have undergone transitions provides a cautionary note. Any assumption that a transition from a repressive to an ostensibly less authoritarian regime, even when accompanied by a heightened involvement of women in politics, will by itself lead to an improvement in political processes, appears naive when set against the reality of lived experience.

NOTES

1 The re-emergence of these other divisions may weaken a women's movement.
2 Women's wings of parties can be seen as supportive of traditional roles and marginal to true political power (Geisler 1995).
3 The word 'given' is used deliberately here. As I discuss below, part of the problem is that progressive women's rights were imposed from 'the top down' as part of a programme of repressive measures.
4 Not that a 'pragmatic' orientation to women's issues should be denigrated. Rather, the lack of a philosophical background to the movement has limited its potential for feminist analysis and action.
5 While this volume does not contain a chapter from a Latin American society, it is noteworthy that the evolution of women's movements from grass-roots organizations to more explicitly feminist groups in Northern Ireland as described by Porter, and in South Africa as described by Meintjes, in many ways seems to parallel developments in Latin America more than in Europe or North America. The existence of armed struggles in these two societies only serves to underline the parallel.
6 Similar arguments can be made for the development of feminism in other parts of the developing world; see Jayawardena (1986), cited in Stivens (1991).
7 'Popular' in the sense that it is used in writing on Latin America, i.e. having to do with the interests and beliefs of the general population.
8 One should note that the right-wing governments in Latin America and elsewhere see women who join the left as acting 'against nature' and are thereby liable to torture and sexual assault without violating patriarchal assumptions about special protected status for women (Kirkwood 1983: 629–631).

BIBLIOGRAPHY

Abdo, N. (1993) 'Middle East Politics through Feminist Lenses: Negotiating the Terms of Solidarity', *Alternatives* 18: 29–38.
Anthias, F. (1989) 'Women and Nationalism in Cyprus' in N. Yuval-Davis and F. Anthias (eds) *Woman-Nation-State*, Basingstoke: Macmillan.
Fisher, J. (1992) *Out of the Shadows: Women, Resistance, and Politics in South America*, London: Latin American Bureau.
Fukayama, F. (1992) *The End of History and the Last Man*, London: Hamish Hamilton.
Geisler, G. (1995) 'Troubled Sisterhood – Women and Politics in Southern Africa', *African Affairs* 94: 545–578.
Jayawardena, K. (1986) *Feminism and Nationalism in the Third World*, London: Zed Press.
Kirkwood, J. (1983) 'Women and Politics in Chile', *International Social Science Review*, 35, 4: 635–637.
Lobao, L. (1990) 'Women in Revolutionary Movements: Changing Patterns of Latin American Guerilla Struggle' in G. West and R. L. Blumberg (eds) *Women and Social Protest*, Oxford: Oxford University Press.
MacAulay, F. (1994) 'Review of *Engendering Democracy in Brazil – Women's Movements in Transition Politics* by Sonia E. Alvarez', *Journal of Latin American Studies*, 26: 518–519.
Manderson, L. (1991) 'Gender and Politics in Malaysia' in M. Stivens (ed.) *Why Gender Matters in Southeast Asian Politics*, Clayton, Victoria: Monash Papers on Southeast Asia, Number 23.
Miller, R. L., Wilford, R. and Donoghue, F. (1996) *Women and Political Participation in Northern Ireland*, Aldershot: Avebury.

Molyneux, M. (1990) 'The "Woman Question" in the Age of Perestroika', *New Left Review*, 183: 23–49.

—— (1994) 'Women's Rights and the International Context: Some Reflections of the Post-communist States', *Millennium: Journal of International Studies*, 23, 2: 287–313.

Racioppi, L. (1995) 'Organizing Women Before and After the Fall: Women's Politics in the Soviet Union and Post-Soviet Russia', *Signs*, 20, 4: 818–850.

Rai, S., Pilkington, H. and Phizacklea, A. (1992) *Women in the Face of Change: The Soviet Union, Eastern Europe and China*, London: Routledge.

Saint Germain, M. (1994) 'Women, Democratization, and Public Policy', *Policy Sciences*, 27: 269–276.

Sternbach, N. S., Navarro-Aranguren, M., Churchryk, P. and Alvarez, S. E. (1992) 'Feminisms in Latin America: From Bogatá to San Bernardo', *Signs*, 17, 2: 393–434.

Stivens, M. (1991) *Why Gender Matters in Southeast Asian Politics*, Clayton, Victoria: Monash Papers on Southeast Asia, Number 23.

Taylor, E. (1993) 'Feminism, Revolution, and Resistance', *Latin American Perspectives*.

Waylen, G. (1994) 'Women and Democratization: Conceptualizing Gender Relations in Transition Politics', *World Politics*, 46: 327–354.

Yuval-Davis, N. and Anthias, F. (eds) (1989) *Woman-Nation-State*, Basingstoke: Macmillan.

Index